Jack Olsen's frightening s[...]
most wanted fugitive in [...]

"*Give a Boy a Gun* was c[...]
escaped. Now that he is loose again, it becomes more so."
—*Salt Lake Tribune*

"A COMPELLING, AND SOBERING, TALE FROM
START TO FINISH."
—*Newsweek*

JACK OLSEN

Winner of a Special Edgar Award from
The Mystery Writers of America

GIVE A
BOY A GUN

"AT THE TOP OF HIS FORM, Olsen . . . demon-
strates how well he has refined the art of nonfiction writ-
ing. The painstaking research . . . is conveyed in the
fluid narrative style that virtually pushes the reader from
one page to the next."
—*Spokane Chronicle*

"A FINE STORYTELLER, OLSEN KEEPS THE
PAGES TURNING, but more important, he makes the
Dallas case a truly significant tale of 'law and disorder in
the American West.' "
—*Newsday*

Books by Jack Olsen:

GIVE A BOY A GUN (1985)
"SON": A PSYCHOPATH AND HIS VICTIMS (1983)
HAVE YOU SEEN MY SON? (1982)
MISSING PERSONS (1981)
NIGHT WATCH (1979)
THE SECRET OF FIRE FIVE (1977)
MASSY'S GAME (1976)
ALPHABET JACKSON (1974)
THE MAN WITH THE CANDY (1974)
THE GIRLS IN THE OFFICE (1971)
SLAUGHTER THE ANIMALS, POISON THE EARTH (1971)
THE BRIDGE AT CHAPPAQUIDDICK (1970)
NIGHT OF THE GRIZZLIES (1969)
SILENCE ON MONTE SOLE (1968)

GIVE
ᴬBOYᴬ
GUN

A True Story
of Law and
Disorder in the
American West

JACK OLSEN

A DELL BOOK

That li'l boy, I've got his baby picture. I got all my boys' pictures in my room. *I got 'em all!* I look at that li'l boy. He was a beautiful child. I adored all of 'em.

—Claude Lafayette Dallas, Sr.

. . . The use of the firearm, particularly in the shooting of the officers in the head, was atrocious and outrageous.

—Judge Edward J. Lodge

People like killers. And if one feels sympathy for the victims it's by way of thanking them for letting themselves be killed.

—Eugene Ionesco

Published by
Dell Publishing Co., Inc.
1 Dag Hammarskjold Plaza
New York, New York 10017

For Su forever

Dell ® TM 681510, Dell Publishing Co., Inc.

ISBN: 0-440-13168-5

Reprinted by arrangement with Delacorte Press

Printed in the United States of America

September 1986

10 9 8 7 6 5 4 3 2 1

WFH

1

THE WIND OFF Steens Mountain hits the skin like cold steel darts. Horses show the whites of their eyes and shelter flank to flank. On the slopes, sage and juniper and bunchgrass tilt to leeward. When common herds of cattle roamed this high desert country, cowboys had no trouble separating out the Steens animals; they stepped on their hay as they ate.

On a cool spring day in 1968, Bob Wallace was driving along the dirt road that runs for sixty miles under the jagged bluffs of the massif. The wind blew from the 9,354-foot peak and the rain came in bursts and gusts. As usual, the huge volcanic lump was creating its own weather.

In his time on the mountain, Wallace had seen far worse blows. Sometimes the wind drove snow and sleet off Steens faster than the wipers could handle. Electrical storms played across the face and the mountain hummed like a turbine, filling the air with ozone. Bob Wallace, a gritty young cowboss, kind of enjoyed it. The rain made the grass grow sweet and tall.

Up ahead he saw a man approaching on foot in a steady, rolling gait. In this bleak part of Oregon, where neighbors lived twenty or thirty miles apart and the drive to market took two hours at highway speed, pedestrians were an unexpected sight, especially in rainstorms. Wallace braked and rolled down his window. "You lost?" he called out.

The stranger blew a raindrop off his upturned nose and said, "Nope." Wallace looked into the brown eyes of a teenager, built sturdy and low to the ground. "I'm heading for the Alvord ranch," the kid said. As he spoke, water beaded up on his steel-rimmed glasses. His pack hung almost to his knees.

Wallace told him he was headed right. The Alvord was his home ranch, the biggest spread in the Steens area, owned by timber millionaires named Wilson. The kid hitched up his pack and asked if anybody was hiring.

"Check in," Wallace answered in a friendly voice. As a top hand on the 300,000 acres, he knew that the Alvord could always use a good man, especially in the spring, but the work was hard and the drifters who popped up these days—draft evaders, hippies, winos, malcontents—were seldom worth the trouble it took to sign them in. He asked the kid where he was coming from.

"Burns." The voice was barely audible. "Took me two days to get this far."

Burns, Oregon, was seventy miles away in the middle of mixed grazing lands and moonscapes. Wallace asked how he'd traveled. "Mostly walking," the kid answered, stepping away.

"How much does that pack weigh?"

"Oh, maybe fifty pounds."

"How far can you walk in a day?"

"About forty miles, if I run a little."

Several hours later, two women were chatting in a small red house on the Alvord ranch when the doorbell rang. Mary Wilson cast a surprised glance at her mother-in-law, ranch owner Constance "Coco" Wilson, a middle-aged woman of aristocratic mien. The older woman mused aloud, "Now who in the world—?"

"I can't imagine," Mary Wilson interrupted. No one ever rang or knocked. The ranchhouse was a mile from the dirt road, and folks who drove this far back toward the mountain were usually friends or ranchhands who "howdy'd" and walked in western-style.

The women opened the door on a clean-shaven young man who introduced himself as Claude Dallas. He seemed a little embarrassed, so soft-spoken that they had to strain to hear his words. His clothes looked neat and so did he. When he asked if the ranch and wire on his back, and returning for fresh supplies. "How many miles you been clocking?" Wilson asked.

"I wasn't counting," Dallas said.

"Looks like you got yourself a job."

2

AT FIRST SOME of the other men made fun of the new hand. "That name Claude Lafayette Dallas—he stole it from a movie." "He's a Polack from Chicago and his name's Dumbrowski." "Wait'll that dude sees his first garter snake." The men thought he might be on the lam like so many others who showed up asking for work— surly men with six or seven names and a pack of Social Security cards. They collected their pay and slipped away. It was the newest Wild West tradition.

For a long time the camp's weathered old outhouse had been in danger of collapse. In addition, the hole was uncomfortably close to being full. As the buckaroos rode off the mountain, Bob Wallace called over his shoulder, "Hey, Claude, dig another outhouse before we come back."

The men returned a week later to find a deep new two-holer in the back. "How's the location, Mr. Wallace?" Dallas asked politely. "I can always dig a new one."

Hoyt Wilson told his mother, "That's some kid. He came riding off the top of the ridge in wind so high I was half frozen in my down coat, and he's got on a T-shirt. I really don't think he was uncomfortable."

Coco Wilson wasn't surprised. There was something about the new man. The proprietress of the big ranch had seen all types, from the bird-watchers who'd once helped her log two hundred and fifty species in Central Park to the coarsest laborers in her husband's logging camps. As a young socialite she'd skiied at Kitzbühel and ridden to the hounds in Ireland, then headed west in 1939 with a timberman named Robert Wilson. Together they'd logged in Oregon's Deschutes River valley and other remote places and made their fortune. Coco Wilson knew quality, and Dallas was it.

That summer she confided to her daughter-in-law Mary that Claude almost seemed like one of her own children. "I have the feeling that he might have a very bad temper but that it takes a great deal to get him angry. But he's steady, level, a pleasure to talk to and be with. He's very well mannered, really intelligent, reads a lot of interesting books. And he's the hardest worker I'd ever known."

Mary Wilson agreed.

The teenager seemed fascinated by tradition. Coco could understand that, too. He confided that he'd always wanted to be a buckaroo. She remembered when she'd felt the same. In the I-O-N country where Idaho, Oregon and Nevada touched, the old ways were dying, but a few remnants remained. Mexican vaqueros had punched cattle here a century before the first herds of longhorns in Texas. The oldest I-O-N tradition was that a man worked hard from "can see to can't see" and thanked God for the privilege. In the branding and roundup seasons a crew might work a month of sixteen-hour days, spend three days in Burns or Winnemucca, then return to work. The pay was four hundred to five hundred dollars a month and each man supplied his own gear, no small expense in a place where equipment was tied up with pride and machismo, and a proper saddle might sell for a thousand dollars.

The young Ohioan blended in, and the talk about him stopped. In mid-June the Alvord's four thousand head of cattle were turned into the upper pastures. "They like the nice green grass up there," a jigger boss explained to the new hand. "The higher the elevation, the longer it stays green in the runoff from the snowfields. When grass turns dry, it don't have near the food value." Dallas listened as though cattle were the most important subject in the world.

7

When someone told him he was a born westerner, he acted flustered. Then he seemed pleased.

As fall approached he asked Bob Wallace if there was an opening for a rider. The other buckaroos were dubious. The kid had ridden before, but he was too green for the Alvord's high-spirited horses. When a flighty quarter horse threw him he punched it in the ribs and climbed back on. The ranch hands laughed when he was bucked off again, but the colt gave up before Dallas. Wallace assigned him a couple of elderly nags, one to ride and one to haul his fencing materials.

The new man went to town and bought an outfit that looked like a lift from a Frederic Remington portrait. "He's playing cowboy," one ranch hand told another, "and he plays it *hard.*" Disparagement turned to grudging admiration and respect. With money saved from his first paychecks, he bought a centennial Winchester Model 94 rifle, "the gun that won the West," and took it with him as he rode. He kept to himself, asked nothing of others, and was as good as his word on the petty trading deals that were always going on. When arguments broke out, he slid away. He drank but didn't get drunk. Once in a while he would punch a cow in the nose, but everyone lost his patience with the danged things.

One day his fellow riders noticed that he'd picked up another old western habit. There was a pistol on his hip.

3

FOR TWO YEARS, Claude Dallas served his apprenticeship as a buckaroo. He seemed to delight in taking on the jobs that no one else wanted. When a half-starved foal was grafted to a new mare, he stood watch night and day till the newborn was accepted. He learned how to rope, how to brand without burning through the hide, how to castrate and dehorn calves, shoe horses, give injections, assist at difficult births. He learned to keep gates closed, how to work with the mean little cow dogs misnamed "dingoes," how to herd cattle without "chousing" or rushing them, how to steer them toward white sage and fescue and away from foxglove and water hemlock, how to cut a slit below the tails of steers that had grazed on poisonous larkspur, to let the thick black blood ooze out in lumps and drips, an ancient Steens Mountain remedy.

Every day he edged closer to an old definition of a cowboy: a bowlegged fella who hates any work that takes him off his horse. He went out of his way to use the two-century-old vaquero lingo of the region: *oreanna,* an unbranded cow running loose; *caviata,* the band of workhorses; *tapaderas,* ornate leather covers over the stirrups; *riata,* braided rawhide used for roping animals (variant of *reata* or *la reata,* which became *lariat).*

9

He bought a high-fork saddle with a bucking roll and a horn for dally roping, a technique in which a riata is looped around the saddle horn to slip or hold the quarter-ton of steer at the other end. He read that early cowboys used copper-inlaid bits to hold moisture in the horse's mouth, so he bought one and put it to use, explaining to a tenderfoot that early vaqueros had been forced to ride hot-blooded horses and the "cricket" on the bit gave them something to roll around in their mouths and calmed them. He became a walking compendium of such information, although he didn't share it unless asked. He seemed to be thriving.

But the idyll couldn't last. After twenty months at the Alvord, Claude confided to the Wilsons that his Ohio draft board was after him. He bought two buckskin horses from the family and loaded one with provisions. "Hold my mail, okay?" he asked Hoyt.

"Where ya headed?"

He pointed toward Steens Mountain and rode off.

A month later he reappeared at the upper camp. His high-heeled boots and oversize tapaderas were a little the worse for wear, and there was a haunch of venison strapped behind his rifle. "Can I borrow some salt?" he asked. He explained that he'd made too many mistakes packing. He'd run out of flour the second day out.

He hung around the cabin for a week or so and then told Hoyt Wilson that he wanted to hook up with one of the big open-range outfits that still fed their hands out of chuck wagons. He said, "I like sleeping on the ground. I like riding horses that're so wild that you don't dare get off even to take a leak 'cause you might have to walk home. That's the life for me." Hoyt Wilson told him not to bother explaining.

4

DALLAS REPROVISIONED AND headed south past bare skulls of steers on the high plains of the Great Basin, the desiccated trough that once was called the "Great American Desert" and includes parts of Nevada, Oregon, Idaho, Utah, Wyoming, Colorado and California. Moving from job to job, he rode one buckskin and led another: an Old West painting on the hoof. Instead of the low-crowned cowboy hat of the discotheques and ad agencies, he wore one with a tall rounded crown, a thin leather band and a flat brim. An army surplus overcoat amplified his frame. Hand-made tapaderas protected his Levi pants, and silver spurs jangled from his high-heeled boots. It was no trouble at all to mistake him for Valdez in the book by Elmore Leonard.

He crossed into Nevada at the misspelled town of McDermitt, where brittle balls of tumbleweed piled up against the doors of the White Horse Inn and the Say When Cafe and the State Line restaurant with its Will Rogers calendar, two slot machines, three-dollar hamburgers and late hits like "The Tennessee Waltz" on the juke. He made a side excursion into the dry Owyhee Desert, named for three Hawaiian fur trappers who went in and didn't come out. Barren, treeless, cold and hot, the Owyhee was once described by Washington Irving as "the ruins of the world," a wasteland so remote that earlier this century parts of it were marked unexplored on maps.

He camped near abandoned gold and silver digs in the Tuscarora Mountains, then rode east to Elko and Wells and south to Ely and Tonopah before heading north toward the glitz and grit of Reno. Tourists waved and Dallas waved back, the inscrutable cow-country nomad once played by Alan Ladd, whom he slightly resembled. A motorist spotted him alongside Interstate 80, crossing an alkali flat called Fernley Sink. "That salt's so white it hurts your eyeballs," the man told a friend. "He was right out in the middle of it, riding one horse and leading another. There were three or four cars parked, and folks were talking to him and taking pictures. Took a few m'self."

At various stopping places, Dallas made lasting impressions on his elders. A rancher named Richard Holbrook was checking line in the snow when he saw the mini-packtrain approaching across the foothills. "I went down and waited," Holbrook said later. "Claude stayed around for three weeks working my ranch. He was one of those people you treated as family. We went away and left our house in his care and didn't worry about it."

In the fall of 1970, the lone rider came into sight of the neon glow of Winnemucca, a rowdy town of some 4,000. He bypassed the whorehouses and casinos and rode on north. On a bright Sunday afternoon, he reined up at a place called Paradise Hill.

5

MOST OBSERVERS OF the Paradise Valley and its environs assume
it was named by someone who was too long in the desert sun. The
accepted folklore is that a disgruntled prospector climbed the
rocky slopes of the Santa Rosa Mountains in 1863, saw the long
valley below and said, "What a paradise!" He didn't add, "Rela-
tively speaking."

In a wet year, eight to ten inches of rain fall in this paradise. The
Little Humboldt River begins with mountain runoff, builds up a
flow and then vanishes in the briny flats. Ponds become so saline
that only a few specialized life forms can survive. Humboldt
County's few serious farmers are kept in hock by a three-month
growing season; they pray for rain and wallow in mud when it
arrives. The rest of the time, the wind lifts curls of ocherous yellow
dust and blows it up the nearest nose. After working in the nearby
gold mines, Mark Twain wrote: "The delicate scales used by the
assayers were inclosed in glass cases intended to be air-tight, and
yet some of this dust was so impalpable and so invisibly fine that it
would get in, somehow, and impair the accuracy of those scales."

Mountains and hills ring the valley: the Santa Rosas, the Bloody
Runs, the Krum Hills, the Osgoods. Wild animals work nights and

sleep days, out of the sun. Oily-black crows perch on fences and wait for road kills. Red-tailed hawks and golden eagles feel out thermals with their wingtip feathers, sometimes hanging motionless to view the table d'hôte. Pack rats and ground squirrels run fast and look nervous.

The Paradise Valley is forty miles long and twelve across, wide enough so that shadowgraphs made by clouds can be seen moving from west to east, momentarily darkening the small frame houses and weathered corrals and trailers and sheds and junked cars that have replaced the sod houses and adobe cabins of the past. The locals say you can look to the west and see until next week's weather and look to the east and see until last week's. The dry air smells of sage and salt and impalpable dust. And cows . . .

In this high desert country it takes fifty football fields to support a steer. The dominant flora is the blue-gray sage; with its tough stringy bark and ranging root systems, a plant can live a hundred years. Rabbitbrush, *Crysothamnus nauseosus,* tastes like its name and resembles leafy sage; cattle will eat it in hard times but dislike its bitterness. Thorny pickle brush is another meal of last resort. In among these unpalatable specimens are outright killers like larkspur and hemlock.

Inhospitable as the desert may seem, the countryside is dotted with beeves, usually called "cows" regardless of sex. There are Herefords and Angus and mixes including a cross called Black Ballys or Baldys that look like black minstrel-cows in whiteface. A few Charolais and Brahmas and Durhams are stippled into the landscape, but the lineage of most Paradise Valley steers is too murky to chart. They eat mountain greenery in summer and white sage and valley hay in winter. Cattle have grazed this high desert ever since vaqueros drove them across the border to the Nevada Territory. They have been the main financial support of the area since the silver mines played out and the railroad picked up its tracks.

Except for certain big-city retirees who arrive in new Winnebagos and leave when they discover the lack of golden arches and Taco Bells, the valley residents tend to be hard-bitten, leathery, resilient—typical Great Basin survivors. Visitors are granted a little leeway in discussing a man's mate, but none whatever in discussing his pickup truck or his dog. Many of the residents pack

14

guns, pronounced "wheapons." Local lawmen estimate that there are five wheapons for every resident. Metro-type crime barely exists here at 4,600 feet. Lawbreakers usually turn out to be from somewhere else. Says a cowboy, "We get a lot of California debris up here." The most popular bumper sticker is the old faithful WHEN GUNS ARE OUTLAWED, ONLY OUTLAWS WILL CARRY GUNS, followed by AMERICA LOVE IT OR LEAVE IT and its local variant IF YOU DON'T LOVE AMERICA YOU AIN'T SHIT.

On the afternoon of Claude Dallas's arrival at the cluster of houses called Paradise Hill, puffs of raw sienna dust marked a roping competition in a corral alongside the highway. The visitor politely declined offers to take part. Later, at a barbecue, he confided that he needed a job. He caught on with the Quarter Circle A, part of the huge Nevada Garvey spread. "I didn't ask no questions," foreman Larry Hill explained later.

A few cynics reckoned that the stranger had outfitted himself from the Buffalo Bill show catalogue. They gathered around to admire his new silver-inlaid spade bit but wondered if he wasn't overworking the vaquero motif. These days many buckaroos rode in blue jeans and tractor caps. When word got out that the new hand's experience consisted of two years on the Alvord ranch, the older cowpokes shook their heads. To those who'd never been there, the Alvord was too much like a dude ranch: a rich owner with a funny accent, an airstrip, comfortable living quarters, modern equipment. Here in Paradise Valley, buckarooing meant fresh manure and muck, dust devils and hailstorms, sore muscles, blistered feet and perpetual hand-to-hoof combat with free-running steers that were just a kick or two from being wild.

Dallas was accepted fast. There was something disarming about his shy smile, his reticence, the way he cocked his head and listened like an acolyte. Paying close attention was high tribute to men who usually talked across the backs of cows.

Given a choice, he seemed to prefer his elders to his contemporaries. An older man named Frank Gavica lent him a compressor to sandblast an old truck, and when Dallas was finished, he asked, "How much do I owe you?"

"Nothing," Gavica said in his slight Basque accent.

Later Gavica found a fifty-dollar bill clipped to his compressor. Dallas always insisted that someone else had left the money. And Gavica never forgot.

In camp with his peers the young cowboy sometimes seemed a little lost. Around the campfire one night a buckaroo told a new-comer, "Claude projects as the orphan. It's yes sir, no sir and thank you. When you meet him, you want to do something for him. But underneath I'm not sure a one of us really knows him."

Champion roper Cortland Nielsen felt he'd known Dallas for years. "I'm already a Christian, but talking to Claude brings out the depth of my own religious feeling, because he's *such* a good listener. He never uses foul language. He could have dinner with the governor tonight."

But instead the kid from Mount Gilead was eating out of a cookwagon parked in the middle of the cheatgrass and wheatgrass and Idaho fescue, eating dust, and listening to bawling cows and calves that never seemed to shut up. He seemed to thrive on the mixture. Even though he'd been on his way to Alaska before the detour to Great Basin country, he let it be known that he'd always wanted to be a cowboy, a remark that pleased those who'd had less choice. A jigger boss reported on the new man: "We were camped at Calico, gathering cattle, still branding calves, had 'em on the forest lands then. Mostly the work was riding circle or roping or branding, and Claude more than held his own. There was six or eight buckaroos on the wagon, but he kinda kept to himself, a little bit hard to know. A loner, not a partier. He'd listen and smile real nice, but he wouldn't offer nothing."

To a few of the cowboys, he seemed like a drop-in from space, a historical blank. When the others reminisced about their child-hoods, he listened and offered nothing. After an all-night drinking session, he confided that his father had been a strict disciplinarian —"had to be, to raise six boys and three girls." But he didn't elaborate, and the next day he acted as though he shouldn't have shot off his mouth.

He made a vivid impression on Irene Fischer, a graying woman who lived with her husband Walt in a weathered old house in the village of Paradise Valley. At thirty she'd been the ranking beauty of the high desert, a raven-haired woman with soft, twinkling ro-mantic eyes, her only loves the gangly Walt and any good cutting horse in sight. Now, a few years later, she was still pretty enough to turn cowboys in their saddles, but she'd spent so many years on horseback that she'd become a little stoop-shouldered and walked like a broken-down cowboy. She carried a pistol loaded with bird shot for the rattlesnakes that still shook her up after a lifetime on the range. Once her friend Jeanie Babe asked her in a bar, "Irene, does that thing shoot?" Irene shot a hole in the ceiling. Jeanie Babe said, "Gee, that's pretty good," grabbed the pistol and added another hole. Soon afterward, Irene quit drinking.

Claude Dallas entered her life in December 1970, and before he'd left, he made her cry so much that "I near wore out my handkerchief." She was still buckarooing in those days, but mostly she ran the cookwagon and painted pretty pictures on the calcified steer skulls she picked up on the desert. "The way I got to know Claude," she said in her soft voice, "the other hands went away somewhere and he stayed in camp. It was Christmastime. So I had one guy to cook for besides my husband. I felt so sorry for him because he just seemed so lonesome. I told Walt, 'There's something really deep in that guy. He's gonna be famous one of these days.' But I meant in the way of something good."

6

IF THE ALVORD ranch was Claude Dallas's basic training, his work on the 2-million-acre Nevada Garvey spread was the graduate course in cowboying. One day, miles from the wagon, his horse spun around and he found himself roped to four hundred pounds of terrified calf. He impressed his colleagues by getting out of the predicament without damage to himself or the stock.

But he was hard on other animals. A campmate took note: "He never walks around a dog that bothers him—he cracks it with a stick." He knocked out a Labrador. He attacked a stallion with a shoeing hammer and had to be pulled off. When a cow fell in a loading chute, he clubbed it with a two-by-four. "He'd've killed it if we hadn't stopped him," a cowboss reported.

He seemed oddly contemptuous of the game laws. Another buckaroo complained, "He sees nothing wrong with shooting any animal any time. He'll drag in a young deer or an antelope and leave it at the chuck wagon. Well, we have all the prime beef we want, and the wild meat just goes to waste. It puts the rest of us on the spot. Government men and game wardens are always dropping into camp."

He killed a quintet of deer out of season and took the hides to a seamstress for a deerskin outfit. He embarrassed a friend by driving up with a yearling in the back of his pickup. "Why don't you cover up the deer?" the friend asked. "People driving down the highway'll see."

"Well, they're not gonna take it," Dallas responded. The friend wondered what that meant, but decided against asking. Instead he discreetly slid a tarpaulin over the carcass.

When others asked Dallas why he was so aggressive about poaching, he explained that game laws didn't apply to subsistence hunters. He said that his family had depended on wild game while he was growing up. "The warden knew it, too," he said. "Everybody poached where I grew up." He rode proud whenever he came into camp with a kill.

Some of the other riders wondered if his contempt for animals carried over into a contempt for humans. If so, he kept it well covered, not by conviviality, but by talking respectfully to the older hands and working harder than anyone. He took old-fashioned pride in his gear, polishing and oiling and repairing while the others killed time with cards or beer. Night after night he worked on a rawhide hondo for his lasso. Rawhide was the choice of traditionalists; it didn't fray rope the way a wire hondo did. He filed his spurs till they were almost too sharp by the other buckaroos' standards. Irene Fischer told her husband, "That kid's a perfectionist."

He insisted that he asked nothing of his fellow countrymen and therefore owed no taxes, no military service, no obligation to obey the law. Irene Fischer thought, He's cold. People have to show a little feeling for one another, a little love and affection. When men drink and party, they get friendly and lovey-dovey. But never Claude . . .

Once in a while he showed up in a spectacular outfit, like a ten-year-old kid playing cowboy. In aquamarine sheepskin chaps and high-domed trapper's hat, he was as conspicuous as a runway model. He didn't seem to notice the attention. Sipping beer with other buckaroos, he posed for a picture that appeared in a *National Geographic* study: "The American Cowboy in Life and Legend." None of the cowpokes looked more authentic.

The hands partied in Winnemucca, a town where a visitor could buy liquor, odds and women but couldn't see a movie or buy a hardcover book. The dusty place had come into being as a Humboldt River crossing and flourished for a while as a railhead for cattle on the old Central Pacific main line between San Francisco and Salt Lake City. In later years its inhabitants celebrated "Butch Cassidy Days" to honor the outlaw who robbed their bank.

Once every month or so the cowboys descended on this self-proclaimed "new frontier of the Old West" in their battered pickups and four-wheel drives and sometimes on horseback. They piled their saddles and bridles against the fronts of saloons like the Reckon Bar, Pepper's Club and the Gem Bar and proceeded to rest and rehabilitate themselves at breakneck speed, mostly drinking and carousing with whoring thrown in if it didn't take too much time from the drinking and carousing. Five or six storefront brothels with names like the Pussycat Saloon and Simone de Paris formed a sad little plexus in the riverfront hollow at the foot of Bodd Street. One of the gaudier establishments was owned by a group of California rice farmers who toned up their yard with a penis carved from a railroad tie.

A campmate reported on Dallas's playtime behavior. "The rest of us do a real professional job of raisin' hell, but not old Claude. He might get high, but not very. Won't get near a whore. He seldom goes on a real toot."

The buckaroos noticed another idiosyncrasy: he treated all women as ladies. In the bunkhouse, he sat out the nightly clinics on breasts and butts and pubic hair. He laughed politely at dirty jokes but added none of his own. Irene Fischer liked to tease him about women. "He turns beet-red," she told her husband. "It's easy to embarrass him about gals."

He enjoyed discussing firearms and had an intimate knowledge of muzzle velocities, throw-weights, calibers, even the histories of famous guns. He knew knives and kept his Sod Buster honed so sharp it was dangerous to touch. He spoke about weapons in shorthand. The 94. The Python. The 20. The Bowie. The buck . . .

He would glance at a holstered gun and say, "That's a two-and-a-half-inch Model 19 Smith." *Smith* was short for Smith & Wesson; a cowboy would bite off his tongue sooner than use the full name. It was part of the buckaroo image to know guns whether you carried or not.

* * *

The .22 trap pistol that Dallas had worn on his narrow hips was soon replaced by a stubby .357. When he wasn't sitting on his bunk rawhiding or working leather, he was filing down pistol grips to match his hands, or melting lead for bullets. After a rare night of drinking in a cow camp on the Little Humboldt River, he pulled out his revolver and pranced around the bunkhouse shouting, "Me Apache, me Apache!" The men ducked under the table as a shot rang out. When the spiral of smoke drifted away, everyone laughed. It was so unlike old Claude.

7

AFTER THAT UNCHARACTERISTIC burst of high spirits, Dallas seemed to drink less and draw in upon himself. It was as though he'd decided never to lose control again. At sight of a camera, he would turn away; no one was indiscreet enough to ask why. A deputy sheriff explained later, "On these intermountain ranches, there's a lot of guys runnin'. They don't stay any one place long enough to get caught. I knew one that had fourteen ID cards— he'd work two weeks and get his pay and leave at midnight."

Dallas was as willing a worker as he'd been on the Alvord, but he seemed to be going backward in time. In the winter doldrums, when he lived in his trailer, he told friends he was "in camp." He buried his turned-up nose in Mark Twain's *Roughing It* and other western books. He stared at the Charlie Russell prints in one of the Circle A bunkhouses, giving a campmate the eerie feeling that "he thinks he's in the painting." He made a vacation pilgrimage to the Russell museum in Montana, a seminarian going to Lourdes, and when he returned he raved about the master's work. Nothing western seemed alien to him.

Now and then he spent a few days in the nearby Owyhee Desert, nosing around Defeat Butte, Devils Corral, Starvation Springs,

Poison Creek, Skull Creek, places whose names were their descriptions. An early sheepman named Gorham Gates Kimball had crossed the Owyhee and observed, "I was brought up and educated to believe there is a hell where all had to suffer for their sins. I now think there was one once and the country over which I have just passed must have been the place where it was located."

Something in the barren landscape seemed to appeal to Dallas—and to many another wanderer who saw it as a haven of freedom and stark beauty. As always, he moved in a rolling gait with feet splayed slightly outward, but his Chaplinesque style didn't keep him from covering ground. In the off-season, he would hike from one mountain to another, then catnap under a tree or a bush. Another buckaroo described him admiringly. "Claude does the things that folks talk about but don't do. It's hard out there on the Owyhee, but he loves it. A great feeling—the quietness, the distances. He isn't afraid to walk fifty miles through hard country carrying a pack."

Said the champion roper Cortland Nielsen, "Claude is true Old West. A lot of guys try it, but the first time they have to shave with cold water they change their mind. Claude keeps going after it and after it. He should've been alive in the old days—a scout, the guy you send a day or two ahead to tell you how things are. He'd been perfect."

8

IN THE CHILLY fall of 1973, the other buckaroos learned why Dallas had kept so quiet about his background. In July, he'd been secretly indicted by a federal grand jury for failure to report for induction. When agents tried to arrest him in Ohio, they found that the peripatetic Dallas family had moved again, this time to New York State. They picked up Claude's trail in Oregon, lost it at the Alvord, then picked it up again when his picture appeared in a cowboy book. The FBI men were puzzled. Why would a draft dodger pose for a magazine picture? But maybe he hadn't posed; maybe a photographer had just clicked off a shot and sold it free-lance.

Word reached FBI headquarters in Reno that Dallas was working at St. John's buckaroo camp in Elko County. Word also came that he was never without a sidearm, sometimes two, and had become a crack shot with either hand. He often stayed behind practicing when the other cowboys left for town.

In November the St. John's buckaroos were spotted in a saloon, and FBI agents Eric Meale and George Schwinn made their move. With Deputy Sheriff Noel McElhany, they dressed in old clothes and drove to the camp in Schwinn's well-worn Chevrolet pickup.

On the way, Meale briefed the others. He said that bringing men like Dallas to justice had become an irritation; the agency had more important things to do. "Most likely he'll try to run," the agent said, "but he may try to shoot it out. We'll have to shut him right down."

They pulled into the camp and spotted a shabby bunkhouse with two doors. In the corral, a colt showed the whites of its eyes and tugged against a tether. No one was in sight. Schwinn covered one door and McElhany the other. Meale walked inside and spotted a sleepy-eyed man getting up from a bunk. "They hiring around here?" the agent asked.

The man wiped his brown eyes. He was wearing Levi jeans, cowboy boots and a western shirt. Meale stepped closer. The man looked to be a few inches under six feet, lean and tanned and sturdy. As they stood face-to-face, the buckaroo's face broke into a half smirk. Meale said, "You're Dallas, aren't you?"

"Yep."

"You're under arrest." Schwinn made a body search while the others checked for weapons. They found a loaded rifle under the mattress.

"I got a green horse tied up outside," Dallas said. He spoke in a soft western drawl. The officers were surprised; they'd been told he was from Ohio. "I've been breaking some colts," he added.

"By yourself?" Deputy McElhany asked.

"Sure," Dallas answered.

"Little dangerous, isn't it?" the deputy asked. Dallas didn't answer.

McElhany turned the colt loose in the corral. Dallas seemed friendly on the drive to Battle Mountain. He was booked in Lander County jail and flown to Ohio for trial.

He returned to Nevada early in 1974 and told his friends that the case had been dropped because of improper procedures by the Mount Gilead draft board. He said the U.S. marshals had marched him through airports bellyshackled and handcuffed. He'd been thrown into drunk tanks with common criminals, "a bunch of thieves." He claimed that he was roughed up by lawmen and that when the case was dropped, an FBI agent whispered, "I'm gonna get you, Dallas, even if it's just for tax evasion." No one doubted his word. He was known as a truthful man.

He seemed defensive about being arrested without a struggle. He said, "They wouldn't've took me like that if they hadn't got the drop on me." Friends were puzzled; had he intended to shoot it out with the FBI? He was publicly heard to swear that no one would ever outdraw him again—*no one*. One of his closest friends asked how he felt about the draft and the Vietnam war. He said he would fight for his country if he were asked in a nice way, but "nobody's gonna order me around."

9

RANCH OWNER CONSTANCE "Coco" Wilson hadn't heard from Dallas in four years when he phoned and told her he needed nine hundred dollars to pay off his lawyer. She sent him the money without hesitation; she knew she could trust the young rider who'd made such a good impression a few years back.

Her life had changed. The marriage that had converted her from a socialite easterner to a buckarooing rancher was defunct. In the divorce settlement with logging baron Robert Wilson, he kept part of the Alvord and Coco wound up with a chunk called the Mann Lake ranch—22,000 acres of deeded land atop Steens Mountain, grazing rights to tens of thousands of acres more, and a thousand cows. Her son Hoyt and his wife Mary continued to run the operation, and Mrs. Wilson, in her fifties by now, began spending more time in nearby Idaho.

Early in 1974, Hoyt Wilson picked up the phone at the Mann Lake ranch to hear a familiar voice. "Hoyt, I got this nine hundred bucks to work off for your mother. When do you want me?"

Wilson was pleased to hear from his old ranch hand. "Well, Claude," he said, "we'll have you ride the mountain for us this summer."

"Fine. When?"

"How about the first of May?"

On the afternoon of April 30 Wilson was driving up the road when a lone figure came into sight riding one horse and leading another. Dallas was right on time as usual. He worked as hard as ever, but some of the riders noticed that something seemed to have gone out of him. He'd never been the playful sort, but now he appeared glum, preoccupied. In the old days he'd studied everything he could find about the West, but now he concentrated on works about guns, self-defense, quick-draw, military tactics, police techniques. "We don't hear no more about Charlie Russell's paintings and Luke Short's books," a campmate noted. "This new Claude, he's all wheapons." He slept with a gun. A few observant cowboys took note and steered clear. Maybe he would dream he was in a gunfight. . . .

He was still hard on animals. "First thing he done was ride a soft horse over the top of the mountain and damn near broke it down," a buckaroo reported. "He's as tough on stock as he is on himself. And that's goldanged tough."

After a few weeks an ugly prospect developed. Hoyt Wilson told his wife Mary: "A couple trout fishermen have been driving through our fence to Kiger Gorge, up on top. Claude took boards with seven-inch spikes and put 'em in the road to blow their tires. I don't like it; I have the feeling if he catches those guys he might bury 'em someplace. Makes me uneasy." He was relieved when the fishermen stayed away.

Toward the end of summer, Dallas said a few words about his arrest. He said that from now on he wanted nothing to do with the government. To Hoyt Wilson he seemed almost paranoid on the subject. "I just don't want *anybody* to mess with me. That's why I came west in the first place."

He talked about a sixty-year-old man he'd met in Paradise Hill: George Nielsen, a bar owner who apparently exerted a strong influence. From time to time he quoted Nielsen's aphorisms, uniformly misanthropic and cynical, especially on the subjects of guns (good), game wardens (bad), and women (extremely good in their place).

* * *

No one was surprised at summer's end when Claude loaded his packhorse and headed south toward Nielsen and Nevada. The loan had been paid in full. The next time Hoyt and Mary Wilson would see his face, it would be on a "wanted" poster.

10

FOR A FEW more years Claude Dallas lived the tough outdoor life of the buckaroo, working cattle on the mountain slopes in summer and in the lower pastures in winter, but he gradually soured on the job. So did most of the other Circle A hands. Night after night they popped their Coors and griped about the way the cattle business was swirling down the drain.

Unimpeded by fence or regulation, they'd once driven cattle seventy-five miles across the painted desert called Owyhee and turned them loose to graze on the bunchgrass and fescue and squirreltail that were watered by thawing winter snows on the mountainsides. To the buckaroos, the open pastures were a metaphor for freedom, especially their own. But the Bureau of Land Management had moved its bureaucracy into place, issuing blizzards of rules and dividing the desert into fenced "fields" measured in hundreds of square miles, each to be grazed one year and rested two. The cowboys hated the system. A fence was a fence.

"Then came the trucks," former cowboss Walt Fischer lamented one night. He was a large man with a blondish moustache that drooped to his chin and thickets of whisker that stuck out at right angles. "Ranchers drive fifty miles into the backcountry and set up pens and chutes and load the cows up on trucks. Right out on the desert!" He said it as though he were cursing. "Pretty soon there won't be no more buckaroos, just teamsters. Why, you hardly ever see a chuck wagon anymore. We used to say we had two rules: we won't ride mares, and we won't ride with women."

His wife Irene grinned ruefully; she'd fought the prejudice for years. "Now," said Walt, "we don't ride much at all."

Claude Dallas had to climb off his horse or go hungry. He began hanging out at the Paradise Hill bar, nursing drinks and smiling at the ribald stories of owner George Nielsen. All his jobs seemed to be temporary. He dabbled in a fertilizer scheme, worked on a well-drilling rig, fixed machinery, drove trucks. Along with other landlocked buckaroos, he did hourly day labor. Sometimes it was semi-skilled, but often it was the kind of seasonal scut work that farmers couldn't handle themselves—or didn't want to. Wetbacks competed for the same jobs.

Still he clung to his personal work ethic. "Everything he does has to be perfect," said an admiring potato farmer. "He won't rush anything. He'll stay late on his own time till he gets it right."

Lowell Dean Taylor, a farm laborer and welder and all-around handyman, spread the word: "I'd trust that boy anywhere. I'd trust him with my daughter, my sister, my wife. He's honest down to the last nickel. When we work together he always does the lion's share."

A construction worker named Lloyd Gibbons introduced him to his daughter, Rhonda Michelle. "Claude's about as good a bunkie as you ever meet," Gibbons told friends. "Sharp, on time, always there. Quick to learn. Won't steal, never heard him tell a lie. Don't cheat, pays his bills." Gibbons added the ultimate western compliment: "When he goes through a gate he closes it."

Rhonda Michelle Gibbons was one of the few women who caught Dallas's eye; the two of them camped together once or twice. Faster females cruised Winnemucca saloons and gambling halls, but Claude seemed as uninterested as he'd been on the R&R trips as a buckaroo. He went fishing with a bartender named Mary Jo and asked his friend Irene Fischer to paint a skull for her, but that romance fizzled.

To the amusement of his friends he had a brief involvement with a peroxided tourist. "Her and her fiancé viz'ted here, and boy, did

31

she come on to Claude!" an observer reported with great glee. "Cute li'l gal name of Bonnie. She was forty 'n' looked twenty. She told Claude, 'You really intrigue me.' Old Claude, he just set there, never said a thing. A week later she come back alone and Claude took her out a few times. They got to be a short joke around here: Bonnie and Claude. Then she went home. Claude's women, he treats 'em like they was queens. I don't believe he takes any of 'em to bed, but if he does he calls 'em 'ma'am.' "

At work or play, the former cowboy packed his gun. "Claude carries even he's just driving a tractor or a truck," said a fellow farmhand. "It's a .357 magnum, and, oh, I wouldn't want him shooting it at me. He can hit a pole seventy yards away and a bottle at fifty." Some said he'd become the best shot in Paradise Valley.

Farmer Everett Miles wasn't surprised when he spotted Dallas wearing his gun while welding; he'd never seen him without one. "I'll say, What you got today, Claude? And he'll say, Oh, it's a model twenty-seven or a twenty-nine, something like that, a Smith & Wesson, a Ruger. I don't know guns myself. I think he has a forty-four magnum with black rubber grips. He owns something like twenty guns."

Dallas made some of his friends nervous with his incessant practice, mostly at human-shaped targets. "He does it the way others hit a bucket of golf balls," said one acquaintance. "He loads his own shells. Him and his friend George Nielsen, they're up on that. Don't seem to have much respect for anybody who don't know guns. I watch Claude by the hour drawing and shooting. Or he'll throw a can out, turn his back to it, then turn and keep it rolling."

Dallas began to be seen with a pair of speedloaders, used by law officers. He would fire six shots, reload in seconds, squeeze off another six, ram in the other speedloader and fire six more—eighteen rounds so fast it almost sounded like automatic fire.

Friends asked why. He said that everyone should be prepared for the future—"People with the right equipment will be able to go into the mountains and protect themselves." But he also admitted that he just loved guns. His father had given him a shotgun at age nine or ten back in the Upper Peninsula of Michigan, and he'd owned at least one firearm ever since. He'd killed his first deer soon after, and his family had been proud. George Nielsen beamed from behind his bar as Claude related the story.

Like so many older inhabitants of the Great Basin country, a sagacious Nevada rancher named Benny Damele had come to know and admire Dallas, and he developed his own theory about the ordnance. "Claude carries a gun so no one'll kick the shit outa him," Damele explained to friends. He found little agreement among the others. Dallas wasn't big, but he was wiry and strong and he'd proved his courage working cattle; surely he could take care of himself in a fight. Come to think of it though, no one had ever seen him in one.

Then a tanked-up mill hand challenged him in a bar. Dallas walked to his pickup truck and pulled out a pistol. The fight was over.

11

GEORGE NIELSEN, SALOONKEEPER and new confidant of Claude
Dallas, never tired of mentioning that Mark Twain had roamed the
area back when Paradise Hill was a stage stop in the mid-1800s.
Drivers changed horses there, and a few miles to the south the
pony express route followed the Little Humboldt River before
slanting west across the dunes.

"This old bar of mine has had two artists working on it," Nielsen told a customer. "Mark Twain wrote on it and I fucked on it."
In his raspy voice, lubricated by constant applications of Early
Times and Seven, he would provide details of his bygone sexual
gymnastics, varying from time to time. He was twice Claude Dallas's age and his memory might have been slipping. Then again, he
was an old-time storyteller, mostly about himself, and his "facts"
didn't come guaranteed.

Nielsen's own history was a little fuzzy. In his wallet he carried
a card that confirmed attendance at the University of Southern
California. His father, a contractor, had built the first two-story
building west of La Brea in Los Angeles. Nielsen told folks that
he'd first come into the Paradise country as a cattle buyer, dealing
in such big lots that he became known as "Traincar." He traveled

34

six or seven states in an old Lincoln Continental and employed a unique advertising scheme: whenever he arrived in town he would select the meanest son of a bitch around and pick a fight, thus letting everyone know that Traincar was available with his super-sweet deals. He told the unlikely story from his perch at the north end of his bar, chortling with the others. Around 1960 he was in an automobile accident and met an Irish-born nurse named Liz, married her and bought the Paradise Hill Bar. But he still enjoyed wheeling and dealing in cows—or whatever came to hand.

The Nielsens lived in a one-story white frame house on Highway 95. The adjoining bar was done in pseudo pueblo: fake rock slapped on a concrete shell. A sign at the top of a twelve-foot pole stated the establishment's entire name, BAR, in a plastic orange-and-black sign with a dim light inside. A pair of locked gas pumps advertised "regular" and "ethyl" at sixty-five cents and seventy-three cents in rusted old numbers. A stubby school bus and an aging Cadillac sedan sat in a driveway. Just north of the bar, in fenced trailer park, six or seven battered trailers squatted in t dust or the mud, depending on the season.

The proprietor was said to have been a handsome man in his youth, but age and alcohol had wrought some change. Like all men of action, he was best observed at work:

On a typical business day, he stops what he's doing to rub out a spot on the bar with a cocktail napkin dampened with gin. A flap of reddish skin hangs iguana-like from his chin almost to his collar as he peers at customers through thick black-frame glasses that seem to film his pale green eyes. His black-and-silver hair is combed back in greasy waves, '40s style. The tip of his nose is a pale purplish blue.

Perched on a stool, he wears a bartender's special white dress shirt, and below his bowling-ball belly an old pair of Levi pants is cinched tight around his waist. When he turns to reach for a bottle, the outline of an automatic pistol shows in one back pocket and a wallet in the other. Regular customers are aware that the weapon is a small Smith and that a backup automatic is under the bar. Like Claude Dallas and many other citizens of the area, the proprietor feels undressed without a touch of steel.

A tourist takes a seat at the far end of the bar and asks for a Coke, interrupting Nielsen's muted discussion with four or five customers in jeans and boots and soiled old cowboy hats raked sharply from front to back. "Pepsi all right?" he calls in his gravelly voice.

"Sure."

"Drink it here or take it with you?"

"Probably both."

"Probably both," Nielsen echoes. He seems eager to get back to the story he's been recounting to his cronies—something about pulling a Jeep out of a mudhole with a bus.

The visitor looks around. The saloon's aesthetic focus is a poster of a bare-bottomed woman flanked by fully dressed men on bar-stools. Another work of art shows a woman sectioned for butchering like a beef. A picture of a bulldog, captioned *Bullshit,* balances atop an old piano. A cigarette machine stands against one wall near a worn red-felt pool table. A jukebox is unplugged; Nielsen detests both music and pool. Electric signs blink MILLER and COORS. An attempt at hominess is provided by an antique wood stove lacking a chimney. The tile floor is spattered with Paradise Hill mud. Signs on the bathroom doors warn, CUSTOMERS ONLY. THIS MEANS YOU! A visitor comments on the signs, and a young cowboy, glancing down the bar to make sure he isn't overheard, explains:

"George is an actor. His stage is this bar and his audience is his cronies. When some poor fool walks in, George likes to say, 'Here comes some son of a bitch that wants to use the rest room. Now watch!' And he'll tell 'em you can't use it unless you buy a drink. That usually starts the fun.

"He had a lady and her family pull up in a motor home. Her husband bought a drink, so George let the kids use the toilet. When they were finished, he said, 'You folks got any disinfectant with you?'

" 'Well, no. Why?'

"Now everybody at the bar turns to watch. Act One is beginning. George says, 'Syphilitic Indians from the McDermitt Reservation urinate on the rest room floor when they're drunk. Your children have it all over their feet.' "

The cowboy can't help laughing. "That woman took those kids out and bathed their feet with iodine before she let 'em back in the

Winnebago." He snickers again. "Ol' George lived off that one for a month. *Still* tells the story."

The narrator accepts another drink and continues in his hushed voice. "George makes a bad enemy but a good friend. Do anything for you if he likes you. But don't push it! And don't pry! They got a rule around here: 'Don't stick your nose in my business and I won't stick mine in yours. *Don't even ask my name!*' If you ask a man his business, four people'll turn around and stare at you. They say, 'Stranger, you don't ask questions like that.' Right out of the 1800s! Some folks down in Winnemucca, they call it 'Robbers' Roost.' But it ain't really. Jes' a buncha boys gettin' together."

A couple of preteeners start roughhousing around the pool table, and Nielsen yells at them with such force—*"Play pool or don't play at all!"*—that they slink out the door. "Why do people bring their goddamn kids in a bar, anyway?" he asks his cronies. "What's a guy gonna think when he comes in here to pick up some pussy?"

He pours himself another Early and Seven and returns to story-telling. Fragments are audible: "I said I'd give her five dollars for a blow job. She said, 'My husband's outside in the car. He'd kill me if I did it for less'n twenty.' . . . So I said, 'I've gone to bed with two women, but I've never done it with another man and a pigmy.' . . . Coupla Indians come in. I says, 'What'll it be for you sagebrush niggers? . . .' "

After a while the proprietor separates himself from his captive audience long enough to exchange words with a newcomer he seems to know slightly:

Nielsen: "We've got the best whorehouses in the country around here."

Visitor: "How expensive are they?"

Nielsen: "It all depends on how good you are. The other day I was in one and it didn't cost a thing."

Visitor (after slight pause): "What's it cost if you're any good?"

The boys at the other end of the bar break into cackles, but George doesn't smile. He's the comedian here. He returns to his colleagues, reestablishes his authority with a couple of quips, then returns to the visitor:

Nielsen: "Well, John, how ya liking it here by now?"

Newcomer: "Tell ya the truth, George, I don't think I could live in this country."

Nielsen: "Why not? All a man can ask is a good fuck, a good steak and a drink of whiskey. We got 'em all right here." His face suggests that he is serious.

This was the man who became Claude Dallas's surrogate father and silent partner in the trapping business. For a while, no one understood the mutual attraction.

12

THE TWO MEN had met in 1970, but their friendship didn't jell till Dallas moved into Nielsen's trailer court five or six years later. Night after night they sat at the bar, the proprietor sipping his Early and Seven, Dallas nursing a beer or a soft drink. Nielsen seldom got drunk; it was a point of pride with him that others got drunk trying to keep up. Dallas didn't try.

The new friends discussed guns and horses and game wardens and the way the West was sinking into the mire of liberalism and bureaucracy. At the small Winnemucca hospital where she was head nurse, Nielsen's wife Liz began telling people, "That boy is just like a son to us." Coco Wilson had used the same words up at the Alvord.

Years later, a man who'd observed Dallas's career in Nevada said, "What Claude didn't bring to this state, George taught him." Dallas began packing a pair of pistols, one in sight and another concealed in a shoulder holster or strapped to his leg. When friends mentioned that the practice seemed unfriendly, he shrugged. Some thought he was still playing dress-up, but why did he spend so much time shooting life-size targets behind Nielsen's house and practicing quick-draw and oiling his pistols? A ranch hand claimed that he'd peeped inside Dallas's trailer and spotted gas masks and military paraphernalia. Where did they fit into playing cowboy?

In the evening he walked into Nielsen's bar like a size thirty-eight Clint Eastwood, leaning slightly to the right. Not all the patrons found him as admirable as those who knew him by his work. The proprietor's antisocial house rules seemed to suit him a little too well. "Sitting at that bar," one rancher told another, "if somebody starts talking to Claude and he doesn't want to talk, he'll just up and leave." A farmer named Jim Stevens found him likable but "cold-steel quiet." An off-duty lawman said, "Claude's attitude is, I'll tell you what I think you should know, but don't ask questions. And that don't go over with everybody."

When Dallas became animated on a subject other than guns, it was usually when government rules and regulations were being decried by the local mix of ranchers and hired hands. When he repeated his claim that he asked nothing of the public and owed nothing in return, a rare critic observed, "You went to public schools. You spend most of your time on public land. You kill public animals. You drive on public roads, and you're protected by public armed forces and police and firemen. I believe you're the most public son of a bitch I ever seen."

Such criticisms were uttered seldom and softly. The cowboys and ranchers who frequented the Paradise Hill Bar were proud of Claude and shared his views. The proudest was Nielsen. One day he confided to cronies, "Some day that boy'll kill somebody." No one took him seriously.

It wasn't long before a few of the more insightful locals began to fathom the strange attraction between the woman-shy gunslinger and the bibulous saloonkeeper who liked to brag, "I get more pussy than any man in the state of Nevada." Irene Fischer confided, "I've known George for twenty-five years. He's always saying things like, Well, shoot the so-and-so! He'd never do it himself, but he's the type who would love to see somebody else do it. An agitator. He really works on Claude. And Claude seems to like it."

Jerry Sans, congenial owner of another outpost tavern eighteen miles away in the movie-set village of Paradise Valley, made a similar evaluation. "George is a great guy, but he loves to stir shit, to get something going and then slide out of it himself. And he hates cops, hates authority." No one knew exactly why, but the way to set George off was to praise a law officer, and especially a game warden. It was plain that Dallas felt the same.

Nevada Fish and Game agents had their eyes on Nielsen and his bar but couldn't figure out how to make a case. At first the wardens had tended to agree with Jerry Sans that "Whorehouse George," as Nielsen liked to call himself, was mostly hot air, but then they began hearing reports that he was selling venison to migrant workers and giving away wild game—a fat chukar for a friend from Reno, a bobcat pelt, a double brace of quail. Word was that fresh venison was available in George's cooler. "He uses it as a gimmick," said an informant. "Winning friends and influencing people."

Late in the 1970s word went out that Nielsen was now into fur, mostly bobcat. Odd, the wardens thought. He was past sixty and had suffered a series of heart attacks. Once his buddy Claude Dallas had had to give him mouth-to-mouth behind the bar, and he'd had two or three seizures since then. Where was he getting the stamina to run traps?

It turned out that Claude Dallas had resumed an old enthusiasm. He explained to friends that he'd started trapping at the age of seven in the fur-rich Upper Peninsula of Michigan. His family had needed the fur for cash and the meat for food; with nine Dallases living on a failing dairy farm, extra provender was welcome.

From 1975, when he quit buckarooing for good, Dallas's traps were almost always set. Once or twice he ran lines across southeastern Oregon or southwestern Idaho, but mostly in Nevada. His main kill was bobcats, worth about two hundred dollars apiece at the fur auctions. He also trapped foxes and coyotes, and one night he surprised friends with a mountain lion that had dragged one of his traps through the sagebrush, finally falling off a low ledge and strangling in the chain. A former government trapper, Santy Mendieta, gave his rival a clean bill of health: "We trap the same areas, and he never bothers any of my traps and never picks up any of my coyotes. If he's not an honest man he has plenty of chances to clean me out."

In his neatly ordered trapping camps Dallas was quietly hospitable, offering tea and draping the used bag on the nearest bush, but he preferred to be seen by appointment. Few took him by surprise.

"Every time I go to see him," one cowboy told another, "he walks out of the brush from my left or my right with that same smile on his face, as though to say, 'I got you covered!'"

After a while his friends got the message. "He traps to be alone," said Walt Fischer. "That's why he works on foot, doing it the old-fashioned way, just like he does everything else."

An older trapper was puzzled by Dallas's technique or lack of it. "I can't understand the mistakes he makes. He works hard, on foot. But he saturates the mountain with traps, and when you do that, you're gonna catch what's there, period, and trapping's gonna be over in that area for a long time. It's like he's more interested in killing than he is in trapping."

The old-timer paused. "He doesn't have the ability to look at a range and say, 'If there's a cat around he'll have to cross right *there*,' and put down a trap or two and pass on to the next mountain. That's the way the long-liners work. They'll put eight hundred traps out and cover maybe three hundred miles round-trip. They'll take a week to run the line. It's hard work, skinning at night, sleeping three or four hours, then back to runnin' the line. Claude'll look at a range and say, 'I bet there's a bunch of cats up there,' and put out two hundred traps. That's his idea of trapping. He just doesn't understand.

"Another thing. I see a lot of his sets. They're carefully done, but if he moved 'em just a foot or two he'd be ninety percent more effective. I'll come on a good set with a lot of brush and rocks moved—hard work!—and there'll be a rabbit hanging over it. Well, that's illegal. He coulda moved the set two foot, put it in this cubbyhole with a legal attractor and not had to move a rock. But he doesn't understand and he won't let anybody show him. Some of the other fellas offer to go out with him, but Claude always says no, he'll do it on his own."

Dallas trapped in ranges like the Santa Rosas, Bull Runs, Snowstorms and Tuscaroras in northern Nevada and the Monitors to the south. He killed far more wildlife than he kept. Sometimes he used monofilament line to tie a sage grouse wing to a branch so that it would flutter in the breeze, the white underside catching moonlight. A curious bobcat would bat at it like a kitten and step into the trap. But so would eagles and hawks. "He doesn't use spacers," a friend explained. "Eagles and hawks have hollow compressible legs, and with spacers they don't get broke. You can throw a coat over 'em and release 'em unharmed. It's easy to obey the law, but to Claude a golden eagle's just an annoyance."

No one knew exactly when he began shooting wild mustangs for trap bait and food. For several months he lived on horsemeat while camped near a place called Council Rock. He raved about the meat and tried to talk his friends into trying it, but none wanted to risk a big fine or jail. Sometimes he would cut down a wild horse with a single rifle shot and ring the carcass with traps. It seemed a poor trade-off: a wild mustang for a couple of ratty coyote pelts. Even some of his oldest admirers shuddered at the practice. Dallas told them not to worry about it.

13

AFTER A WHILE the overworked Fish and Game agents got wind of a working arrangement between Dallas and Nielsen. "Claude hunts and traps, and George does the rest," an enforcement warden was told. "George is a benevolent guy with a lot of pals. And Claude—well, he likes to kill."

The Nevada desert was a conservationist's dream and nightmare, teeming with animals from tiny kit foxes to mule deer. Game birds abounded: pheasant, chukar, partridge, sage hens, mourning doves, quail. Hawks and eagles and vultures flew cover. But the wide open spaces were so wide and so open that a clever poacher could work unmolested. The place was made for Claude Dallas and his ground-covering stride—"forty miles a day if I run a little." His leghold traps clinked in his pack and his small brown eyes gleamed with excitement as he scratched in the dirt to make his sets.

In March 1976 Nevada F&G Agent Dale Elliot heard that an unknown trapper was working the upper end of the Simpson Park mountain range. Like most wardens, Elliot was fighting a losing battle against poaching. His beat covered 6,500 miles, and the most he could do was teach an occasional object lesson. He went into the desolate range southeast of Winnemucca and found a line of traps baited with wild mustang hair, jackrabbit fur, bones and other illegal lures. The word was that the trapper had been shooting mustangs, eating the meat and using the hide for trap bait.

The warden waited at the poacher's empty camp till a man walked up. "These yours?" Elliot asked, pointing to nine or ten traps he'd thrown into the back of his state pickup.

"They're mine," the young man answered. He introduced himself as Claude Dallas and asked what the problem was. When Elliot told him that the traps were illegal, the trapper didn't argue. But he emphatically denied shooting mustangs.

"I'm gonna have to give you a citation for baiting your traps," the warden said.

"Do I get 'em back?"

"Yeah. After you post bail." Dallas went to town, put up a hundred dollars and retrieved his equipment. Elliot wished that all violators were as reasonable.

Months later the warden encountered the soft-spoken trapper again, this time dead center in Nevada and sixty miles from the nearest town. The pine-cloaked Monitor Mountains reached to 9,000 feet and sheltered mountain lions. Variously known as panther, puma, catamount and cougar, the great tawny cat was one of the last western trophy animals for hunters. But trapping them had been illegal for years. It was too easy, and populations were down.

A trusted informant had reported that a man named Dallas had five lion pelts in his camp on Savory Creek. Dale Elliot and his partner visited the camp and came up empty, but Dallas invited them to stay for tea. The wardens noticed a greasewood bush festooned with used tea bags and marked it down as a Dallas trademark. They helped him start his sagging old pickup truck and left.

Months later a rancher recounted a conversation he'd had shortly after the tea party. Dallas had confided that he'd allowed Elliot to cite him for illegal traps only because he hadn't wanted to make trouble for the landowner. "Otherwise," said Dallas in peculiarly cool tones, "I'd have shot him." He was also quoted as saying that Elliot and the other warden were lucky they hadn't found lion pelts on their second visit or "I'd have killed them both." The rancher didn't know what to make of the strange comments.

45

Soon the loquacious George Nielsen began popping off about his own prowess with big game. He told an off-duty state trooper named George McIntosh and several other friends that he intended to take trophy animals like cougars whenever he had a chance. McIntosh warned him that he was going to be caught. "That's okay," the trooper quoted Nielsen later. "I'll just do away with the warden." Everyone laughed. Old George was blowing smoke again.

One Saturday morning Nielsen told McIntosh and several others that he and a partner had killed two lions in the nearby Owyhee Desert and sent the hides to Idaho for tanning. If anyone was interested in making a purchase, he added, he had two beautiful skins from the year before, completely rugged out. He ushered the uniformed trooper and another man into his living room and showed them the pelts of a full-grown male of about 180 pounds and a smaller female. "Fifteen hundred dollars for both," the former cattle buyer announced.

McIntosh couldn't see the required Nevada seals; usually they were crimped into the paws. Toes were missing from both hides, indicating that the animals had been trapped, another violation. McIntosh tipped the Fish and Game Department. A computer readout showed that no one named Nielsen had applied for a mountain lion tag or validated a hide.

On a warm April morning, two F&G enforcement agents drove to Paradise Hill with a search warrant. Nielsen took them inside and showed off the pelts, now serving as rugs in the living room. He said that an Idaho big-game hunter had traded him lions for guns. The intermediary was a truck driver. He didn't recall the driver's name.

"We'll have to confiscate these," one of the agents said.

Nielsen became excited. "You're not taking those lions!"

"Yes, we are."

"No, no! Those are in my house. You can't take 'em."

The wardens handed him citation number 10280 for "possession of mountain lions (2) without validation seals attached." But the Nevada tag law was flawed, and a few months later he was acquitted in Winnemucca and the rugs returned.

Within a few weeks the inside story of Nielsen's coup was told and retold to his clientele. The lions, he said, had been trapped by Claude; Nielsen had assisted by shooting one in the trap. There'd been at least five kills. Two of the soft golden pelts were east with Claude's father.

The wardens were doubly frustrated. Notoriously underpaid, they valued their jobs because they loved the wild country and detested its enemies. But in Humboldt County alone there were 11,000 square miles of desert to patrol, some as inaccessible as Nanga Parbat. When the familiar F&G trucks hove into sight, poachers yanked their traps and moved, sometimes into Oregon or Idaho, thumbing their noses at the green uniforms.

No one was surprised when Dallas began poaching in Idaho. A hot report to Fish and Game Department headquarters in Boise said that he'd shot a mountain lion near Riddle, Idaho, on the road to the Duck Valley Indian Reservation. Conservation officers were a few hours late. Later they received an anonymous call: "That guy Dallas has killed everything from lions to trophy rams to kit fox. Tell your men to be *very* careful."

Soon after, Dallas returned to Paradise Hill and began trapping on the sere flanks of the Bloody Runs. There were already two hundred trappers in Humboldt County. One more wouldn't matter.

14

ON FIRST ACQUAINTANCE Gene Weller seemed less than perfectly cast for his role as enforcement warden with the Nevada Fish and Game Department. A young thirty-five, he had warm brown eyes, neatly combed short dark hair, and a stiffly trimmed moustache that looked borrowed. By avocation he was a Sunday School teacher, by profession a fisheries biologist, but in the short-handed conservation business he mainly chased poachers. Out he went, faintly smelling of formalin and fish, to tromp Humboldt County with a .38 on his hip.

Weller was too pleased with his job to complain. He was bright and sensitive, most often described by his fellow Winnemuccans in the all-purpose phrase "a good Christian." When he spoke of wildlife and man's obligations to the birds and beasts, he sometimes sounded like an evangelist. But out in the field the visionary faded and the lawman appeared. He could walk nonstop at least as far as Claude Dallas, and did it day after day. To the poachers of northern Nevada, he was known as tough but reasonable—"not a one-way son of a bitch, like some of them agents," as one trapper put it. "But a hard man to shake." The consensus was that the Sunday School teacher was doing his impossible job as well as possible.

* * *

Weller had friends who trapped, but he'd never romanticized the craft. "There's a higher percentage of maggots among trappers," he said, "maybe because they're commercially harvesting a non-commercial resource. Hunters hunt for the sport; trappers trap to catch something to sell. They'll tell you, 'I go out there because it's a challenge to catch a bobcat.' Maybe so, but when they catch it they also peddle the pelt. That makes them . . . different."

Though he'd learned to live with it, Weller didn't like to think about the way trapped animals suffered. Nevada had a ninety-six-hour visitation law, meaning that sets had to be checked every four days, but like most conservation laws it was almost unenforceable. Nor did he like to think about certain other cruelties—for example, the way some trappers stomped on their prey to burst its heart. No matter how vigorously the wardens enforced the law, trapping remained a hard business.

At 10:00 A.M. on an unseasonably warm December day in 1978, the sometime fisheries biologist was prowling the Bloody Run hills. There was a thin crust of snow, but as the sun rose higher the footing turned sloppy. That's our weather for you, Weller said to himself. T-shirts in the daytime, parkas at night. The oldest story in the high desert. . . .

He tromped several dry gulches and found nothing untoward. In a draw east of Nate Smith's isolated potato farm, he spotted bootprints. He followed them up one canyon and down another and came to a rabbit dangling over a trap—"hanging bait," a violation.

He knelt. The trap lacked a spacer, another violation. But it wasn't tagged; there was no way to write a citation unless the poacher showed up and acknowledged ownership. Normally he would have staked out on a nearby hill, but his F&G pickup was parked in the open and gave him away. In a variation of a city cop's "street justice," he yanked the trap loose—it would cost ten dollars to replace—and pinned his business card to the rabbit. On the back he penciled, "Please contact me." A little chat might benefit both humans and wildlife.

He followed the footprints over a hill and down a fork, up a canyon, then down an arroyo in a big S. He found a second untagged and unspaced trap, then a third. Any minute he expected to come across a dead hawk or eagle. Once their legs were broken, they were finished. Altogether he found five traps, three of them

49

baited. He wrenched out the illegal equipment, left business cards and hiked out. It was 4:00 P.M. He'd been walking for six hours.

The next morning he returned. As he drove up the deserted valley road he noticed a reddish-orange Jeep ahead. He pulled off, climbed to a ledge and watched. The Jeep stopped on an alluvial fan at the mouth of the same canyon where he'd parked the previous morning. A silhouette in a high-domed trapper's hat walked toward the trapline. "Ah hah!" Weller told himself. "I've snatched the elusive trapper!" He felt a rush. This was what the long hours were all about. This was better than payday.

When the mystery man had vanished up the canyon, Weller pulled his truck alongside the old CJ-5 Jeep and waited. Noon passed, then two o'clock, then three. He was bored but didn't intend to leave. For every poacher cited, hundreds slid by. An occasional hot surveillance was good public relations. Trappers talked.

He wondered what was taking so long. In another hour or so the sun would go behind the 8,000-foot peaks. There was no place as dark as the lees of these mountains in winter. By four-thirty Weller had waited seven hours. He began to worry. The canyons were steep. He thought, It's frozen and slick up there. *Maybe the poor guy's busted his leg!*

The light flattened down from yellowish-white to violet to purple and went out. Weller radioed the sheriff's office in Winnemucca. Two old friends, Deputies Al Lyons and Noel McElhany, arrived at five-fifteen. In the high desert country, lawmen from different agencies were almost interchangeable. McElhany, a dedicated naturalist who spent most of his free time backpacking the desert, had helped the FBI arrest Claude Dallas five years earlier.

"I'd like to go up and take a look," Weller told the deputies.

Lyons called from the red Jeep, "Hey, there's a rifle in here!" He paused. "It's a .300 Savage Model 99 with a round in the chamber." Weller made a note: *Loaded weapon in vehicle.* Another violation.

Lyons fired into the air three times: the old emergency signal. There was no answer. The deputy replaced the weapon and Weller pulled the coil wire to immobilize the Jeep. The three men began picking their way up an icy old cowpath, stomping their bootprints atop the earlier ones. The dark and the silence were a little unnerving. In this agoraphobic place, the man on the high ground ruled.

In fifteen minutes they reached the first hanging bait. Rabbit, wire and card were gone. They cast their lights about but couldn't tell if the poacher's tracks continued up or turned back. Then Weller found a set several yards from the trail and parallel to it. The poacher had slipped back down the canyon.

About five hundred yards from the bottom, the tracks ended on a south-facing sidehill bare of snow. Weller was puzzled. Trapping violations called for light fines, and there were dozens of ways to beat them in the friendly local courts. "He must've sat up on the hill yesterday, watching me till it got dark," he said.

The three lawmen agreed that flight was an overreaction. Weller thought, At least he's not lying in his own blood at the bottom of a cliff. The Sunday School teacher in him was thankful for that.

They hiked back to their vehicles and the deputies drove off. Weller grabbed the Savage rifle and a Ruger Blackhawk .357 pistol and replaced the coil wire. Then he gunned his engine and left. Seven or eight miles out of the valley, he doubled back with his lights off. The Jeep was still there. He watched from the shadows for another hour and a half, but he had paperwork to do, and even if he left now he wouldn't be finished before midnight. He had logged in at 8:01 A.M. As he left the Bloody Runs he thought, Another normal day . . .

Everett Miles heard the knock around 8:30 or 9:00 P.M. He'd been taking it easy. The harvesting was done; a hardworking farmer deserved a break between seasons.

"What's the matter, Claude?" Miles asked when he saw who was there.

Dallas was breathing hard. "I want to call George," he said.

"Did the Jeep break down?" Claude had been using George Nielsen's red Jeep lately.

"Naw."

"Well, what do you need?" Like other Paradise Valley farmers, Everett Miles liked to help the young man.

"I need George to pick me up," Dallas said. "I just ran three miles down the mountain."

The good-natured Miles said he would be glad to drive him to the trailer court. En route Dallas muttered about some illegal traps in the Bloody Runs and how the wardens were lying in wait for him. He said, "Let 'em set there all night if they want to. If they want me, they know where to find me."

At nine-thirty the next morning Gene Weller pulled up on the same alluvial fan. The red Jeep was gone. All he could do was go home and wait. Eventually the poacher would try to reclaim his guns. They were worth five or six hundred dollars, a high price for a few violations that were probably unprovable anyway.

Three days later the Humboldt County sheriff's office called. "Gene?" a deputy said. "A guy here wants to talk to you about a rifle."

Weller thought, The old waiting game works again! He felt like the Maxwell Smart of the desert. He drove from his home to the sheriff's office and found a young man in the lobby kneading his hat. He said his name was Dallas and that he understood that "the Fish and Game" had two of his weapons.

Weller took a good look. It was the same silhouette, all right, but up close the kid looked more like a cleaned-up hippie than a hard-bitten poacher who would pack all that artillery into the mountains and set a line of trash traps. His short ponytail was bound so tight it pulled his hair away from his forehead. Underneath his lightly tinted glasses his eyes looked small and dark. He wore high-heeled boots, jeans, and a shirt that looked like one of Eddie Bauer's chamois-skin specials: $19.95 apiece, the garment of preference for ranchers and dudes alike.

The young man stared, then tilted his head and smiled. Weller relaxed. The guy didn't look like the new breed of mad-dog hermits. There'd been a few Charlie Manson clones around lately, and once in a while they shot someone just to relieve the boredom.

"Can I get my guns back?" Dallas asked.

"Let's sit down first," Weller answered. They went into an interrogation room, where he expected to administer the Miranda warning and a lecture on the law, then listen to the poacher's tale of woe and turn him loose. There wasn't much else that could be done without a little help from Dallas. He couldn't be connected to the unmarked traps, and the loaded-gun charge was a joke in a county where guns were as common as magpies.

Weller got a surprise. The accountant wasn't in a confessional mood. Yes, he'd been in the Bloody Runs the other day, but only to look for a place to trap. How would he know anything about illegal sets?

Weller was irked by the lie, but more so by the smirk. "I don't understand you, Dallas," he said. "I was raised by the system that if you were caught with your hand in the cookie jar, you took your slap and were more careful the next time."

"Nobody caught me with my hands in a cookie jar."

"We found your traps and your tracks and your guns."

Dallas stared behind his wire-rimmed glasses. The lenses were clear now. Pretty fancy for a trapper. But then so was the rest of the outfit. You didn't see many trappers in chamois shirts. "You know, Claude, I'm really disappointed in you," Weller said. "I don't understand anybody who acts like you're acting."

Dallas said in that same soft voice, "Can I have my guns back?"

Weller thought, It's like a game to him. He knows that I know and I know that he knows and he knows that I know that he knows, *but he's not gonna talk.* Well, that's what the Miranda says: "You have the right to remain silent."

A change of approach was in order. No game warden could hope to keep up with a poacher like Dallas in the badlands of northern Nevada. An image of the Snowstorm range crossed his mind; the only way in was on horseback, and nine days out of ten the trail was too muddy or icy. Snowstorm trappers laughed at the law and picked sage hen from their teeth. And the Snowstorms were just one range of many.

He decided that the best way to protect the local wildlife from this cold little man was to appeal to his pride and his conscience. "You could trap legally and do just as well," he began. He mentioned some techniques that Dallas hadn't known, judging by his sets. He ended his little instructional on a semijocular, semifriendly note: "Hey, look, Claude, I got enough problems out there without having to worry about you. You can be legal and be a good trapper. *So do it!* Get off my back!" It was an approach that worked more often than not, especially when accompanied by a soft ecclesiastical smile.

Dallas said, "If I have any bad traps in the Bloody Runs—which I don't—give me a week and I'll clean 'em up. In one week you won't find a bad trap set in those mountains."

Weller offered his hand. "It's a deal."

As the poacher was signing for his rifle and pistol, he turned to Weller and said, "You're welcome in my camp—"

"Well, thanks."

"—on one condition. Leave your badge outside."

Not long afterward, the Paradise Hill Bar buzzed with news of the incident. "Claude said he won't be caught again," one of the regulars told another. "He emphasized that. He will *not* be caught again."

15

GENE WELLER ENCOUNTERED the young trapper several more times and was pleased to see that he was polite, even friendly. One night he visited the warden's home to have some bobcats tagged, and apologized for his lateness. On balance, Weller thought, he seems decent enough. Most poachers were so set in their Mesozoic ways that they would still be hanging bait in the hereafter if they could get their hands on a No. 3 trap and some rabbit fur. But Dallas appeared capable of change, well worth the time spent on his case. This was the positive side of the job, turning someone around before it was too late.

Others thought they detected a capped volcano. At the bar one night Dallas mused, "It'd be fun to be on the run, going from one cache of weapons to the next and fighting it out." He gave the impression that his caches were already prepared.

Another trapper ran into him at a cattle camp and couldn't get away fast enough. "It was the way he talked, the way he handled his gun," the man confided. "He spooked me good."

An Idaho warden named Bill Pogue wrote a note on the back of a business card and left it in the screen door of a trapping cabin

Dallas had frequented. According to Dallas, the note said simply, *I'll check on you later.*

He reacted angrily. "That's a hell of a way to introduce yourself," he complained.

His attitude toward game wardens was making some of his best friends edgy. Farmer Everett Miles told his wife, "Claude seems to have a thing about game wardens. I think he might be dangerous to them." Mrs. Miles agreed.

At a fur sale in Winnemucca a Fish and Game official named Terry Crowforth took a good look at the man who'd kept his department so busy. "Mr. Dallas was in a large group laughing," Crowforth reported later, "joking and carrying on, which was out of character. When I was called to the group to answer a technical question, Mr. Dallas observed my badge, became sullen, quiet, and left the group."

Dallas visited Walt and Irene Fischer in their little frame home in Paradise Valley. Over dinner, they leafed through catalogues to select a new hunting rifle for Irene. Claude had an encyclopedic knowledge of the subject and had a favorite weapon all picked out for his friend. The conversation turned to the Bureau of Land Management and its fences and "fields" that were changing the cattle business. The three old friends were of one mind: the range-cattle business was doomed.

Claude mentioned that maybe it was time for Walt to buy a new rifle, too. "Why?" the rangy cowpoke asked. "The way the hunting's going, pretty soon there won't be anything to shoot at."

"Well," said Claude, "shoot a BLM man!" The host and hostess laughed politely.

He went driving with his friend Benny Damele. When they reached an area of volcanic rocks and rubble, Dallas commented, "That would be a good place to hide." As they passed a cave he said, "You could hide in there for a long time." After a third such remark, the rancher turned and asked, "Claude, why play hide-and-seek when nobody's it?"

Dallas didn't answer. To Damele, he seemed lost in a world of his own, a world of unreality. But a great kid all the same.

16

By THE END of the 1970s, Claude Dallas seemed more restive than ever. A pickled prankster stole his trapper's hat and he turned white with rage and frustration, causing a friend to observe, "That hat's abnormally important to him." He worked hard on his traps but sometimes pulled his lines to go off on trips and tangents. He canoed a few wild rivers and backpacked into the Owyhee Desert. The boys at the bar thought he might be getting ready to pull up stakes. But where next? When they inquired about his plans, he said the Paradise Valley was the finest place in the world and he would never leave. Every day he sounded more like George Nielsen.

In the summer of 1979 he headed north to float a river in the Yukon with his friends. Just on the U.S. side of the border, Claude ducked into the woods while the others cleared Customs with their canoes and camping equipment. A mile into Canada they picked up Claude and his armload of contraband guns.

On the trip, he shot a Dall sheep, breaking several Canadian laws in the process. It wasn't his first mountain sheep; he'd killed others in the United States. His campmates joked that he was poaching his way to the prestigious Grand Slam, which required record-class heads from four different kinds of sheep. Dallas seemed proud.

Back home in Nevada, he resumed his trapping, sometimes across state lines. An Idaho rancher reported that a bearded young man with a ponytail was trapping out of season a few miles north of the Nevada border. By the time the understaffed Fish and Game Department arrived to investigate, the route into Dallas's camp had been closed by the spring thaw. What had been true in Nevada was now proving true in southern Oregon and Idaho. The poacher held the cards.

In the 1979–80 season, Dallas trapped out of George Nielsen's yellow school bus. He drove the old Ford bus so far into a canyon that it looked as though it would have to be abandoned, but friends pulled him out with their four-wheel-drive vehicles. Good old Claude, they said. Who else would get into a pickle like that—and out of it?

His reputation as an eccentric began to spread, encouraged by George Nielsen and his friends at the bar. The colorful local trapper was pointed out to tourists, who tried to draw him out with little success. To his friends, he seemed more misanthropic than ever, especially toward anyone who showed emotion or got hurt or appeared weak. He called them "leppys" or "those leppy son of a bitches." Leppys were rejected calves that ran around bawling; he'd never been known for his sympathy for them or any other animal. No one was sure if he'd always felt this way about humans and had kept it concealed, or if it was something new.

"The only folks he was cordial to, the only folks he allowed out to visit him in his camps, was us old friends," one of them said, "and he was really using us as packhorses. He'd say, 'Did you bring stamps and envelopes? Did you bring cartridges?' He never asked if we brought food because we *always* brought food. We had standing orders to drop by the Nielsens' before visiting Claude in camp. George and Liz would load us up. Everybody thought old Claude was some kind of mountain man living off jerked venison, but he loved his cake and pie."

Dallas stepped into the role of mountain man as comfortably as he'd stepped into the role of buckaroo ten years earlier. In some ways the title seemed to fit. Except for his sweet tooth he seemed to be an ascetic. He'd drunk nothing but grapefruit juice since blowing a winter's income in one night of boozing and gambling in Elko a few years before. A friend heard him say, "All the good buckaroos I know are either dead or alcoholics." He seemed strong, tough, impervious to extremes of heat and cold. He dug a hunter out of a snowy canyon and accepted the gift of a portable heater in return, but as far as his friends could tell, it remained a decoration, like the unused stove in George Nielsen's bar.

"He doesn't acknowledge discomforts," said a Winnemuccan who'd known him for ten years. "He's always trying to toughen himself up. He'll walk ten miles for groceries, rest a minute and walk back. He sleeps on the floor of his trailer. He'll refuse lunch—he'll say, 'I don't need it. I ain't worked a lick today.' He's cheap. His grapefruit juice always ends up on your tab. He told me he's going north and needs a grubstake. He likes books about Alaska and the Yukon, especially Jack London and Zane Grey, and he reads each one four times. I guess that's gonna be his next adventure. Is he a genuine old-time mountain man? Well, no, but he's trying."

Nielsen and the Paradise Hill regulars talked up their folk hero, his ability to prowl the desert in sandstorm and hail and never get lost, and his philosophical disdain for comfort. They said he was the best trapper in the whole I-O-N country; he thought like a bobcat and sold more hides than anyone. One year, they said, he turned ten thousand dollars in the short season—thirty-five cats at three hundred dollars per.

Former government trapper Santy Mendieta disputed the claims. "I ran into him at the Winnemucca fur auction and he had fourteen cats," said the old Basque. "He told me that was his total for the season. Some folks say he sends hundreds of pelts to Seattle, but I never heard that from Claude. He doesn't brag." The veteran trapper added, "Claude will be a good trapper in time. He enjoys it. All he needs is a little encouragement and help."

With Dallas trapping full-time, there were ugly confrontations. He showed strong territorial instincts, treating certain public lands and wildlife as personal property. Two veteran trappers laid lines in the Bloody Runs—it was all BLM land—and Dallas yanked them several days running. They dropped into the Paradise Hill Bar and instructed George Nielsen, "Tell your trapper to leave our sets alone."

The proprietor peered through thick glasses. "I don't have a trapper," he said. "I don't know what you boys are talking about." The discussion grew heated, and the partners went off to find the law.

Over coffee, Gene Weller told them, "Dallas is a strange case. For one thing, he's always armed." He leaned across the table and lowered his voice. "I don't think he'd hesitate to snipe you off a ridge. Leave Claude Dallas to us."

Other complaints came in. There was a tip that Dallas had taken bighorn sheep in the Deep Creek drainage of Idaho. He was said to have killed a mountain lion and two cubs in central Nevada. Several informants swore they'd seen him shoot wild mustangs on the Owyhee Desert.

Late in 1980 Weller and his fellow warden Rick Davidsaver decided that the bloodbath had to be stopped whatever the cost in manpower and money. The word around Paradise was that the mountain man planned to add to his fame by wintering alone in the wilds of southern Idaho. When he came back, Nevada would be ready.

17

It was an excited group of men who piled into the three over-loaded vehicles and lumbered out of Paradise Hill toward the terra incognita of the Owyhee Desert, seventy miles away if they'd been crows but more like a hundred by the bumpy route they were forced to take. No one had greater expectations than a farmer named Jim Stevens. He'd finished the year-end chores on his 1,800 leased acres near Winnemucca and sorely needed a break. What better way than to help a friend set up camp?

Not that old Claude ever lacked for helpers. Half the crowd at George Nielsen's bar would have dropped everything to spend a few days in the open with "the mountain man." Stevens didn't necessarily buy the description, but his fifteen-year-old son Scott thought so much of Claude that it bordered on hero worship.

Personally, Stevens preferred to deal with Dallas one-on-one rather than with the drinkers at the Paradise Hill Bar. The Stevens family was from Idaho, but most of the barroom habitués were Nevadans. Jim was a potato farmer, a "spud person," while the others were mostly cattlemen, or claimed to be. Stevens was sensitive about such things. Folks in Paradise had welcomed farmers in good years, but now profits were declining and the locals complained that all they got out of the farmers was five hundred wetbacks at harvest time. Spud people were respected up in Idaho, where your license plate said FAMOUS POTATOES even if you drove a Rolls.

Claude and Jim had met four years before, when the farmer was running a combine and Dallas was driving a truck. Dallas had mentioned that he liked to trap. Stevens had a hayseed look and manner, with bulging brown eyes and dark hair worn well above the ears, but he was a business graduate of Idaho State University, a sometime schoolteacher, a Boy Scout leader, and an open-minded man who was curious about many things, including the way his fellow men earned a living. He asked some questions about trapping but soon realized that Dallas was putting him off with yep, nope, and maybe. This guy, he decided, will take a while to know.

The snap judgment proved out. Each time the two men ran into each other at the Paradise Hill Bar, Claude thawed a degree or two. They spent hours commiserating about the fading potato and cattle markets. By 1978 they'd become friends, not exactly "ass-hole buddies" in the local terminology, but close enough to share a few secrets.

Of course Stevens knew about the poaching—everyone at the bar did—but he rationalized it. Everyone did that, too. "Claude shoots bucks, not fawns or does," he explained to a friend. "I've seen him come in with two antelope and four deer. Now, dang it, that's a little greedy, but he gives the meat away. He told me, 'People are always doing nice things for me and this is the only way I can pay 'em back.' "

One day Claude asked Jim and Sandra, his wife of seventeen years, to help wrap venison. They wrapped for hours; neither of the Stevenses had ever seen so much illegal meat. Dallas seemed to get a kick out of killing. He raved about a book on African hunting and gave Jim a copy, but the potato farmer couldn't get through it. "All those dead elephants," he told Sandy. "It makes me sick."

In the fall of 1980 Dallas confided to Stevens that he planned to hole up in the nearby mountains if an enemy ever occupied the United States; he had five thousand rounds of ammunition and a stash of survival tools. The two men had long discussions about law and lawmen; Claude respected neither. He was resentful about taxpaying. Jim wasn't happy about taxes either, but he explained that with no taxes there would be no government. "That'd be perfect," said Claude. "No government, nobody to bother me, nobody snooping around my camps." He sounded as though he might be talking about game wardens again.

It occurred to Stevens that Claude might have a touch of paranoia, but it had been a long time since he'd taken college psychology and he didn't feel qualified to judge. He had a vague idea that Claude was weak in one of the three personality components he'd learned about in school—the ego, the superego and the id—but he'd forgotten which was which. There was no doubt that George Nielsen was a strong influence, with all his bluster and bull. If Claude was a real paranoiac, then inflammatory rhetoric like Nielsen's could only make him worse.

One day the two friends ran Claude's trapline together, and Jim reported to his wife, "Claude saw cat tracks crossing a road and he could tell the cat passed through yesterday afternoon. He showed me a bare spot in the snow and said, 'The sun woulda melted that spot around noon, and the cat walked through it. If you look in his track, there's a little dirt in his paws.' I asked him how he knew it wasn't the day before yesterday. He said it'd been storming in the Bloody Runs the day before. He keeps track of the weather and everything else. A trapper has to know the dangdest things!"

Now it was Wednesday, December 3, 1980, and they were on their way to another Dallas trapping adventure: three months in the Owyhee Desert. He'd floated the Owyhee River the year before and admired a place called Bull Basin. It was five or six bonecracking hours from Paradise by four-wheel drive. Claude described it as "maybe the most remote place in the United States, as far away as you can get." His eyes gleamed as he said it.

Jim's own eyes had gleamed when he read up on the place. Bull Basin had been abandoned since the late 1800s. For years the Tuscarora Mountain miners had wintered cattle on the flats by the river. Ore freighters had changed oxen at Bull Camp; rusty bullshoes and hand-wrought square nails were buried in the sand. Indians had roamed the region before the miners, and prehistoric man before the Indians. Broken pots from a cave had been carbon-dated to 10,000 B.C.

The scholarly farmer had a collection of arrowheads and other artifacts: boxes and boxes from Paiutes and Shoshones, Snakes and Bannocks and Washos, maybe a thousand specimens altogether. There were heavy pressures in his business, notably the pressure not to go under like one of his potatoes, and collecting helped him unwind. Both Jim and Sandra Stevens enjoyed history, but he preferred tickling his history from the soil with a metal detector and other specialized gear like shovels and rakes and trowels. On an average day he could figure on one find per hour: utensils, buttons, arrowheads, a rare axhead or hammerhead. When Dallas told him that there were deserted rock cabins at Bull Camp and not a decent road for miles, he couldn't wait to go.

The six of them drove steadily northeast: George Nielsen, Nielsen's grown son Randy, old Frank Gavica from Paradise Valley, a young fence-builder named Craig Carver, and the two friends Dallas and Stevens. A small bus and a pickup truck were loaded with tents, tarps, traps and provisions; Nielsen's Chevy Suburban station wagon pulled a trailer with two borrowed mules in it. Jim thought, Who but Claude would trap with mules? Isn't that pure Claude?

Dallas had prepared himself for the winter's trapping with self-inflicted privations, including a few that seemed capricious. He'd refused salt for months "so I won't have the craving in camp," but it seemed to Jim that he could have carried three months' needs in one pocket. He'd turned down free potatoes because the crop had been sprayed, and bought expensive items at a health food store in Winnemucca. He'd grown a beard for warmth and practiced sleeping on the floor. No wonder folks called him the mountain man!

After an hour or so the expedition passed the natural-gas pumping station near Greeley Crossing and began following the pipeline northeast toward the Owyhee River. They soon ran out of good dirt road. Parts of the desert were pockmarked with badger digs and prospect holes. Jim imagined the work that had gone into each new search for gold, silver, antimony, lead, zinc, opals, manganese, nitrates, diatomaceous earth, the jackpot minerals of the Great Basin. How many earnest young men had mistaken the smell of alkali for the smell of gold and left behind their chalky skulls as playgrounds for the ants and mice? The I-O-N country had lured footloose Civil War veterans looking for a stake, homeless husbands waiting to send for the family, runaway slaves and deserters, vagabonds and dreamers and hustlers and fools—and sent most of them home broke or boxed or both.

Jim sensed the bygone presences as he peered out the window of the little bus at the clouds streaming off the Santa Rosa peaks like pennants. He wondered if he and Claude and the others would ever reach Bull Basin and what they would find when they got there. On most of the route there were no indications that man had ever existed: no markers, no corner posts, no fences, just miles and miles of volcanic ruins and sage. A stray cow with xylophone ribs blinked from atop a crumbling ridge. Jackrabbit ears popped up like semaphores. Stevens watched and wondered where the hell they were.

Just before dark, the trail died in sagebrush and finely ground geological rubble. Claude and Randy Nielsen signaled the station wagon and bus to stop and drove ahead to scout. They returned in Randy's pickup with bad news. The expedition had penetrated almost to Don and Ed Carlin's "45" ranch. They would have to double back in the morning.

They camped at a livestock water reservoir while coyotes yipped like Indian scouts. Dallas fed and hobbled the mules. Then everyone assembled in the school bus. A bottle materialized, followed by a few stories and a couple of George Nielsen's ribald jokes. The temperature dropped; Claude said he smelled a storm. One by one the men fell silent in their sleeping bags.

It was snowing when they reached their destination late in the morning. Jim looked out and saw that they had stopped on a rim above a canyon. Not a minute too soon, he said to himself. For the last few miles the bus had bounced so hard that its springs had lost their zip.

He squeezed his top-heavy frame through a door built for schoolchildren. Claude was already out, batting at snowflakes and grinning behind his darkening light-sensitive glasses. "Ain't this sumpin'?" he asked.

At first Jim saw the same old sights. Low desert hills. Sage, greasewood, bitterbrush. Rust-colored earth turning dirty gray in the snow. Lava buttes in the distance and a top line of mountains behind them in the haze.

His excitement grew as he walked toward the rim with the others. He might never again see a place like this. He remembered the forbidding notations on the maps: "numerous potholes," "reservoir (dry)," "no vehicle crossing," "no water," "dry lake," "danger." He remembered something that the Canadian explorer Peter Skene Ogden had written: "A more wretched country Christian Indian or Brute ever traveled over or more will." But that was exactly the point. That was what had preserved the Owyhee Desert. He couldn't wait to unearth its mysteries, one arrowhead at a time.

He reached the edge and looked down. The river had carved out a basin a mile or two long. To north and south the rushing water poured through rocky gorges, but here, just briefly, it bubbled and gurgled across sagebrush meadows. The place was a natural corral, an amphitheater, sheltered from the winds and storms. He saw two small structures, but no trace of a road or trail. He thought, I've been dreaming about this all my life. . . .

Claude was busy with a fractious mule. He'd always had problems with animals. The older men, Gavica and Nielsen, decided to stay on top while the others packed loads into camp. Jim and the two younger men, Randy Nielsen and Craig Carver, hefted backpacks and followed an old wagon trail that angled down off the rim. One of the maps had shown an altitude difference of seven hundred feet between rim and river, and a horizontal distance of a mile. It didn't shape up as much of a hike, but the cutbank off the top was steep. Jim was six one, weighed 225, and he'd gone a little soft in the two months since harvest. He wondered how Claude would get his tents and equipment back up the hill when the trapping season was over; the mules couldn't haul everything. He wouldn't want to be on that trip.

He passed a wooden axle poking through the snow cover. He thought, That must have been a runaway years ago. I'll bet it tore up the whole wagon. A chukar flushed. A deer splashed across the river in water up to its withers.

When he reached the bottom he saw two rock cabins across the river, both open to the sky, the larger one with walls intact, the smaller crumbling. Claude had said something about stretching aluminum tent poles across one of the roofs and moving in. A wind-blasted wagon wheel leaned against a wall; it could have come off the northbound freighter to Boise or Butte a century before. He wished he had a metal detector, his "coin shooter," but that would have to wait till next time. My God, he thought, Sandy and the kids will swear I'm lying. . . .

Just before they headed back to town, Gavica confided that he didn't feel right about leaving Claude. "His camp isn't even set up," the old man said. Boxes of food and equipment were stacked on the rim; Dallas planned to pack them down in the next few days. "And this storm's getting worse," Gavica added.

George Nielsen said, "Nobody ever has to worry about Claude Dallas."

Jim took Claude aside and told him how fascinated he was with Bull Camp. "Then come back," Claude said. "I'll be needing a few things. You can bring 'em in." He hesitated. "Maybe you can camp here a few days." The two men shook on it. As the caravan moved out, Jim looked back and saw his friend waving. It was snowing harder. Claude looked small.

There was no news for a few weeks. Then Nielsen and Gavica returned from a supply trip and reported that things were progressing at Bull Camp. Claude had "hung up some camp meat"—a euphemism for killing deer—and was already trapping bobcats even though the Idaho season didn't open for a month. He and George had promised Liz a fur coat.

Just before the Christmas holidays, a Department of Motor Vehicles agent named Duane Michelson drove his teenage daughter in for an overnight adventure, stopping first at Nielsen's to make the obligatory pickup of provisions and extra gear for the mountain man. Michelson described himself as a "truck cop," a job equivalent to a state trooper's, and he and Dallas had come to know each other through guns and shooting. Just for fun, he'd brought a pistol with him.

When he returned to Winnemucca, the lawman told mutual friends that Claude had made some odd statements. He was living in a tent on the west side of the river and said he wished he'd pitched camp elsewhere because he felt he was being watched. He said the location made him feel "down in a hole," and added, "Someone could roll a rock on me." Michelson figured his friend had seen too many westerns.

Otherwise old Claude seemed to be keeping well. He'd packed in a small heater and the tent was cozy and warm. He said he thought he would last the winter. Then no one heard from him for a while.

18

DALLAS HADN'T BEEN wrong about being watched. Around the time of the Michelson visit, Don Carlin and his son Eddy J. had been hunting coyotes above Bull Camp. They reined up on the east edge and saw a tent below.

The Carlins were concerned. Their 45 ranch headquarters was twelve miles north, and Bull Basin was on their winter range. All the surrounding land, thousands of square miles, was owned by the people and administered by the BLM, but like most open-range cattlemen the Carlins treated their allotments as though they owned them. In bad weather they sheltered cows in Bull Basin. When the water holes went dry on the mesa, they herded their stock to the river, the "live water." Bull Basin was vital to their cattle operation, and there were gates that needed opening and shutting.

Don and Eddy J. Carlin also trapped. At two hundred dollars a pelt, there was three or four times as much net profit in a bobcat as there was in a steer. On January 9, when the Idaho season opened, they intended to make their sets.

For years the Carlins had been drawn to the Owyhee Desert. Don, a heavy-equipment operator from Snake River country, and his son Eddy had recently leased the 45 and run in 220 head of cattle: purebred Durhams and Herefords and desert-thriving crosses like Limousin bulls on Durham cows. They had only 250 acres of deeded ground but 200 square miles of BLM allotment. Ranch foreman Eddy and his bride Joann planned to spend the rest of their lives in the little house where the South Fork met the East Little Owyhee River. But everything had to break just right.

As father and son sat their horses above Bull Basin, Eddy aimed his .25–06 rifle at the tent. Through the scope he could see a bearded man almost a mile away. He couldn't be anything but a trapper. Eddy was twenty-eight and he'd been coming to these parts for half his life, but this was the first winter camp he'd ever seen in the basin. To his knowledge the place had been deserted since the last Tuscarora drover had pulled out in 1885.

His father said, "You'd think the guy would've stopped in to say hello, maybe found out where we're gonna run our lines this year."

"He knew where we was," Eddy said angrily. "We're on every map." Not long before, he'd turned some cows into the basin and someone had run them out and locked the gate. Maybe there was a connection. He decided to pay the camp a visit.

Nearly two weeks went by before he got a chance to saddle up for Bull Camp. On the morning of New Year's Eve, December 31, 1980, he rode south, following the river upstream. Directions could be confusing around the 45. The Owyhee and its branches flowed north; going upstream meant traveling south toward the Nevada border. Summer kayakers and canoeists who thought all rivers flowed down the map sometimes got twisted around.

It was four hours of hard riding to Bull Basin, in and out and up and down, but the skies were clear and Eddy didn't mind. Most days he rode till dark, fifty or sixty miles, nursemaiding moony-eyed calves that didn't have the sense God gave a stick. He was a big man on a big horse, six feet and 190 pounds on a 1,200-pound Appaloosa, and he'd strapped on his Ruger Security 6. He didn't usually carry a gun, but he thought it might be wise.

When he reached the rim above Bull Basin, his eyes were drawn to a bright orange tarp in one of the crumbling rock cabins. A pair of mules grazed on the slope. One seemed to be picketed.

He urged his horse Danny across a shallow barranca and down a faint trail that zigzagged toward the flats north of the campsite.

The river came up to the Appaloosa's knees. In the ruins of the smaller rock cabin Eddy saw a deer head against a wall. In the larger cabin he lifted a plastic orange tarp and found two small deer hanging like beef in a market. That made three deer in all; he wondered why anyone would kill more than one at a time when they were so abundant. He also spotted a sawbuck packsaddle, a stock saddle and some packing gear and bags.

After a while he recrossed the river for a closer look at the tent. Several stretching boards and a flushing board leaned against an outer wall. On the other side of the tent an unturned bobcat hide was on another stretcher. A deer's hind leg hung from a corner post; someone was slicing meat as needed.

Ten feet away, the turned hide of a bobcat was spread across a greasewood bush. Eddy was surprised. The Idaho season didn't open for nine more days and the turned pelt looked at least a week old. Folks got careless this far from town, but jumping the season by two weeks was unfair. He took another look at the pelts. They represented four hundred dollars that the 45 would never see when the season opened, and they'd been poached in his own backyard.

He wished that Bill Pogue was here. The conservation officer's district was up north, but he took a personal interest in the Owyhee Desert and dropped in often, usually unannounced. The Carlins believed in game laws, but that hadn't kept Pogue from slapping Eddy's father with a citation for untagged traps, a minor offense in the outback but one that the superstrict warden had refused to overlook.

Eddy thought, Where's Pogue now that somebody's turning our canyon into a butcher shop? He considered a trip to the nearest phone, but this far out a man was supposed to take care of his own problems. Anyone who'd read Louis L'Amour knew that.

He wanted to check the tent, but it was tied shut. He heard a droning noise and looked up. A light plane circled the camp and flew back toward Nevada. He wondered what *that* was all about. The 45 had once been described as the most remote ranch in the United States, but the whole Owyhee was turning into downtown Boise. The other day he'd seen chukar hunters on the bluff. Five hours in and five hours out to shoot birds. He thought, Those dadgum new pickups are making things easy that ought to be hard.

A splash made him look up. One of the mules bore down on him like a mare in heat. It nuzzled him, blinking sappy brown eyes like

70

an inhabitant of the Saturday morning cartoons. Eddy tried to shoo it off, but it stood fast. His horse Danny was an easygoing gelding—"plumb absolutely gentle" was the way Eddy usually described him—but the muscles in his flanks were twitching. Any second now, one mule was going to be kicked into the next canyon.

Eddy spurred his horse to the east side of the river, and the mule followed. A few well-placed rocks had no effect. He headed north toward home at a trot. The stubborn animal would give up before long.

A few hundred yards downstream the mule was still nose-to-tail with Danny when Eddy spotted a man walking south on the camp side of the river. He had a tight ponytail, a full beard and a rolling walk. He carried a small green pack, a pistol in a holster, and a rifle cradled across his left arm. Eddy reined up and waited till they were abreast. Then he called across the ripples, "How do you get rid of a mule you don't want?"

The man stared. From fifty feet away he looked anything but friendly. Eddy ended the High Noon staredown by urging Danny across the river. "Who was in that plane?" the man asked. It wasn't as much a question as a demand.

"Dunno for sure," Eddy answered. "Maybe the BLM." He introduced himself and explained what he'd been doing.

The stranger said, "I'm—" then interrupted himself before a name came out. "I'm Dallas," he said.

Eddy recognized him now and wondered if he'd been recognized in return. Two years before, he'd run into the man at a cow camp called Star Valley, ten miles west near the Oregon-Idaho border. Dallas had given the impression of being short-fused and itchy-fingered. Last year Eddy's father had encountered him at the same place. "The season ends in January, but he's still trapping in March," Don Carlin had reported when he got home. "I started talking to him about trapping and he said, 'I don't think it's anybody's business in the world where I trap or when I trap.' He was armed and he made me uneasy. He's just a guy you don't color to cater to."

Eddy was surprised when Dallas invited him into his tent for tea. He hobbled Danny while the trapper went to the river for water. When he returned, the two men chatted about Bull Basin. Close up, Eddy saw that the small rifle had an old-fashioned look

71

to it, like a centennial model. Inside the tent he noticed a heavier rifle and a shotgun. Dallas mentioned that he'd canoed the South Fork the previous spring and decided to come back to Bull Basin for some winter trapping. Eddy blurted out, "That's a nice bobcat you got outside."

"Yep," Dallas said, pouring tea. His dark glasses were clearer now. "That cat thinks it's January ninth, and don't you tell him different."

Behind his lenses, he didn't appear to be smiling. He said that he liked to take his cats when their coats were prime. He also said that he kept his venison in sight because he wanted ranchers to know it wasn't prime beef. Something about him made Eddy uneasy. There was no warmth to him. He was Peter Lorre in jeans.

They talked about trapping in Canada and Alaska, and Dallas said he was heading north for good in June. As they talked, Eddy found himself peeking at the revolver. It was square-cut, stainless, maybe a .38 or .357. As a trap pistol, it would have torn a pelt in half. He thought back to their first meeting, Dallas washing dishes at Star Valley, a heavy gun on his belt. He thought, A man who carries a weapon like that must be thinking about larger game. Out here, who would know?

He was afraid his nervousness was showing. When Dallas stood up, he stood up. When Dallas moved, he moved. Early that morning, Joann had said, "That son of a gun, you just go down there and tell him to leave!" Strong language for her. But the custodian of all this weaponry didn't look that easy.

Eddy decided to drop a hint. He mentioned that Fish and Game agents came into the area each year and checked everyone. "You can just about figure they know you're in here, and they'll probably be in to check you before the winter's over."

"All right," Dallas said calmly. "I'll be ready for them." Eddy took that to mean he would hide his kills.

They got around to the delicate subject of territory and spent a half hour working out an agreement: Dallas would run his lines north to Coyote Springs, more area than anyone could trap effectively on foot. Eddy wondered how the deal would be enforced. "You know," Dallas said as though he were a mind reader, "I'm not a government man. I don't believe in law enforcement. If we have any trouble over trapping, it'll be personal trouble. I don't believe in man-made laws."

At last Eddy understood. That's where the guns came in.

Riding out of the basin, he couldn't believe how twitchy he felt. He was built on the order of one of his own Durham bulls and Dallas would have been a pushover in a fight, but he sensed that it wouldn't come to that. It would come to a bullet fired from a hilltop, a house-burning, an ambush—something sudden and silent, over as soon as it started. That's the impression Dallas gave— not tough, but mean. Eddy remembered characters like that in cowboy stories. They were called renegades. He thought they were out of the bloodlines by now.

As his lathered horse worked his way up the steep bank, he tried to piece out what kind of a man would never be seen without a gun. He thought, Maybe he's scared, but he don't talk scared. Scared men are dangerous, especially the ones that're scared so deep they don't even know it themselves.

And yet the guy was out here in winter on foot, by choice, just him and a couple of mules. Nothing scared about that. Poaching wasn't new to the Owyhee Desert, and he'd been right up front about it. He had guts and he was no hypocrite. You had to give him that.

When Eddy told Joann about the meeting, she said, "Eddy, I don't want that creep up there." He thought, She's all alone in the dadgum sticks while I'm riding. She's got a right to be upset.

"Well, he's not a guy you want to fool with," he replied.

Joann seemed surprised. "You're not gonna run him off? You're . . . afraid of him?"

"Well—"

"He must be something if he scares *you.*"

"He's somethin', all right," Eddy said. Then he told her he'd had enough Claude Dallas for one day and they dropped the subject.

The operators of the 45 soon ran into other problems. They thought they had a territorial agreement with a couple of Oregon long-liners, Don Carter and Sam Shaver, but four days after the meeting with Dallas they found Carter-Shaver traps north of the ranch house. To make matters worse, the sets were baited with sage hen. Don Carlin told his son, "We gotta do something or the wardens'll think it's us." One encounter with Bill Pogue was enough.

Eddy's nightmare was coming true; the 45 was turning into the hub of the universe. Dallas was a serious enough problem, but Carter had been a government trapper and knew the business backward; he and his partner could lay two or three hundred traps and wipe out the local fur for years to come. And that might turn the Carlin operation belly-up.

The nearest phone was fifty-five miles across broken terrain, in the home of an Indian friend named Delbert Jim. It was a jolting two-hour drive to the village on the Duck River Indian Reservation. Father and son arrived around ten Sunday night and phoned the warden.

19

DEE POGUE KNEW the signs. A handsome woman of not quite fifty with straight straw-colored hair, she listened to Bill's end of the conversation. "Trappers?" he was saying into the phone. "Sage hen parts? Near the 45? . . . Yeah . . . Yep . . . Well, I'll be down that way in the next day or two. . . . *Huh?* . . . Okay, I'll leave tonight. Be there before daylight. . . ."

Like a fireman's wife, Dee had learned to hear between the lines. Obviously someone was baiting traps with sage hens. Well, the informant had called the right place. Bill had a weakness for trappers; one of his most frankly sentimental pen-and-ink drawings, "The Trapper," depicted a man in a high-domed flat-brimmed hat dropping a bug in a baby bird's mouth. But when trappers and birds collided, Bill always sided with the birds.

Dee closed her book; there'd be plenty of time to read after he left. The violations must have been committed on the Owyhee Desert. That explained his eagerness to spend the night behind the wheel of his Fish and Game Dodge with the license plates denuded of paint from driving through brush and sand. The Owyhee was his favorite place on earth; he'd asked to be buried there. He liked to browse the desert, looking for passerine birds that he knew by their flight patterns, colors, and songs. He'd banded thousands of these "dickeybirds," photographed and sketched them in meticulous detail with Rapidograph pens and india ink. His birdcalls were so impressive that fellow wardens insisted he must have been a dickeybird in another life. He always laughed and said he hoped to be one in the next.

Following old established ritual, Dee asked, "Do you have to go? Can't it wait till morning?" Of course he had to go; he *always* had to go. The phone would ring at 3:00 A.M. and he would leave to put an injured deer out of its misery or pull some fool out of the mud or help find a lost horse. If the call was from his old district, the Owyhee, he went twice as fast for half as much reason. He considered himself the personal bodyguard of every bird and bug and rattlesnake.

He told her, "If Carlin drove that far to get to a phone, I feel like I should go." He didn't mention that Owyhee County was now another warden's territory. That never mattered.

He grabbed the phone again, trying to find a partner for backup, standard procedure now that so many crazies occupied the wilderness. These days wardens were required to carry the sidearms that once had been optional—Bill had lobbied for the change. He wrote as many tickets as anybody in Idaho and he'd carried a pistol since his days as a police officer, although his bad eye made his range record a joke.

She heard him on the phone with Michael Elms, the conservation officer assigned to the Owyhee, and then with Gary Loveland, a senior C.O. like Bill. She could tell that neither was free. She was afraid Bill would decide to go alone. There was no radio contact with the lower desert and it was the kind of place where a sprained ankle could be fatal.

When he phoned Mike's younger brother Conley, Dee felt better. If that big lovable bear was home, he would be ready in five minutes. He was as eager as Bill.

She watched her husband as he cradled the phone on his shoulder. At fifty he was still a lean six one and 175 pounds. His stomach had pooched out an inch or two in the four months since he'd given up smoking and tried to eat all the food in Boise, but no one else would have noticed and she didn't care. He looked just like the curly-haired Marine she'd married twenty-nine years before. Together they'd raised four children, although his take-home pay had never exceeded a thousand dollars a month and there'd seldom been more than fifty dollars in their savings account. He'd been squashed by a truck, bitten by a rattlesnake, stung by hornets, attacked by rabid dogs, shot at, poisoned, and almost lost an eye, and she figured his stomach deserved to pooch out. He was the best damned game warden in the state of Idaho.

Best damned husband, too.

He pulled on his dark green uniform pants, gray shirt, and green jacket, and headed for the door. It was 10:30 P.M., a fine time to go to work. She caught sight of his gun and holster on the piano. "Bill," she called, "you forgot your gun."

He picked it up and said, "I'll be at the Forty-five ranch. Back tomorrow night or Tuesday morning." Then he added, "Don't worry about me." That was another part of the ritual, equally silly. She would miss him, yes, but she never worried about him. There was no situation he couldn't handle.

In another small frame house a few blocks away, C.O. Wilson Conley Elms, Jr., a quiet bearded man of thirty-four years and 265 extremely firm pounds, had gone to bed after checking duck hunters till 9:00 P.M., but he jumped right up when the telephone rang. His schoolteacher wife knew the signs as well as Dee Pogue, even though she and Conley were newer to the business. "You can't leave, Conley," Sheri warned her husband. "You're on jury duty."

He was already pulling off his pajamas. "I can't let Bill go alone," he answered.

She asked what was so important that he had to leave a warm bed on a cold Sunday night in January. "Some Oregon guys are hanging bait on the Owyhee," he said. "Bill's afraid they'll jump the state line. Gary and Mike can't go. That leaves me."

"And a lot of others," she said.

"Bill called *me.*"

His faraway look suggested that he was already halfway there. He was hard to turn once he'd made up his mind. If he wasn't stubborn he might still be working in a log mill. He'd walked into the lobby of the Idaho Fish and Game Department in Boise, flashed his fresh degree in geology and game management, and asked if they had any work. No, they said. Okay, he said, I'll just sit here till something opens up. Three hours later they'd offered

77

him a part-time job in the fish department, and three years after that, in 1977, he was promoted to conservation officer. Now the big kid from a little outhouse ranch near Crater Lake, Oregon, was fulfilling his lifetime dream. He would have worked for nothing—in fact, Sheri thought, he almost did. So did every game warden. There were other payoffs, fleeting and ephemeral but just as satisfying.

She helped him with his double-extra-large jacket. Blue ambled in and licked his master's brand-new rubber boots. He was a black Lab, fourteen years old, Conley's companion in his frequent attempts to catch and release every trout in the Boise River. Then the other dog, the nine-year-old, came into the room, followed by the fourteen-year-old cat. Friends suspected that the Elmses had so many pets because they couldn't have children. Well, that would soon be corrected. They'd just completed the paperwork to adopt a girl from India; all the baby had to do was get herself born. Conley had gone to the library and picked out a Hindi name: Allia Kiran, "ray of sunshine."

She asked him who would be driving tonight. There wasn't any part of the lower Owyhee that could be reached from Boise in less than four or five hours on bad roads. He told her that Bill would drive, of course. He was the senior man and they would be using his assigned Dodge pickup truck.

"Will you spell him?" she asked. "You know he's got that problem." One of Pogue's hazel eyes was damaged and he wore dark glasses. It had something to do with a plug flying out of an air mattress fifteen or twenty years ago; surgery had left the pupil permanently dilated. Everyone knew that Bill had trouble with his depth perception. The right rear of his truck was dented and the bumper was twisted up from backing into trees and stumps and rocks. He managed fairly well frontward, though.

"Nobody helps Bill," Conley was saying. "He'll drive all night and then run you a footrace."

Sheri said, "Well, it wouldn't hurt—"

"Don't worry so much," he said gently. He gave her a short semi-official hug, the one that meant, I love you but this is business. He said, "We'll be fine."

He left and then came back for his revolver. She thought, Isn't that just like him? He hated to carry a gun because he was sensitive about his intimidating size. He hid it under his jacket in a shoulder holster. He'd never fired or drawn it on duty, probably couldn't hit anything with it if he'd tried. Except maybe a trout . . .

He called, "I'll be back tomorrow night." For thirteen years, ever since their junior year at Oregon State, they'd been man and wife. Best friends, too. She couldn't wait till he got back. She never could.

20

EDDY J. CARLIN was helping Joann make breakfast when the kitchen wall lit up. His father said, "They're here." It was 6:30 A.M., still dark outside. Eddy looked out the window and saw a Dodge pickup with a bubble-gum light on top.

Bill Pogue looked about the same as last year—a few more gray hairs, maybe. He introduced his sidekick, a younger warden built like a Charolais bull, with brown hair and a brown beard. Both were in uniform, but the big man was bareheaded and Pogue wore a narrow-brimmed cowboy hat. Elms wore rubber boots with a distinct tread—you could see the print in some mud he'd tracked in—and Pogue had on work shoes that laced to his ankles. They both looked rested and ready to go. Eddy was glad about that. There was work to be done.

Joann served coffee, bacon, eggs, steak and pancakes, the everyday cowboy breakfast. Pogue said that they'd pulled in about 3:00 A.M. and dozed in their truck up at the gate. They talked about trapping and cows and the mild winter. Eddy's father Don said there was great fly-fishing in the Owyhee. The big warden looked up from his third plate of flapjacks and said he'd rather fish than eat.

Pogue said, "Some of us aren't so sure about that, Conley."

Elms laughed louder than anybody. Eddy thought, They seem like good old boys.

After a while Eddy said he'd be glad to guide the wardens through the Spring Creek drainage and on over to 45 Butte and the illegal sets. The wardens were pulling on their down jackets in the front room when Pogue asked, "Any other trappers around?"

"You bet," Eddy told him. "There's a boy by the name of George Poland, and there's Delbert Jim." He tried to think of more names. He wasn't going to mention Dallas. Some situations were too hot to handle.

Joann handed Pogue a thermos of coffee and said, "What about the trapper up the canyon? That man . . . Dallas." Her voice had an edge; Eddy could tell she was still annoyed. He threw her a shut-up look, but it was too late.

"Dallas?" Pogue asked. "Who's that?"

Eddy told about the tent at Bull Basin, the deer and the cat hides, keeping the details skimpy. Pogue asked for directions to Bull Basin. The discussion lasted a few minutes, but still too long for Eddy.

A gray winter day was breaking as they stepped outside. Don Carlin said, "Bill, I have all my traps tagged this year." Eddy thought, poor Dad. He's embarrassed. He trapped all his life and never had a ticket till he met Pogue.

The warden smiled. "You knew better last year, Don," he said. "Only you were lazy. I won't be checking your traps again." They shook hands on it.

In his own pickup, Eddy led the green Fish and Game truck north. It took about an hour to reach the first set, downstream from the ranch house. Pogue looked at the name tag. The season opener was still four days away and the trap was baited with sage hen. "Can you follow the trapline back toward the ranch?" he asked Eddy.

"You bet."

"Pull any bobcat sets you find," the warden ordered. "We'll pick 'em up later."

Eddy asked if they wanted him to help them find the trappers, Carter and Shaver. Pogue thanked him for the offer but said it was against department policy. "We're big boys, Carlin," he said. "We can handle it."

It was 9:00 A.M. when the wardens went north and Eddy south. He spent an hour uprooting illegal traps and then spotted one of his Herefords lying motionless in the bottom of a draw. As he was starting to investigate, Pogue and Elms pulled up and told him they'd cited Don Carter for trapping out of season, possession of game-bird parts, and hanging bait.

Eddy thanked them, then pointed and said, "Look there. That's one of my strays."

The three men ambled down the draw. Pogue had a smile on his face; he seemed to be enjoying himself. When they got close the animal ran. Eddy thought, Dadgum cow! Now he'd have to ride in on Danny to collect the blamed thing.

He led the wardens to the fork in the road near the branding corrals, opened the gate, then walked over to the Dodge pickup. Pogue asked again for directions to Bull Camp and Eddy sketched the route in the dirt. "If you want to see Dallas's deer," he advised, "one of you's gonna have to wade the river."

"Is the trail open through Devils Corral?" Pogue asked. "I haven't been there in a while."

Eddy told him it was, and Pogue smiled again. Devils Corral was a sinkhole big enough to shelter cattle. It was full of odd volcanic shapes, mineral encrustations, peculiar seams and lines and cracks. Looking down its sides was like looking into a smashed crystal egg.

Pogue asked, "What kind of a man is this Dallas?"

Eddy stopped to think. He didn't know Dallas well and it wasn't his place to badmouth him. But these men had driven a long way to do their job and they were entitled to the truth. "I don't trust him," Eddy said. "I wouldn't turn my back."

"We'll keep each other covered," Pogue said. He didn't sound nervous or scared. Eddy thought, Facing down poachers must be routine to him. Anyway, they were both armed; Eddy had noticed Elms's shoulder holster at breakfast.

"You'll come back for dinner, won't you?" he asked as he turned back toward his truck. "And stay the night?"

Pogue smiled. "You bet," he said.

21

WHILE THE WARDENS made their way south, someone else approached the Dallas camp from the opposite direction. Jim Stevens was so far from civilization that his car radio had gone dead. Fog draped the tops of the mountains and sealed out the sun. The day was humid and gray, uncommon in the high desert, but Jim didn't find it depressing. After four and a half hours of driving he still felt like a kid on the way to the circus. His last words to his wife had been, "Send somebody if I'm not back in three days."

He thought about the backasswards way the trip had worked out. His leased farm wasn't paying off. Jackrabbits had eaten his wheat crop, and when he'd put out poison, he'd killed hundreds of jacks plus crows and magpies and coyotes and other animals that ate the tainted flesh. He didn't want to stay on a farm that required him to slaughter wildlife to break even. So the family was in the first stages of leaving for central Idaho. For a month he'd thought about driving to Bull Basin for one last fling with arrowheads and broken pots, but the solo trip was just too dangerous. "One mistake and you're shaking hands with the goldang buzzards," he'd told Sandy, only half joking.

Then he was invited to accompany George Nielsen and a friend on a reprovisioning trip. Just when he was fully committed, the others had to cancel. Now here he was, bumping and bouncing and rearranging his shorts and doing front-seat isometrics and peering through the side windows of his blue-and-white 1977 Blazer trying to figure out where the hell he was.

He felt like yelling when he spotted the rim just over a low rise. He had his coin shooter, a shovel, a fishing rod, a shotgun, a sleeping bag and plenty of gas, everything a kid could ever want. He also had mail for Claude and a styrofoam cooler crammed with goodies. Pistachio pudding was Claude's favorite; once Liz Nielsen had made him a big batch for a wilderness trip and he'd driven a hundred yards down the road, parked, and gobbled it up. Jim smiled as he thought about the Cool Whip container full of Sandra's pistachio pudding and the big bag of brownies made by his daughter Stephanie. And there were fruit and groceries from the Nielsens. He'd picked them up at dawn at the bar.

George had insisted that he take a Model 19 Smith and a box of bullets. "You fire two shots, wait ten minutes and fire two more," the bar owner had told him. "Save the used cartridges. I reload 'em." If Claude was in camp he would respond to the signal with a single shot and head for the rim with a pack mule. The system had been designed to spare Nielsen and old Frank Gavica the climb down and back.

It was 11:30 A.M. when Jim reached the rim. A silver haze clung to the high ground, but the air below was clear. There were no signs of life at the camp. He fired two rounds at a rock and flushed a jackrabbit—too bad he'd left his 12-gauge in the car. As he was walking back to the Blazer, a shot sounded from the west, away from the camp. He was surprised. He decided it must be a hunter.

In ten minutes he fired the second pair of signal shots. This time there was no response. He wondered if he'd screwed up. He'd been so eager to get away that he'd only halfway listened to the instructions. He slipped the expended shells into the bullet box and slid them in the glove compartment.

He nibbled at a sandwich and thought about his prospects. Chances were good that neither of the rock cabins had ever been checked with a metal detector. If one twenty-dollar gold piece had fallen out of a drover's pocket a hundred years before, the trip would show a profit. He tried to remember if the Spanish had been through here. A doubloon or two could lift his family right out of their double-wide trailer and deposit them in a nice comfortable farmhouse back in Idaho.

After thirty more minutes he walked to the rim. A deer looked up from the snow fence about a hundred feet down, then returned to its munching. Another chukar exploded into the air. He took it as a sign, rolled his shotgun in his sleeping bag, grabbed the cooler and started his descent.

He'd just reached the first bench below the cutbank when a figure approached in an unmistakable walk. "Hey, Claude!" he yelled happily. Nobody could cover ground like Claude; he almost seemed to be running. He wore a small green pack and his old cowboy hat and a yellow fireman's turnout coat, open in front. He liked to wear the jacket because it cut the wind and his guns didn't show under the rubberized material.

The two friends shook hands and Claude explained that he'd been north of the rim resetting some traps. He asked if Jim had brought fresh fruit. Jim said there were oranges in the cooler, and Claude looked happier than Jim had ever seen him. Living in the boonies was good for some folks.

Claude said that he'd been expecting any of three different visitors and was glad it was Jim. He asked if there was something to be carried down from the Blazer.

"Yes, there is," Jim said. "Mail and groceries."

"Can I get it all in one trip?"

They discussed whether to saddle a mule, then decided that Claude might as well bring down the first load since he was so close to the rim. Jim said, "Don't bother to bring my Geiger counter or whatever. Just the necessities. We can get the fishing rod and the other stuff later." He asked how the trapping was going.

"Two cats is all," Claude answered. "Weather's been too mild. They're not moving around." Jim remembered that he was supposed to take Claude's first batch of furs back to town. Two cats wouldn't be much of a load.

Claude started toward the top. "We're gonna have a good time," he said, grinning.

"I brought pistachio pudding," Jim said. "Stephanie made some brownies."

Claude said, "We're gonna have a *good* time." Jim was sure of it.

* * *

He reached the tent by himself at 12:35 P.M. Everything was neat, the mark of a Dallas camp. Firewood was stacked alongside one wall of the tent. Deer quarters hung from the posts. Jim untied the flap and looked inside. Two bobcat pelts and a raccoon leaned against the back wall.

He walked toward the river, milky with early runoff. The ground was bare. He thought, Why wait? If a storm hits, we might get a foot of snow. He shuffled along, staring at the ground. In five minutes he found an arrowhead. He wasn't surprised. What next? An oxen shoe? A *doubloon?*

He didn't know how long he'd been wandering, his thoughts a century removed, when he heard a shout from the direction of the tent. He looked up and saw Claude with two uniformed men, one lean and one large. Even from a hundred feet away, he could tell there was trouble.

When he reached the tent, he recognized the Idaho Fish and Game patches. The older warden, the one in the Stetson, asked for his pistol. At first Jim didn't comprehend, then handed over the Smith & Wesson that Nielsen had lent him.

The warden popped the cylinder open. He was middle-aged with a long face and a square jaw, his general appearance about midway between an elk hunter and someone you'd see in the stands at a girls' basketball game. After he'd pushed out the cartridges, he reached over and dropped them in Jim's shirt pocket, then returned the gun. The heavyset warden, the one with the beard and glasses and soft brown eyes, watched quietly. Except for his size, he put you in mind of Claude; he was Claude multiplied by two and subtract the ponytail.

Jim introduced himself and the men gave their names; you could read them anyway on their nameplates. The one called Pogue seemed standoffish. Jim wondered if he'd had a few words with Claude. Or maybe he just knew how Claude felt about wardens and game laws.

Jim tried to soften the situation with the kind of friendly chatter he'd used as a farm equipment salesman just out of college. "Where ya from? Oh, Boise? Say, you're a long way from home."

Claude mentioned that Jim might know one of the officers. "Mr. Pogue here," Claude said, "he was chief of police in Winnemucca a few years back."

86

"How long ago?" Jim asked.

"Sixty-four, sixty-five," Pogue answered.

"Before my time," Jim said. He smiled, but the older warden didn't smile back. Apparently he was the honcho. The other kept watching. Maybe he was a trainee. He looked young enough.

Jim found the silence oppressive. "By the way," he asked, "how far are we into Idaho?"

The older man gestured toward the border. "About three miles," he said. Then he got right down to business. He pointed to the venison; Claude said that he was a hundred miles from town and had to hang up meat. Pogue said the law didn't differentiate; Claude said he'd starve to death if he obeyed the law this far from civilization. Pogue said the law didn't care about that, etc. etc. He began to sound a little like a drill sergeant, but Claude didn't act annoyed—just kept trying to explain his way of life. If there was anything different about him, it might have been his stare; Jim thought of Wyatt Earp and his "eyes that showed no fright." But mainly he just felt embarrassed for Claude and relieved to be on the sidelines.

After a while Claude opened his wallet and showed his Idaho trapping license. Pogue said if he had Idaho papers, he should have known that the bobcat season didn't open till January 9. Jim wasn't sure, but he thought he heard Pogue say that he'd have to make an arrest.

The word took him by surprise. *Arrest?* For game violations? He thought, What ever happened to tickets?

Claude said evenly, "I guess you know I'm gonna tell the judge I got those hides in Nevada." Jim had heard him sound more excited drinking grapefruit juice at the bar.

Pogue said, "You're still being cited for possession of illegal cats." Jim thought, Why doesn't the guy make up his mind? There's a hell of a difference between *cited* and *arrested*. If Claude was arrested, it was good-bye arrowheads and doubloons. All that trouble driving in. He turned away and faced the river.

He heard Pogue say, "Are you going in there and get those hides or am I?" There was talk about search warrants. Jim turned around to see what a search warrant looked like; he'd never seen one. A muffled voice came from inside the tent: "There's a raccoon hide in here also."

Elms emerged with a fur stretcher in each hand and laid the pelts on the ground. Dallas was facing the tent, with Pogue off to one side. The three men stood in a triangle, not more than five or six feet apart.

Jim turned toward the river again. He heard Claude say, "Are you gonna take me in?"

A few seconds passed. Then a shot made him jump. He turned and saw Claude firing from a crouched position, both hands on the heavy gun, police style.

Pogue's arm dropped and Jim heard him say, "Oh, no!" Smoke curled from his chest as he started to fall backward.

Claude whirled and fired at the other warden in one continuous volley, then back and forth till the hammer fell on a click. Elms went down on his face. Pogue lay on his back, twitching. His head lifted an inch or two and then dropped as the last reverberations died against the canyon walls.

Jim had backed eight or ten feet away without realizing it. His ears rang. He kept asking himself, What happened? *What happened?* His thick farmer's hands were shaking.

Claude went inside the tent and came out carrying a rifle. When he pointed the muzzle a few inches from the big man's head, Jim shut his eyes hard.

The shot sounded like a .22. A few seconds later he heard another.

He looked back at Claude. The rifle was still in his hands and he was standing directly over Pogue. The only sound was little sucks and burbles from the river. The canyon wind had quit for a change. It hadn't been five minutes since he'd first seen the men in the green uniforms. He didn't know what else to do, so he walked toward Claude.

22

"WHY, CLAUDE?" JIM asked. *"Why?"* He was embarrassed to sound so shook up.

Claude said something that sounded like, "I swore I'd never be arrested again. They were gonna handcuff me." He spoke faster than usual.

Jim stared at the wardens. One faced up, one down. There was little blood and no movement. He squatted for a closer look. Dead, both. He asked himself, What did they do? What did they say? He tried to remember if they'd threatened Claude's life in any way.

No. He'd heard every word.

Claude interrupted his thoughts. "I'm sorry I got you involved in this. I've gotta get rid of these bodies and you've gotta help me." Jim said to himself, He doesn't seem mad or even upset. He's acting like he's got a minor problem and if I just help him, it'll be solved. *And then what'll he do?*

Claude was saying, "I know that what you think is right and what I think is right aren't the same. But nobody has the right to come into my camp and violate my rights. In my mind it's justifiable homicide."

Jim didn't argue. Claude said, "Maybe we should hide them up on the rim." Then he frowned as though he disapproved of his own idea. "Nope," he said. "They radioed in when they came here. They'll send planes, dogs, find the bodies sure. We'll have to haul 'em out." He turned to Jim. "I'll get the mules. You cover the bodies with brush. There was a plane around here a couple days ago. There might be somebody up on the rim."

Jim grabbed an armload of sage from a pile behind the tent and carried it to Pogue's body. Something reflected the light eight or nine inches from the outstretched fingers of the right hand. "My God," he called out, "he's got a gun in his hand!" He wondered why he hadn't noticed it before. The warden must have drawn while he was reeling backward. A lawman's galvanic reflex. His last.

As Jim laid the branches in a crisscross pattern atop the body, he noticed a small hole behind the left ear. There was a similar hole in Elms's head; something white oozed out. The two men had been finished off trapper style.

He watched Claude chasing a mule on the other side of the river. At any other time it would have been funny. The midday sky was thick with clouds, but they were skidding off toward the Owyhee Mountains. "God dang," Jim said half aloud, "I gotta wake myself up." He pinched his calf muscle till it hurt. He closed his eyes hard and said to himself, When I open 'em those guys aren't gonna be dead. He opened his eyes and said to himself, Jesus Christ, it's real, it happened. His heart thumped. As he walked in circles he realized that he was the only eyewitness. *I'd better be ready to defend myself. . . .*

He lurched to the river and slumped on the upper bank. Several cartridges squirted from his hands as he tried to reload the gun. He thought, Why, hell, if Claude draws first, I'm not even gonna get this thing out of the holster. I won't even bother. If he's gonna shoot me, he's gonna shoot me.

Claude called from across the river, "Hey! Get some feed. It's in the tent. I can't catch this damned mule." The big mule was picketed, but the small one was bounding away like a scared dog.

Jim poured oats into a dishpan, spilling some on the ground cloth. He told himself to calm down and think. What's the best way to get out of this place alive?

Shoot Claude?
No way.
Run?

90

The nearest cover was a mile uphill. He'd softened in the three months since harvest and Claude was the best shot around.

He thought, If I can't kill him and I can't run, then what choice do I have?

No choice. I'll have to go along with him till I can break loose.

He waded the river. "Here," he told Claude, offering his car keys. "It'll take me two days to walk out. You can get wherever you want to go." *He had to open up some space.*

Claude said, "I'm not gonna leave you out here this time of year." He glanced skyward. "You never know what the weather's gonna be like. I wouldn't feel right about it."

"You sure?"

"I'm sure."

Claude shook the oats and the mule edged sideways toward him, its eyes showing white and its nostrils flared. "Okay, Claude," Jim said. "Whatever you want to do, I'll help you. You make all the decisions." He was thinking, He's my friend but he scares hell out of me. Above all I don't want any conflicts. This is his territory. He's just killed two men over nothing. I'd be a lunatic to take him on out here. Folks will understand. . . .

Claude was saying, "Jim, I'm really sorry about doing this to you. I mess up everybody's life. Everybody's always doing stuff for me and all I do is cause people trouble." Jim thought, He's so apologetic about me, but he doesn't say a word about the dead men. Where's the remorse? *Something about this isn't natural.*

"They checked my twenty-two up on the rim," Claude said. Jim assumed he meant the little trap pistol that he carried in a shoulder holster so he could work with his hands free. Why hadn't they checked the revolver on his hip? A fatal mistake, but understandable. Who would expect a wilderness trapper to be packing two guns?

"I woulda took 'em up there, but they woulda killed me," Claude was saying. "They had no business in my camp." In a businesslike tone, he added, "We gotta get these guys out of here."

With both mules now at the campsite, Claude emptied Pogue's pockets. He held the warden's pistol and said, "This gun is going into the ground with this guy." He dropped Pogue's wristwatch in the pocket of his yellow turnout jacket, then began tearing off emblems and service stripes. He shook his head and said, "I can't

91

imagine anybody working that many years with the Fish and Game." He seemed genuinely puzzled.

He hobbled the jenny front and back, tied the hobbles together and rigged a packsaddle. As he worked he told Jim, "I may not get caught for seven or eight years. And maybe when I do, I'll only get seven or eight years." Jim thought, My eyes must be bugging out a mile. If he makes it to trial without getting hung, he'll be lucky.

The two men raised the body to the crosstrees of the packsaddle and Claude roped it down. Jim was surprised there was still so little blood. Death was as neat as Claude.

"Follow me," Claude said. "Take everything you brought in with you. I don't want you connected with this." He shouldered a big load and started up with the mule.

Jim tied his shotgun inside his sleeping bag and grabbed the styrofoam cooler. The damned thing weighed a ton; he wished they'd eaten a few meals. He tried to catch Claude and the mule, but they were climbing much too fast.

He'd just reached a bench near the top when he met Claude coming back down alone. "Put your stuff right here and come with me," Claude ordered. He sounded very much in charge. "I'm gonna get the other guy."

On the way back to the tent Claude said, *"Stop!* Hear that?" Jim heard a dickeybird. Claude said, "There's somebody driving up above."

They walked faster now. "They're coming," Claude said. Jim was convinced his friend was hearing things.

At the tent, Claude muttered, "The only man that knew I had those cat hides was Carlin. He was here a few days ago." Jim didn't know who Carlin was and had no intention of asking. Don't antagonize him, he told himself over and over. *Don't antagonize him. . . .*

Claude rigged a harness on the big mule, still tethered to a drag. The two men rolled the heavyset warden on his back. The sand under his massive chest and shoulders looked as though it had soaked up gallons of blood. Claude reached inside the down jacket and pulled a pistol from a shoulder holster. The jacket was halfway zipped. Jim thought, There's no way the guy could have won a quick-draw contest with Claude or anyone else. Those wardens just hadn't been ready.

92

* * *

When they had Elms nearly in position, his green uniform pants caught on the packsaddle and the heavy body fell to the ground with a thump. Claude slashed the seat of the pants with a pocketknife so they wouldn't hang up again.

Jim looked at his own clothes; they were sticky with clotting blood. When he pressed his hand against his mouth, Claude said, "Don't throw up in front of the tent. Go over in the brush."

Jim said, "I'm all right." He knew how Claude felt about physical weakness. This was no time to act like a leppy.

The mule kept rearing back and jerking out from under the body. The big man's belt buckle tore loose and his pants fell down. Claude said, "The only way a guy could get this body out of here is to quarter him."

Quarter him? Jim looked at Claude and blurted out, "I can't do that."

Claude said, "Oh, there's no way I could do it either." Jim studied his face. Thank God, he said to himself, he didn't mean it.

Claude led the mule to a ledge above a washout. "We'll lower the body," he told Jim. On the third attempt the animal sagged but stayed upright, and Claude roped the load. "You take this guy to the rim," he ordered. "I gotta burn out some of the evidence and the blood spots."

Jim started up with Elms and the mule. A large bird circled overhead. He guessed it was a buzzard.

He hadn't gone a hundred yards when the warden's body rotated and the mule fell on its side, its hoofs clawing air. The cinch had pulled loose. Lying atop the dead warden, the animal snorted and gasped. When its pupils rolled back in its head, Jim thought it must be dying. He untied the straps and the mule revived.

Now what?

He looked toward the camp. Greasy black smoke obscured the view; it looked like the sack of a miniature city. He assumed Claude was trying to scourge his camp from the earth, but that was plain impossible. Jim thought, He should run for one of those survival caches he's always talking about—the old mine shacks, the caves, the charcoal cabins near Tonopah. Forget about the evidence, forget about the bodies—just run! It'd take an army to dig him out. *And I'll get away.*

He kept his advice to himself. He wanted to see Sandy and the kids again.

Claude ghosted out of the smoke, moving upward. He carried a full pack, a double-barreled shotgun, two rifles, an orange tarp, the bobcat hides and a gunnysack. The two men tried to reload Elms, but it was hopeless. Claude threw a lariat around the warden's legs and tied the other end to the packsaddle on the mule. "I'm gonna drag this guy to the river," he said. "It's getting dark. We've gotta get out of here."

The dead man's boots caught on the hardscrabble terrain and pulled off. His uniform pants kept sliding to his ankles. His blood-soaked shirt and T-shirt tore into shreds and left him almost naked. Then the lariat broke; Claude retied it under the arms and dragged the heavy body, head facedown, toward the river. Jim felt sick again. No one should be treated like this, dead or alive.

"Cover up my skid marks!" Claude yelled. Jim dragged his boot across the trail and Claude said, "No! With your hands." Jim thought, There's blood all the way down the trail. Does he think I can hide it with my hands? He followed orders.

When Claude was out of sight, Jim retrieved the warden's boots and clothing and put them in a sack. He hefted the pack and wondered how Claude had been able to carry it. He threw one loop over his shoulder, gripped the other in his hand and lurched forty feet to the next landing before stopping to rest. The pack was so overloaded that the metal clasps had pulled apart on one side. He jettisoned some weight and climbed on.

Claude caught up. "Take it easy," he told Jim. "I don't want anything happening to you. I don't want you to have a heart attack or anything. Just set down and rest." He said, "I dumped the big guy in the river. This is murder one for me. I didn't weight the body. They'll find it in the morning."

They climbed the rest of the way together. Jim's lungs felt as though he'd swallowed flame. He remembered his first trip to Bull Basin, how he'd said to himself that breaking camp would be a bitch of a job. Now they were doing it in double time.

The sky blacked down as though on a rheostat. In the darkness he tripped over loose rocks that had dropped from the overhang. He was soaked—he couldn't tell whether it was blood or sweat. He kept telling himself, Don't stop! You'll never get started again. He wondered why Claude didn't strain or stumble. He was as sure-footed as a goat. Well, he was a mountain man.

In the middle of the trail through the cutbank, Claude raised his hand and said, "Wait! I hear a motor." Jim thought, It's his imagination again. But what if it isn't? There'll be a gunfight. His arms and hands were numb. He felt like giving up.

Claude went over the top. Jim listened for the shots, but the only sound was the squooshing of his wet socks in his boots. He thought, This damned desert is as humid as the beach. Up above it was silent.

Claude reappeared with a can of 7-Up. "Here," he said. "Drink this. And take it easy." Then he jogged downtrail, returning with some of the things they'd left behind—the styrofoam cooler, sleeping bag, shotgun, remnants of clothes and other odds and ends. He hauled them out and returned for more.

When he came up for the last time, Jim thought, I don't feel safe when I can't see what he's doing. He said he didn't want anything to happen to me, but how the hell can I believe him? His muscles ached as he struggled up the cutbank wondering how a bullet in the back would feel. Not much worse, he decided.

On top, he saw a green Fish and Game pickup. As he approached, Claude yelled, "Don't even go near it!" The Blazer's tailgate was open and Pogue's body lay faceup on the ground underneath. The cargo deck had been cleared and everything piled on the backseat including the tool chest. Claude said, "Help me load this body. We're taking this guy out of here."

Jim couldn't see the point of driving away with one body when the other was in plain sight in the shallow river. A sick thought entered his mind. Does Claude consider the warden a *trophy?* It was inconceivable, but so was the whole situation. He said, "I don't understand why we're taking it with us."

"They'll find it in five minutes," Claude replied, "and I need all the time I can get. Without the body they can't pin the rap on me." He said he wished he knew of a good rockslide. "I could dump it there tonight and come back tomorrow and get rid of it for good."

Jim started the car and snapped on the defroster to clear the ice. Claude had spread orange plastic on the tailgate and cargo deck.

The two men wrapped the stiffened body and slid it inside. The spare tire took up room and made the feet stick out the rear.

Claude said, "Pull up a ways. I'm going to burn this spot where he was laying." Jim moved the Blazer and helped Claude gather brush and wood. They sprinkled kerosene and set it afire, then loaded the last items. "Let's go," Claude said.

Jim squeezed behind the wheel. "Where?" he asked.

"To George's."

Driving off, Jim thought of the sights that had passed before his eyes since arriving with his coin shooter and his expectations. He decided that hell must look a lot like Bull Camp. Now he was on his way from hell to Paradise with a dead man's boots wrapped in orange sticking out the back like a flag. He wondered if he would live to tell the tale, and if anyone would believe him.

23

As THEY DROVE across the desert, the body thumping and bumping in back, Claude kept working on an alibi for Jim. "I don't want
you involved," he said for about the fourth time. Jim thought, My
boot prints and tire tracks are all over the place, there's blood on
my clothes and in my car, and a dozen people know I went to Bull
Camp. *How the hell can I not be involved?*

Claude looked deep in thought. In the pale glow he gave the
appearance of someone in the middle of a great adventure—a little
tired, alert, anticipatory. Jim thought, I've seen folks show more
emotion over dead jackrabbits. And that warden's head is right
behind his.

Claude jerked upright and said, "Is that a car?"

"Where?"

"Up over the ridge. *Didn't you see those lights?*"

"No," Jim said. Claude was seeing things again. What would he
do if they encountered a real car?

Claude said, "Do you still have that pistol?"

"Yes."

"Let me have it."

Jim thought, There was no reason to kill those wardens, but
there's plenty of reason to kill me. . . .

He unbuckled his belt and handed over the holstered gun. Claude put it on the floor near his feet. Then he was quiet again.

"Okay, here's your story," he said after they found the natural-gas pipeline and turned southwest. It took a few minutes to spell out, but the essence was that Jim had driven up to the rim, spotted the empty Fish and Game truck, and sped home to avoid involvement.

"What about my footprints?" Jim asked.

"Oh, yeah," Claude said. Together they worked out a new story: Jim had driven to the rim and fired his signal shots. An answering shot came from the west, and Jim walked back up the canyon to see if it was Claude. When he returned to the rim an hour or so later, the Fish and Game truck was there. He waited on top till dark, then hiked down to see what was going on. Claude met him in front of the tent and said, "Don't ask any questions. I'm going to be gone for a couple of days. I'll follow you up to your car." On top, Claude had collected his groceries and mail and told Jim to leave.

They spent hours on the details. Jim didn't mind; it broke the silence and helped steady his nerves. He knew he wasn't thinking straight, but he was sure of one thing: as long as they were working on an alibi, Claude wasn't shooting him behind the ear.

When the talk turned to hiding the body, Jim became frightened again. The less he knew the better. He could still see Pogue staring at him with glassy eyes, one darker than the other. He could still see Elms being dragged toward the river on his face. And for what? The poor guy had hardly said a word; he'd just done his job. But he'd been a witness. *One* of the witnesses. He tried not to draw the obvious conclusion.

Claude was saying, "I should put this guy in Chimney Rock Dam." Jim hoped he didn't. Chimney Rock was rattlesnake heaven, and rattlers moved by night. If Claude shot him there, his body might not be found till the spring thaw, and maybe not then. The coyotes would do to him what they'd done to his poisoned jackrabbits back on the farm.

"Claude," he said, trying not to sound hostile, "don't tell me where you hide the body, okay? Just do it and then there's no fear of me even telling. I don't want to know. Use my rig if you want to."

Claude nodded. They drove on in silence. From time to time Claude said he saw more lights. A few stars appeared and he mistook one for a plane. Jim thought, Why don't I see the things he sees? Isn't there a name for that?

As the hours passed, it became clear that Claude was serious about taking the body to Paradise. "I don't want to get George involved," he said, "but there's no place else to turn." Jim thought the plan was crazy, but he didn't comment. They were crossing miles of wasteland, passing abandoned mine shacks, prospect holes, cattle reservoirs used and unused, shale ledges and caves and shifting dunes and alkali sinks. And they were going to the Paradise Hill Bar to hide a body?

Claude returned to the subject of protecting Jim; it seemed paramount. Jim thought, Either he's setting me up or he's really concerned; I wish I could tell which. Claude said, "If you get in hot water and things get rough on you, I'll call Duane Michelson and I'll tell him that you didn't have nothing to do with it." Jim had met Michelson. He was a tall, blond lawman who practiced shooting with Claude. He added, "I'll stick around for a while to see if you get charged."

"Thanks a lot, Claude," Jim said, trying to sound sincere. He realized that he'd been kissing Claude's ass ever since they'd left the rim, but he wanted to get home alive.

Claude talked a little about the incident. He said that the Fish and Game truck had just pulled up and stopped when he topped the rim to pick up supplies from the Blazer. The two uniformed men introduced themselves and asked if he was armed. He handed over the .22 trap pistol in his shoulder holster and they took out the bullets and gave it back. They didn't ask for the revolver under his turnout coat. The older warden fiddled around in the green truck for a few minutes. "Probably calling in," Claude said, "reporting their position." The threesome had hiked down to the camp without saying much, and Jim had witnessed the rest.

There was a long pause as the Blazer bumped up a draw, headlights jerking skyward. Jim waited for Claude to fill in one more blank: why he killed the two men. But all he said was, "I emptied my pistol," followed by a mumbled phrase about "justifiable homicide." Jim thought, Go ahead and justify, Claude. You're my friend; I *want* to believe you. But Claude stopped talking.

They passed the pipeline pumping station about halfway to Paradise and were approaching Greeley Crossing, a gulch set off by cattle guards, when they both saw lights in the distance. "Cars!" Claude said. For the first time, he seemed shaken. He said, "I'm gonna get out and run along in the sage alongside you. When they pass, I'll get back in."

Jim braked and Claude jumped out. "If they come up to you," he said, "just put your hands up and don't try anything. Just tell them I held a gun on you and I'm out here in the sagebrush." Jim thought, Are you gonna shoot them? Please, Claude, no more killing. These are just innocent people driving along.

Claude left. "Don't give them any cause," he called back. "Don't take any chances. I don't want you to get hurt." He disappeared in the sage.

Jim drove at a walking pace, intending to speed up when the car passed so no one could get a good look at his cargo. After a few minutes he realized that the lights came from a low-flying airplane. It passed directly overhead and the night closed in again. He got out of the Blazer to look for Claude. In the ruby glow of a taillight he saw the warden's foot. He called, "Claude!"

He decided he'd driven too far. He turned back toward the pumping station. He wondered if Claude had run off, leaving him to explain the body, or was he waiting in the darkness to put one through the windshield? He told himself to knock off the paranoia. If Claude distrusted him, why would he have left him in the Blazer? Claude wouldn't abandon him, and that went both ways. What happened at Bull Camp didn't change the fact that they were friends.

He called again, "Claude?" My God, he thought, he must have cut across to the Greeley road. The way he covers ground, he's probably over there cussing me out.

He was turning the Blazer again when he heard a shot. In a minute or so Claude jumped in and slammed the door. "You okay?" he asked.

Jim sighed. "I'm okay," he said. They arrived in Paradise Hill around ten-thirty.

24

"PARK IN BACK," Claude ordered. He climbed out, stretched, and walked to the door.

Jim recognized the raspy voice of George Nielsen. "Whatta you want?"

"George, open the door!"

The door opened and Claude said, "Well, we're in trouble." Nielsen squinted and led them to the kitchen. They gathered around a small table and Claude said, "I dusted two Fish and Game."

George's head jerked. "They came into my camp," Claude went on. "We got one in the Blazer. I put the other guy in the river. I need your pickup, George. I'm gonna take the body out and cache it someplace." He looked at Jim and then back at George, still in his nightclothes. "Jim said he doesn't want to have anything to do with it."

George mumbled, "I don't want anything to do with it either." His pomaded hair was in spikes and his face was the color of sliced bread. Jim thought, I bet I look worse.

Elizabeth Nielsen walked in, a slender fiftyish woman with coiffed red hair and tired eyes. After twenty years with George, she blended in so well that it was hard to imagine she'd grown up in

Ireland and England. "What's the matter?" she asked. All three men tried to answer. *"What's going on?"* she repeated. She knows already, Jim said to himself. She's a cop's daughter and she's sensed it. Claude was family to her.

George embraced her and said in a thin voice, "I think Claude shot two men."

She rubbed at her reddened eyes, looked from Claude to Jim and back to Claude again, then left the room in tiny steps like a tightrope walker. George called after her, "Why don't you go lie down?"

Claude sat at the head of the table and Jim alongside. Every muscle ached, every bone. George gripped a chair and listened standing up. The veins on the backs of his hands moved like worms among the liver spots. He seemed to have trouble following the story, forcing Claude to repeat several times. Jim thought, Where's the macho stud that's always saying, "Well, shoot the son of a bitch! *Blow him away!*" Now that two men were dead, he was spaghetti.

Liz reappeared next to George; it was hard to tell who was holding whom. She looked like a nurse who'd just scrubbed up for an amputation. "Claude, we don't want to know anything that happened," she said in an uncertain voice. "We don't want any trouble whatsoever." Her lower lip wobbled; her Irish accent had returned strongly—"any trrrouble whatsoeverrrr."

Claude nodded and said, "Jim, remember to wash off real good. Take a shower. Be sure you wash under your fingernails." He sounded calm. "We've gotta burn some clothes," he said. There was so much blood on Jim's shirt that he could barely discern the pattern. His Levis bore long dribbly stains and his boots were caked with mud and blood.

Liz said, "Whatever you want, Claude." As she spoke, her hand drifted up to her red hair and patted it front and back. After she had it arranged, she reached up and patted it again.

Claude was still giving orders. "Jim, you've got to clean out the Blazer. If there's any evidence in there or any bloodstains, they should be cut out of the carpet or washed out. And wipe all the fingerprints." He told Nielsen to gas up the family pickup truck.

George came back inside and said, "I filled three tanks, Claude. You got enough gas to get you to Mexico or Canada." The three men went to the shed and picked out a spade and other digging tools.

"Let's move the body," Claude said. They backed George's pickup to the rear of the Blazer and took hold of the plastic-wrapped package, Jim at the head and Claude at the feet. Jim thought, Am I really doing this? The body thumped onto the bed of the truck.

Claude slammed the tailgate. Backlighted by the glow from a house window, he stuck out his hand. For the first time he looked a little melancholic. The two men shook, and Claude said, "I hope you have good luck and I hope this isn't too hard on you."

Jim didn't know what to say. Claude squeezed his hand and said, "If you'll do one thing for me—if you see my parents, could you just tell them that I love them?" Then he climbed into the pickup and drove off alone with the body and tools. It was just after midnight.

Jim took a change of clothing from the Blazer and went inside. The living room stove burned so hot that it made the wall look crooked. He piled his old clothes on the floor. As Liz threw them into the flames, she muttered, "We'll all be in jail by noon."

He showered but still smelled blood on his skin. He stepped into the living room as Liz was trying to stuff his boots into the fire door. George snapped, "Don't put those in there!" He took the boots outside. Jim didn't know what he intended to do with them and didn't care.

George came back in and ushered him to the bar like someone leading a sick old man. The long darkened room smelled stale. Six or seven pool balls were scattered at one end as though someone had scratched on the eight. George poured them both drinks. Jim had just started on a second drink when Liz tiptoed in and said, "You better get out of here, Jim. We don't know what frame of mind that boy's in."

It was eight miles to the potato farm on Dutch Flat Road, about halfway to Winnemucca. Jim felt mixed up—exhausted and high at the same time, relieved to be alive, depressed about the killings, grateful to Claude and also sore as hell. He thought, God, what a tragedy, not just for the wardens but everybody, even the Nielsens. Claude certainly doesn't mind implicating his friends.

Then he said to himself, No matter how many caches he's got

hidden away, he's as dead as Pogue and Elms. You don't kill cops and live. They'll probably set the dogs on him if some vigilante doesn't bust his skull. Poor Claude. He deserves better.

He tried to decide what to tell Sandy. After seventeen years of marriage, she could read him like the *Humboldt Sun.* Well, she would be the test for his cover story. If it fooled her, it would fool anybody. When things blew over, he'd swear her to secrecy and tell the whole deal. He didn't want another soul to know what he'd seen, especially his children. Now or ever.

As he pulled up to his double-wide, he remembered the bullets that George had given him for signaling. He flipped open the glove compartment and groped for the plastic box. He thought, The cops'll arrest me in the morning and use these bullets as evidence.

His tires squealed as he backed out of the driveway and sped toward Paradise Hill. But he couldn't bring himself to go to the bar. He buried the box in the sand at the first telephone pole. At daybreak he would dig it up and sneak it back to George.

When he walked in his door, fifteen-year-old Scott greeted him, "Hey, Dad, it's one o'clock."

"Go to sleep, son," he whispered.

He tiptoed into the bedroom and started taking off the clean clothes he'd put on at the Nielsens'. Sandy asked why he was home so soon. He'd barely started to answer when she told him not to bother.

He said, "Listen, go to sleep. I'm gonna take a shower." As he padded toward the bathroom, he said, "I'll talk to you later."

He heard her sleepy voice. "Jim?"

"Huh?"

"You'll never make it as a liar."

He scrubbed his body, scoured under his fingernails and washed his hair. When he returned to bed he could tell Sandy was awake. He felt bad about lying and worse about getting caught. Maybe he'd tell her the whole story after the school bus collected the kids in the morning.

It seemed like hours before her breathing deepened. The room was January cool, but his side of the bed was damp with sweat. He got up and paced, then slid himself under the covers like a board. God, he thought, if people knew what's out on that desert. He saw the big warden's naked body bobbing in the current, the whole scene an eerie green. He thought, It'll sure stand out in the morning. And that poor Pogue. Claude's probably dropped him in a mineshaft by now. Or under a rockslide. I wonder if he has a family. They'll suffer. Oh, Jesus, how they'll suffer. . . .

He wished he could turn off his mind for a while. He was afraid for Claude and afraid *of* Claude. He thought, Maybe he's on his way here. By now he's had time to think. How had he put it to George? *I dusted two wardens.* No, *I burnt two wardens.* No, *I dropped* . . .

What difference did it make?

At 4:00 A.M. something jumped through the open window and knocked out the screen. Jim gasped, "My God, he's back!"

Sandra slept. It was the cat.

At six-thirty he heard the kids stirring and got up to scrub the floor mats in the Blazer. He opened the car's front door and saw George's signaling pistol lying on the floor. He thought, That's *evidence.* The windshield was fogged again and he steered by looking out the side window. He dug up the box of shells and headed for Paradise Hill. He thought, I'll never relax till I get rid of this stuff. In a few hours every deputy in the West'll be on my ass.

He pulled behind the bar and saw a potbellied form standing near the pickup. The last time he'd seen that truck, Claude was using it as a hearse. He got out and glanced in the bed for the warden's body, but it was gone. Look out, he warned himself, Claude might be in the house. "Here, George," he said, handing over the pistol. "Claude forgot to take it. Here's the shells, too."

George steered him inside. "Liz'll be at the hospital all day," he said as he stashed the gun in a bedroom. "We couldn't sleep. Set down and have a cup of coffee." He sounded like a man who'd capped off a night of drinking by getting mugged. Jim wondered how any of them could put in a day's work with so much on their minds.

"Well," George said after he poured the coffee, "are you going to town and tell everything?" He leaned forward and narrowed his pale green eyes. "Or are you gonna stick with that story?"

Jim had a mental picture of Claude listening behind the door, a .357 in his hand. It was odd that George hadn't mentioned him or explained why the pickup was back. Hadn't Claude intended to drive it to Mexico or Canada? "Well, God dang it," Jim said, "I guess I'll try with that story, if I can."

He sipped at the coffee but couldn't swallow. "George," he said, "I gotta go."

The kids were just boarding the school bus when he reached home a few minutes before eight. He went inside and Sandy said, "Jim, what's the matter with you?"

"There's nothing the matter with me."

She grabbed him by the shoulder and gave him a jerk. "Jim, what's happening? *What the hell is wrong?*"

"Nothing!" he snapped as he pulled away. "I'm not gonna tell you nothing. Don't ask me any questions." Then softer: "I don't want to implicate you."

She started crying. Jim thought, She knows it's something bad, but she has no idea how bad. I'm doing her a favor by not telling her. God, it's like a death in the family. You gotta talk about it, but you don't know how to start.

He filled a pan with soapy water and worked on the Blazer's floor. Then he rubbed fingerprints off the doors and windows. As he worked, he said to himself, This is no way to treat Sandy. Hell, this is no good.

He threw down the rag and went inside. At the end of the story she asked him to explain again why Claude had drawn and fired. He said, "I don't know. Maybe I'm just dumb. I didn't even think a fight was brewing. Claude never raised his voice. Nobody made any threats or called any names. Pogue was a little overbearing. You know, like a cop? Then—*bang!*"

Sandy cried and said, "What are you gonna do now?"

"The right thing," he said.

But first he wanted to tip off the Nielsens. "We'll all be arrested," he explained to Sandy. "I don't want the cops sweeping down on them without warning."

"Let's just tell Liz," Sandy suggested. "George might try to talk you out of it."

They headed for Winnemucca. In bright sunlight the party town looked bleached. They found Liz on duty at the hospital. Her skin was the color of Sheetrock. She said, "I didn't have my car last night or I'd have driven in and told the police meself." As she spoke, her fingertips tapped her face. At first Jim thought she'd put on too much powder, but then he realized she wasn't wearing any. Poor Liz. It wasn't just the fear of being involved; it was losing Claude. She'd given him a mother's love and pistachio pudding.

"I'm just—I'm just—I'm going to resign my job," she said in a breaking voice. "I can't work here with this hanging over me." Jim thought, Everybody's being punished. Liz said, "I want to call George and tell him what we're gonna do."

"Sure," Jim said. "Call him." It would be better if they confessed together.

Liz spoke on the phone briefly and reported that George was on his way. It was nine-thirty; he'd be in Winnemucca by ten. While they waited she filled them in on the night before. "After two or three hours Claude came back with the pickup. The body was gone. George told me Claude needed some food. I put some raisins, a couple pounds of beans and some rice in a shopping bag for him."

She halted, and Sandra reached out and patted her thin hand. Liz resumed, "Claude said, 'Come over here and give me a hug and kiss.' He put his arms around me and he said—he said, 'I love you, Liz. Try to be nice to my mother.' He told George to take him down the road and drop him off. When George left, I was afraid I'd never see him again. But he came back home around four and told me he'd let Claude out on Sand Pass Road."

I might have known, Jim said to himself. That's where the Bloody Runs begin. Claude's in his own backyard, and he's already got a six-hour jump.

An hour later George still hadn't arrived. Liz phoned him at the bar and said he'd been on his way out the door when the 7-Up truck arrived. George liked to set up his deliverymen with drinks. They'd be finished in a few minutes.

Jim was annoyed. It looked like a stall to give Claude more time. He desperately wanted to take the killings to the law before the law took the killings to him. There was a hell of a difference.

George showed up just before noon, looking wan. On the way to a lawyer's office, he confided, "Claude said, 'I did a sloppy job, George. Those two guys had it coming.'" Jim wished he knew why.

Attorney Richard Lagarza heard a few words of the story and

raised his hands, palms forward. "Game wardens?" he asked. *"Two* bodies?"

"One in the river and one—I don't know where," Jim said. He glanced at George and George looked away. Maybe he didn't know where the body was, either.

The lawyer made a phone call, then said, "Let's go."

25

A HUNDRED AND fifty miles to the north, Owyhee County Sheriff Tim Nettleton wished he could put the whole day on videotape, rewind it to 6:00 A.M., and start over. He was working three hot cases and drawing blanks. His desk was such a mess that his dispatcher had threatened to plant potatoes in it. He'd completely misplaced his file marked "Legal B.S." His throat was raw from chain-smoking Chesterfields and his checkbook was telling him lies and it was still three hours too early for his first sip of Black Velvet.

Then the phone rang and things turned sour.

It was the Owyhee County prosecutor with a report from Winnemucca. Some nut was claiming that two Idaho conservation officers had been shot by a "mountain man." They weren't sure of the wardens' names, but one sounded like "Pugh."

"Pogue?" the sheriff asked. *"Bill Pogue?"*

"Could be."

Nettleton winced. He'd worked closely with Pogue, shared ponchos with him in rainstorms, manned roadblocks with him, and admired him as he would a wise older brother. He pressed his palm against his forehead. Bill dead? Inconceivable. He'd never heard of anyone shooting a C.O. in Idaho, and when they started, the last one they'd shoot would be Bill Pogue.

If the victim had been anyone else, he would have picked up his phone and notified the next of kin. But Bill was a special case. He'd spent his life getting out of tight spots. Besides, communications with the lower Owyhee Desert were shaky at best and various damn fools reported everything short of Indian massacres down there, when in reality it was a nice peaceful place if you liked lizards and snakes and dickeybirds.

Nettleton lit a cigarette and tried to decide what to do. He was a rangy man, six four and 180 pounds, with sharply sloping shoulders drawn down by a life on horseback. He had thinning black hair, chopped sideburns speckled with white, and a long, dolorous face. His bass voice had a Johnny Cash tremolo and his laugh sounded like an old tractor starting up. A devout Catholic, he tried not to swear any more than necessary, but like most cowboys he found the word *bullshit* useful. "Don't bullshit me," he would say. "I don't want to hear any more bullshit about that bullshit story."

He was a kidder, quick to smile, a natural politician, an unashamed rustic. Low brown hills and sagebrush were all that could be seen from Murphy, the smallest county seat in the United States, but along with forty-nine other residents he considered it a garden of sweet delights. Asked when he intended to go into town, meaning Boise, he had a stock answer: "As seldom as possible." Asked if he'd been to town, he would smile and say, "I hope not."

Four generations back, his Irish ancestors had fled the potato famine, worked their way to northern Nevada in time for the Indian uprisings, then fled north to Sinker Creek, Idaho, a hoofbeat ahead of the scalping knives. Young Tim grew up chasing cows with his father and brothers. When their old Box-T ranch finally went under, Tim drove his pickup truck into Murphy and filed for sheriff so he wouldn't have to leave Owyhee County. He won by one vote out of two thousand.

The new job seemed to fit the thirty-one-year-old cowboy. He'd always worked long hours and saw no reason to stop. He put forty-three thousand miles on his patrol car in his first year in office, learned to fly, borrowed a plane and ended a wave of cattle rustling. On a single October day he handled a fatal accident, caught five men butchering cows, nailed old Cleo Dobbs for housebreaking, righted an overturned wrecker, talked a crazy out of beating up his wife near Jordan Valley, mediated a tavern brawl, and cooked for the boys in the jail. At 2:00 A.M., when the clocks went back an hour to mark the end of daylight saving time, he was chasing a stolen car. When he came home his wife, Charlene, said, "Tim, do you know what you just did?"

"No," he said. "What did I just do?"

"You worked a twenty-five-hour day."

Little by little he improved his department, adding personnel till he'd doubled his manpower. "But when I doubled my manpower I doubled my crime rate," he explained. "We got all kinds of calls we didn't get before." Since it was happening in Murphy, he called this "Murphy's Law." His first election was the only one he didn't win by a landslide.

Now he dialed Fish and Game headquarters in Boise, forty miles northeast of Murphy, and asked, "Have you got any men in the bottom end of my county?"

He was told that C.O.'s Bill Pogue and Conley Elms were expected back momentarily. They'd been out of radio contact, but they were probably in a dead zone. Nothing new about that.

He said thanks and hung up without explaining his call. He didn't want to upset anybody over another bullshit report from the desert. If anybody had to bother with that kind of bullshit, he'd do it himself. That was the way things usually worked out anyway.

He performed one of his death-defying backward tilts in his prehistoric desk chair and lifted his runover cowboys boots to his desk in his cogitating position. His eyes swung to a note he'd chalked on the blackboard: *Draft evaition trial Friday.* The county commissioners had talked about buying him an IBM computer with a fifty-thousand-word spelling corrector. "I can misspell more'n that," he'd insisted.

Now he blew a stream of smoke toward the cracked ceiling and called to his dispatcher in the next room: "Get me the sheriff in Humboldt County."

The source of the report turned out to be a potato farmer, the killer a trapper. One body had been dumped in a river at a place called Bull Camp. Nettleton knew Owyhee County better than anyone, but it was bigger than New Jersey and at the moment he couldn't place Bull Camp. He and Bill Pogue had once worked some California poachers near a place called Bull Basin; he wondered if that might be it. "Exactly where's Bull Camp?" he asked the Nevada deputy.

"We don't know. But it looks like it's in your county."

"How good's your information?" he asked. He still hoped it was bullshit.

"The informant handled the bodies."

The sheriff redialed Idaho Fish and Game and reported two wardens down. He suggested that someone ask the governor's office for National Guard helicopters. His own plane was out of service, so he phoned a rancher who owned a twin-engined Cessna and asked him to drop everything and fly right over.

A few minutes later, Police Chief Allen Bidwell of the Snake River town of Homedale phoned to talk. "Allen," Nettleton barked into the phone, "you just volunteered to go with me on a murder case. Pick up my deputy on the way. You got twenty minutes."

"It's forty miles!" Bidwell responded.

The sheriff hung up.

Dee Pogue was at the bank where she worked. Around noon she'd started to call Bill at home—he'd be back by now—but something had interrupted her. She wasn't worried. He always dawdled on the desert.

Her clear blue eyes lit up when a suntanned man with a Roman nose and a close-cropped beard stepped into the bank. A top Fish and Game official, Jerry Thiessen had been Bill's closest friend since they'd attended trainees' school in 1965. Every May the cronies disappeared in the Owyhee Desert for a week, roaming ancient Indian campgrounds, chipping obsidian, collecting arrowheads, snapping pictures, sharing a nip or two if the cold made it unavoidable. When they came home, they always looked younger. Jerry had several of Bill's drawings on his walls, including an original called "Lady Friends Comin' " showing one old cowpoke barbering another's bald head. With his bad eye, Bill could draw only in brief spurts, and some of his closely stippled sketches took weeks to complete. But if you praised one, it was yours.

Jerry took her arm and said, "Is there somewhere we can talk?" Dee couldn't imagine what was wrong. His voice sounded drowned and he was avoiding her eyes. As she led him into an empty office, she thought, I hope I can help.

112

"Dee," he said, "we think Bill's been shot."

She didn't believe him. "When?" she asked.

"Around noon yesterday. We only found out a little while ago." He wrapped her hand in both of his and said, "Dee, there's a chance Bill's dead."

Part of her mind went numb. She heard herself say, "I better go home." She ran upstairs, grabbed her purse and told her boss she had to leave.

"What happened, Dee?" a voice asked.

"Bill's been shot and they think he's dead."

She teetered toward the parking lot and realized that she wouldn't be able to drive. Thiessen drove her home.

She wondered how to tell the children. Kathi still lived at home; Linda and Jodi were housewives in Boise. She told the girls and then phoned her son Steven, a log-truck driver in nearby Horseshoe Bend. "I need you to come home," she said.

"There's something really wrong, isn't there?" he said.

"Yes. It's your father. But there's no need to hurry."

Rancher Joe Kenworthy painted the Cessna on Murphy's uphill gravel runway at 4:00 P.M. By that time the sheriff had made several more contacts with Nevada. Two Idaho wardens were believed dead, but no bodies had been found and he hadn't given up all hope. Strange things happened on the desert.

He assembled his troops: Kenworthy, Police Chief Bidwell and Owyhee Deputy Sheriff Gary Olsen. The door to the smoky office burst open and Senior Investigator Harry Capaul of the Idaho Bureau of Investigation came in. A six-footer with a swarthy complexion despite Swiss ancestry, he'd averaged a hundred miles an hour from Boise.

The phone rang with more information. The "mountain man" was loose on the desert. He'd last been seen around 3:00 A.M. on a dirt road twelve miles south of Paradise Hill. Nettleton knew enough about the former habitat of his ancestors to realize that it would take men and dogs and planes and a ton of Irish luck to flush the killer out.

He loped to his nearby frame house to pick up a toothbrush and some clothes. "Charlene," he said, "you may not see me for a while." He had the same feeling he'd had a year ago when he and his deputies had tracked an escaped convict for weeks and finally

113

run him down. "I don't know why I'm always getting into these things," he complained. "This is bigger than me."

"Was it bigger than you last year?" his wife asked. "Well, it isn't now."

As he left he thought, That's what wives are for.

He gave Joe Kenworthy the compass heading to the 45 ranch. From there they would sweep the river forks. He didn't bother to look down as they flew. From Murphy you could fly two hundred miles south to Battle Mountain, Nevada, and not pass over a house or village. That was one of the things Nettleton liked about his home county. As they flew, a scene with Bill Pogue kept coming back:

A man had stopped at their roadblock on Poison Creek and pleaded, "Do you have to take the buck? That's the only food we're gonna have in the house."

Nettleton whispered, "Bill, this guy's just been laid off. Five kids and a sick wife."

Pogue frowned. "Is this the kinda guy that's gonna go down to the bar and tell 'em he got away with something?"

"No."

Bill turned to the man. "You go home and feed that deer to your family. Don't waste a bit!" Then louder: "Don't ever break the game laws again!" And finally in a whisper: *"And don't tell any-body."*

Nettleton was thankful that he'd known a side of Pogue unknown to game violators. No one who banded dickeybirds and drew sensitive sketches and trudged through swamp and desert to rescue lost pets could be as stern as Bill sometimes seemed to be. He was a mixture of personalities, of surprises and contradictions, and now they were all dead.

The sun slid down the backslope of 11,000-foot War Eagle Mountain, and by the time the search team reached the junction of the South Fork and the East Little Owyhee River, the sky had turned to a thin wash of purple and violet. At 5:35 P.M. the twin-engined Cessna was flying level with the canyon rim when Investigator Harry Capaul said, "What the hell is that?"

Nettleton looked out the window and spotted something that looked like a blue spark. He squinted his eyes and saw that it came from a single ray of sunshine piercing the lens of a roof-light on a

114

truck. "Oh, Christ," he said. "Bill's gone. No way he'd leave his truck out here."

He found the exact spot on the chart as the plane turned south toward Winnemucca. They were definitely in Idaho, two and a half miles north of the Nevada border and thirteen miles east of Oregon. If earlier reports were accurate, Conley Elms was in the river, but it was too dark to tell. They wouldn't be able to start a search till tomorrow. So far, all the luck was with the killer.

Patrol cars waited with their motors running at the small Winnemucca Airport. Nettleton spent most of the evening talking to Humboldt County deputies and scrounging up aircraft and manpower. He was introduced to Jim Stevens but questioned him only briefly. The red-eyed potato farmer rattled on like a truck driver on NoDoz. Poor guy, the sheriff thought, he won't be worth a damn till he gets some sleep.

Sheri Elms had never claimed clairvoyance about her husband, but they'd spent half their short lives together and were sensitive about each other. When he hadn't returned from the desert by Tuesday afternoon, she'd called his supervisor's office and was told they expected him any minute.

Three calls later, she said, "I'm really worried. Is Ray worried?"

"No."

"Well, I guess I won't worry then." But she knew she would.

At 4:00 P.M. her nerves took her to the supermarket. She raced up and down the aisles. What if he was lost? Or hurt? What if Bill's truck had missed a turn in the pass?

She tried to stop the what-if game and concentrate on her shopping. She filled the cart with Conley's favorite foods, the ones she'd always made him buy for himself—chocolate pudding, syrup, sesame seed rolls, Chee•tos, Doritos, everything sweet or fattening or both. When she got home she had two bags of items she'd never bought before.

She'd just set the junk food down when she saw Conservation Officer Don Beach and his wife at the door. "Have you heard yet?" the woman asked gently.

"No," Sheri said. "Heard what?"

"There's been a report that two Fish and Game officers were shot and killed in Owyhee County."

Sheri felt cold. She walked past the couple into the yard and began raking leaves. "No," she said, raking as fast as she could move her arms. "I don't believe this. I don't be*lieve* this. . . ." The two old friends tried to console her, but she said she had to get up the leaves.

After dark she dialed Fish and Game headquarters again. A voice confirmed that one C.O. was dead and maybe two. No, they weren't sure who. Had she heard from Conley? She wished she could say yes.

He couldn't be dead. Who on earth would shoot a man like him? Just the day before she'd been griping about some money that was owed them and he'd said, "Have a little compassion." Even the folks he ticketed ended up liking him, wrote letters to the Department thanking them for employing such a reasonable man. Everybody liked Conley. *No one would kill a man everybody liked!*

At 10:00 P.M. she called the capitol switchboard and left word. When Governor John Evans returned her call, she spoke fast so she wouldn't take too much of his time. "I don't know if my husband's alive or not but if there's any chance he's alive then I'm the only one in the world he can count on to come find him. So please get somebody to fly me down there in a helicopter and make sure it's got a strong searchlight because I know where to look and *nobody else does!*" The governor assured her that they were already doing everything that could be done.

She didn't sleep.

Dee Pogue, her son and her three daughters stayed up drinking coffee. By midnight they'd been told again that Bill was dead, but they kept hoping. Steven twisted the radio dials for news. The governor's office called and said that a National Guard helicopter would pick up the bodies. Dee said she would believe it when she saw the proof.

One by one her children dozed and woke and dozed again. She thought about the medical checkup Bill was supposed to have in a few days. Lately he'd felt flutterings around his heart. From childhood he'd lived in fear of cardiac arrest. He feared nothing else.

She brewed more coffee. The children stirred. When she heard a helicopter cranking up at the nearby National Guard station, she decided to accept reality. She walked to the window and said, "Well, they'll soon be back with your father."

116

26

LATE THAT NIGHT the mixed bag of Nevada and Idaho lawmen walked to the Winners Inn, a hotel and gambling hall, where the security guard irritated them by insisting that they check their firearms. They bought each other drinks and shared information about the killings and told war stories and complained of low budgets and unpaid overtime—the standard chatter of cops. To hear the Humboldt deputies tell it, northern Nevada was turning into a slaughterhouse. A hermit who called himself "Bristlewolf" had murdered three travelers on the Black Rock Desert. A woman was clubbed to death with a sledgehammer. There were three or four unsolved murders and a couple of murder-suicides. And now—the two game wardens. What was happening to the peaceful old desert?

After a while Tim Nettleton paid up and wandered back to his motel. He was surprised to find his mind still on Bill Pogue despite five or six rounds of anesthetic. He remembered a fall night along the Snake River in 1979, when Bill had mentioned that someone was poaching heavily in the southwest part of Owyhee County and moving fur through a Nevada bar owner. One quote came back: "That trapper's a dirty little mean son of a bitch. If you ever get

117

around him, watch out." He wondered whom Bill had meant; was it the same man who'd killed him?

The sheriff blew a stream of smoke into the light from his motel bed lamp and tried to work up a plausible theory about the killings. But he couldn't. Bill was a family man, an artist, a biologist and a dedicated protector of wildlife, but first and foremost he was a lawman. How in the name of common sense had he let a killer get the drop?

In wilderness confrontations, he'd never seen Bill back down. There was always some asshole full of camp booze who couldn't resist mouthing off at the fifty-year-old man in the green monkey suit. After the third or fourth wisecrack Bill would address the guy as "sir," swell fifty pounds and grow two inches, and in a few well-chosen sentences extinguish him like a drowned match. To Nettleton it wasn't hostility or belligerence; it was what peace officers knew as "command presence." Bill had learned it as a marine and later as a policeman. It was the most peaceable way to shut down violence.

Well, the sheriff said to himself, if he had to go, he found the perfect place. In the ten years of their friendship, Bill had been fanatical about working in the field and especially in the Owyhee. He'd been promoted to a desk job and squawked so much that they'd returned him to his animals and fish and dickeybirds. He fit the outdoors and vice versa. On overnight trips he slept outside. If it rained, he dragged his sleeping bag under a haystack or a tree. He wouldn't permit fires because they might alert poachers. He would wake up at dawn and complain about oversleeping. He was never off duty. Dee Pogue confided to the Nettletons at dinner one night, "When our family goes for rides, Bill'll say, 'Look at that fisherman down there! I'll bet he doesn't have a license.' He's thinking *work* all the time."

He took every violation seriously, becoming equally annoyed at kids stoning birds and hunters killing bighorn sheep. The sheriff had heard him tell more than one violator, "Poaching isn't a game and we're not gonna play it like a game." And he didn't. He played it like a war.

He wasn't faultless. Nettleton remembered kidding him about the prejudice that folks in the wilderness were up to no good. Bill had been a hunter but quit cold, explaining to friends, "There isn't anything I'd rather see dead than alive." Sometimes his love of wildlife made him write citations for infractions that other C.O.'s would have ignored. But he also knew when to back off and when to compromise. He often pulled traps instead of dragging the violators into court; it was less hassle for everyone, and the message got across. Once when he tasted illegal venison in a desert cookout, he stalked out of the camp without a word, making his point without issuing a ticket.

The sheriff remembered long talks about guns almost word-for-word. Bill packed a .38 and never sat with his back to a restaurant door. "I put some people in prison when I was working in Nevada," he explained. But he wasn't fanatical about guns like so many law officers, including Nettleton. He used his sidearm as a tool, a prop. In all his years, he'd drawn it once, when he cornered two car thieves along the Boise River, hobbled them and delivered them to the county sheriff in the back of his pickup. When he made a rare visit to the shooting range, the other C.O.'s ducked. One of his eyes was damaged; he joked that he saw two targets and split the difference.

Maybe that's the explanation, the sheriff said to himself as he shook the last Chesterfield from his crumpled pack. Maybe Bill just got outdrawn. But what kind of nut would start a High Noon gunfight with a C.O. in the middle of the desert? He remembered Bill's description of a certain new type of outdoorsmen: "freaked-out creeps, dropouts with guns on their hips, drug culture bums that aren't eating right and their mind is shot and they're wanted back in L.A. for armed robbery or something."

Bill had argued that wardens should have the right to lay down such characters before frisking them. Nettleton had agreed, but one night at Walters Ferry he asked Pogue, "The way folks dress nowadays, how could you tell you're not laying down a responsible citizen?"

"That's the problem," Bill said. "Can you imagine what would happen if I laid down the head surgeon from St. Alphonsus with a pistol in his back?"

The old friends agreed there was no pat solution. That's what made law enforcement rewarding—the challenges, the frustrations. "That's why we're so overpaid," Nettleton said, and both men laughed at their own expense. At the time, the sheriff was earning fifteen thousand a year and driving a beet truck on his summer vacations. Pogue earned less.

Maybe if Bill had laid Dallas down, Nettleton thought, he'd be alive tonight. It was 3:00 A.M. and his motel room was layered with smoke. He wished he could doze off; in a few hours the manhunt would begin in earnest. But his friends didn't get shot every day and it wasn't conducive to sleep.

He decided that there wasn't much that Bill or anybody else could have done about a crazy son of a bitch who went out and got himself a game warden the way others went out and got a deer. The only way to handle a dude like that was to give him a fair trial and hang him. Then maybe the next "mountain man" would think twice.

But first, of course, he had to be caught.

27

WEDNESDAY BEGAN WITH palaver and planning. The lawmen who trooped into the Humboldt sheriff's office were outraged by the killings and showed it. A Winnemucca cop asked permission to fake a heart attack on top of a hill, then shoot Dallas when he came to help. Someone suggested that the trap line at Bull Basin be rigged to Bouncing Betty mines, the type known for slicing off genitals, in case the killer returned.

Some of the volunteers had driven all night, and each seemed to have the same set of questions: was the killer a cop hater who would shoot on sight or just a hot-tempered fool who'd made the mistake of his life? How angry was he? How *crazy?*

Nobody knew.

The men kept telling each other to take no chances and follow procedure. Sheriff Frank Weston warned, "At *all* times, above *all* else, cover your ass!" Some of the searchers dressed as hunters, even to red caps and Day-Glo jackets; Dallas had had enough easy target practice on uniforms. Everyone agreed that he deserved the same consideration he'd shown Pogue and Elms, but Gene Weller's earlier words to a trapper were widely quoted: "He'll snipe you off a ridge." In the Old West or the new, there was no protection from a bushwhacker.

It was late morning before the planning stopped and Humboldt County deputies hauled tracking dogs to the spot where George Nielsen had reported dropping Dallas off. Some of the officers wore bulletproof vests and a few carried canteens and snacks in case they were pinned down. A Cessna from the Nevada Department of Wildlife droned back and forth, just above the fences. Somewhere in those low hills a wagonload of gold was still missing after a century. Fifty square miles of shifting sand kept secrets.

The thermometer had dropped and Sand Pass Road was frozen hard. Footprints went a short distance into the brush, reversed, then faded. At first the tracking hounds couldn't get a scent, but as the earth warmed they got too many. Northern Nevada's chukar season had opened a week earlier. The hounds yipped and howled and ran in circles.

After three hours sleep, Tim Nettleton had decided to cede the Paradise search area to Nevada authorities and shift his base north to McDermitt, forty miles west of Bull Camp and the closest community of any size. Deputies and game wardens were converging on the wind-blasted little cowtown when the Owyhee sheriff arrived after a high-speed drive up from Winnemucca. One Idaho National Guard helicopter had already landed.

At the outdoor briefing he wished he'd had the common sense to bring along some liquid fortification. The wind howled down from Disaster Peak and hit his face like slush off a roof. A pair of "dingoes" skulked by, scruffy backs arched against the cold. White puffs floated ahead of the sheriff's words as he told the posse, "Dallas is thirty years of age and he's loose down in an area south of here. He's a man of five ten, a hundred and seventy pounds, brown hair, brown eyes, has a cinnamon-colored beard, wearing glasses, a short ponytail, and wearing a down jacket. He's portrayed to us to be a very capable man in the backwoods."

The volunteers, some dressed for the outdoors and some for the office, shuffled their feet and blew in cupped hands. The sheriff recognized men from Nevada, Oregon, and Idaho—state troopers, game wardens, city policemen—all looking like refugees from a three-day poker game. He thought, Word goes out that a lawman's been killed and it's like some son of a bitch shot your brother.

122

Can't sleep till we're on the case. It's one of the traits that distinguish us from humans.

A few of the men looked as though they'd spent their lives indoors. How would they fare against the merciless young mountain man? He had misgivings about sending them on such a dangerous mission, but he knew they'd go with or without authorization. He stressed, "If you make contact, call for backup." Gunfights were out. Animals like Dallas notwithstanding, this wasn't the 1800s.

He started to throw in a final note of optimism, but he held back. It never paid to bullshit cops. Dallas was in his second day on the run; he was desert-wise and heavily armed and was said to have caches with survival tools and ammunition. He could be biding his time in a thousand different mine shafts, shacks, cabins and caves, and there wasn't a one of them that you could approach without being seen a mile away. It would be a miracle if they caught him and a double miracle if he didn't take one of them down before he was captured.

For the second night in a row, Jim Stevens had wrestled his sheets and pillows and lost. He'd been questioned half of Monday and all of Tuesday, and now on Wednesday he and the Nielsens were scheduled to take lie detector tests. He knew his story sounded crazy. Every time he told someone that Claude had drawn and shot the two wardens, they asked, "But why?" That was the problem. There was no why. Then they would ask how many shots had been fired.

"I dunno. He said he emptied his gun. Maybe five or six rounds. I'm not sure."

"Why aren't you sure? *Weren't you there?*"

The questioning was gentle but persistent. No third degree was necessary. The Humboldt County district attorney had called him "helpful and cooperative." He was pleased about that.

But now that the lie detector test was coming up, he was fearful. How could he pass when he couldn't hold a cup without spilling it and broke into a cold sweat every time someone mentioned Claude Dallas? He'd heard that Liz Nielsen had been excused from the tests because she'd taken tranquilizers. He wished he'd gone that route instead of sucking up so much caffeine.

The potato farmer hadn't been strapped to the machine with its skittery styli for five minutes before he realized that he was looking bad. "The operator's expression showed it," he told Sandra later. "I thought, 'This guy isn't believing me.' And that puts you off, too." The longer he was questioned, the jumpier he became. When the session ended six hours later, the Nevada state police polygrapher confided that the trauma had been too great and the tests were inconclusive.

George Nielsen's tests were easier to evaluate. The polygraphist said he was a perfect subject for the machine; all his emotions showed and at times he got so excited that the operator feared for his health. In the end, Claude Dallas's friend and mentor was adjudged to be telling the truth for the most part but "practicing deception" on four questions to which he answered no:

> Are you withholding any important information from us in this investigation?
> Other than what we talked about, have you deliberately concealed any evidence of this killing?
> Do you know for sure where Bill Pogue's body is now?
> To your knowledge, has anyone been in contact with Claude Dallas since January sixth?

In the post-test questioning, the bar owner admitted that he'd slipped Dallas a hundred dollars on Sand Pass Road. He'd previously denied any financial assistance. He also reported that when Dallas left the pickup that night, he'd warned Nielsen not to try to get in touch with him; Dallas would initiate any contacts. Nielsen told the state police polygrapher that he knew his responsibilities under the law—if Dallas contacted him, he would have to turn him in. But he wasn't sure he could.

By the time Tim Nettleton deployed his search party from McDermitt and arranged for more aircraft, it was late in the morning. Everyone except the governor had demanded free transport to the scene, and the sheriff had lost time acting as travel agent and loadmaster.

At last he turned to a helicopter pilot he'd just hired and said, "You got enough gas to go forty miles and back?"

"Yeah," the pilot answered.

Nettleton dozed on the thirty-minute flight over the low northern hills of the Santa Rosa range. When he awoke, they were circling a ranch. "That's the Forty-five!" he shouted over the rotor noise. "We gotta go twelve or fourteen miles south."

The pilot said he barely had enough fuel to return to McDermitt. "Then put me down here," the sheriff said. "Radio the next chopper to pick me up." Now he would be the last man at his own party.

Joann Carlin told him that her husband Eddy and father-in-law Don had left on horseback to help out at Bull Basin. She offered breakfast, but the sheriff stoked up a cigarette instead. A bottle of Southern Comfort materialized on the kitchen table, reviving his Roman Catholic faith in miracles, and when the news helicopter from Salt Lake City picked him up thirty minutes later, he was wide awake and ready.

The Idaho Bureau of Investigation's Harry Capaul had reached Bull Basin via the first National Guard helicopter. Two airborne TV crews were already circling the tent, and one of them advised by radio that a body was snagged downstream. About four hundred yards north of the campsite Capaul got his first view of Conley Elms.

His aircraft lifted back to the rim and landed next to the abandoned Fish and Game truck. A short time later a helicopter marked "KIFI" touched down and let out Sheriff Tim Nettleton. At his order, the IBI agent checked the Dodge Powerwagon for boobytraps while others began searching the area on hands and knees. They found several burnt spots, a pair of Penlite batteries, a plastic drinking cup and a few other items. Bloodstains marked an old wagon trail that led down toward the camp.

Forensic teams from Boise arrived in another National Guard helicopter and began working the trail with evidence bags, tape measures and cameras. Among other things, they found the footprints of four men and two mules, streaks and splotches of blood, a butterscotch candy wrapper, a 7-Up can, a label from a Portland Rose glove package with a price tag of $2.09, a tag from a New Life feed bag, a torn Pillsbury tag, an unfired .357 magnum bullet and two shell casings labeled ".38 cal. P-plus."

The collection job took all day. On Nettleton's orders, everyone steered clear of the sealed tent. Under the law, it was abandoned and therefore no longer private, but the sheriff didn't want to risk contaminating the court case against Dallas. A search warrant was being prepared in Murphy and would be flown down. Too much was at stake to commit any procedural errors in the touchy age of Miranda and Escobedo.

A glum Nettleton led a team to collect the body. Conley Elms floated facedown about eight feet from shore. Deputies waded into the chilly current and eased him ashore. The sheriff took a close look and began repeating to himself, It won't do to get mad. . . .

The warden was naked except for two pairs of socks and a beltless pair of pants around his ankles. His face was puffy, the area above his eyes yellowish purple. There was a large ragged hole in his chest about three inches above the left nipple, a second hole about eight inches below the first, and a small hole in his head. He was badly scratched and bruised.

The sheriff ordered him zipped into a body bag and flown in a sling to the campsite.

The teams finished the day's work by flashlight; sage bushes were ignited against the night chill. A helicopter pilot warned the sheriff that the temperature was twelve and dropping. Nettleton assembled the three state policemen, four IBI officers, five game wardens, two crime lab specialists, and two men from the prosecutor's office, and ordered them to stow their gear and secure the area —"We'll come back and finish tomorrow."

He checked the straps on the body bag, lying in the landing area next to the tent. "Come on, Sheriff!" the pilot called out.

"This goes, too," Nettleton said, tugging at the bag.

"Negative! I'm already overloaded."

The last flight lifted out of the canyon and headed west toward McDermitt.

Early in the evening a reporter called George Nielsen and learned the address of the fugitive's family. By telephone from South Carolina, Claude Lafayette Dallas Sr. entered the case in angry tones. "We're all tore up but we're standing close by him," the father said in a robust Appalachian accent. "We've been hounded by the FBI and local police and I don't want to say anything about that boy." Then he hung up.

His wife, Jennie Johnston Randall Dallas, a pert realtor in her early sixties, told a friend in her rich Carolina accent:

"I heard it on the radio at the office around two o'clock, that the

126

FBI had put out a warrant for my son. They said he was wanted for killing two men. I just sat there. When the fellas came back in from lunch, one of 'em came up and said, 'You don't look too well.'

"I said, 'I'm not.'

"He said, 'What in the world's the matter?' That's all I heard.

"When I felt a little better, I told them what I'd heard on the radio. They said you couldn't have heard that. I said, 'Yes, I did. And I know it's my son because the announcer used the expression mountain man.'

"I phoned my husband, Claude Sr. He said, 'What'll I do?'

"I said, 'Call out there to Nevada, see if it's true.'

"He did, and called me back. Said he'd talked to George Nielsen and it was true. The FBI was with Nielsen right then and they talked to Claude Sr. a few minutes and asked our address and everything.

"The folks in the real estate office wanted to bring me home, but I said no. I had to close a deal with a teacher about a rental. They were trying to tell me, No, you cain't do that.

"I said *I will,* but first I'll go by our house and see how Claude Sr. is. He hasn't been well. When I got there, Claude was yellin' and hollerin' and blamin' it all on me. Why? I guess because I'm the mother. The mother has to be blamed. I wish to hell I knew what I did wrong. I loved my kids too much, probably. But they were *not* spoiled. You can't give a child too much love. And I kep' up with 'em. Well, it's always gotta be blamed on somebody. . . .

"I told Claude Sr. to take it easy, I'll be back in a little while. I was annoyed because this was the second day after it happened and nobody from Nevada had called and told us. Liz could've called, George could've called. They knew how to reach us. It's just like when there's a death in the family—you take care of what you have to do. And that's exactly the way I felt about it: a death in the family.

"I went on over and met my little teacher and rented her the apartment. Didn't say anything about what happened. When I got back home Claude'd already told all the neighbors and they were pilin' in our house and I couldn't stand that—showing things that Claude Jr. had made, and pictures. I came in there and gathered all that stuff up and went back in the bedroom and slammed the door. I didn't want 'em nosin' in there. After that I just kep' busy. That way you don't think about it."

Sheri Elms's friends had stayed with her all day. She refused to accept that Conley was dead. Missing, yes. In trouble, maybe. But dead? Dead was impossible.

The evening newscast showed a naked body swinging in the current. Just like Conley, the man had a thick upper torso and narrowing waist and spirals of fine black hair down his back.

She rushed out the door and banged her head against the side of the house. Then she ran down the street. She didn't want to be home.

Tim Nettleton had asked the Say When Cafe in McDermitt to charge all the law officers' meals to his two-hundred-dollar-limit credit card. When he got in from Bull Camp, some of the searchers were ordering from the cheap side of the menu. "Listen," he told the waitress, "you make sure everybody here gets fed good." Before the night was over, the bill passed three hundred dollars and the sheriff signed with an unspoken prayer that the cashier wouldn't check his card.

He stayed up even later than the night before, talking to the sheriff's office in Winnemucca, his own office in Murphy and the attorney general's office in Boise. He returned a dozen calls from newsmen and law officers who wanted to join in the search. It was 3:30 A.M. when he reported to his wife. "It don't look good," he told Charlene. "They hunted all day and didn't find a trace of Dallas."

"And Bill?"

"Plumb gone."

"Where?"

"Nobody knows."

The frozen body of Conley Elms spent the night by the river.

28

By THURSDAY DAYLIGHT, the eighty searchers had nothing to show for their exertions but blistered feet and frostbite. There were so many canyons to hike up, so many mine shafts to look down, so many cabins to creep up on. "It'll take a goddamn army to find that asshole," crusty Harry Capaul griped to fellow searchers.

The trackers took heart from generous infusions of matériel and manpower. Idaho dispatched a steady flow including National Guard aircraft. Joseph Greenley, director of Nevada's Department of Wildlife, sent in four armed men and the agency's airplane to work full-time in the search. As former Idaho wildlife director, he'd hiked the Owyhee Desert with Bill Pogue. Other volunteers continued to stream toward Winnemucca and McDermitt.

Around Thursday noon, Winnemucca police heard that a man had been seen peeping out a window at a deserted mine north of Paradise Valley. Deputies in bulletproof vests covered one another with shotguns and semiautomatic weapons and searched the old buildings. Humboldt Sheriff's Investigator Stan Rorex was belayed on several fruitless drops to the watery bottoms of nearby mine shafts and wells. Others wallowed in clammy tailing dumps looking for footprints; Dallas had left a distinctive crosshatch track at Bull Camp. But he wasn't at the Cinnabar.

Elko County deputies crept up on a cave where the fugitive had entertained a woman years before. Word was that he'd boasted he would hide inside "and shoot any cop that comes near." The cave contained nothing but bear droppings.

Mounted officers swept canyons and gulches and creek bottoms for miles around Paradise Hill and Sand Pass Road. Helicopter crews made gunship raids on deserted cabins and flushed out skunks and pack rats—"the wrong kind of rat," a searcher complained. Ground parties searched fissures and ledges and caves in the Bloody Runs and the Humboldts, the Slumbering Hills and Santa Rosas. Patrol cops drove the back roads buttonholing residents and looking for tracks along the frozen shoulders. None appeared.

The biggest problem was that Dallas's escape route was a guess. From Sand Pass Road, geographical logic suggested that he would continue west to the Black Rock Desert and thence into California, but he also could have headed east to the Tuscaroras or the Owyhee Desert, or south across the Krum Hills toward Reno and Las Vegas, or north to one of his famous caches in the Bloody Runs. It was also possible that he'd strolled two miles to heavily traveled Highway 95 and stuck out his thumb, in which case he could be a thousand miles away. Duane Michelson, the Nevada truck agent who'd visited Bull Camp with his daughter, ventured the opinion that his friend had fled to Steens Mountain and the Alvord. The advice was ignored on the grounds that Dallas's favorite shooting companion might be lying.

Some of the searchers gave up on Dallas and turned their attention to finding Bill Pogue. Reservoirs were dragged with grappling hooks; a ramp was bladed to an inaccessible pond so that a rescue team could put its boat in the water. Fire engines pumped out a hot pool ten miles west of the Paradise Valley. Helicopters looked for telltale tire tracks where Dallas might have backed George Nielsen's truck to a mine shaft. Deputies raced around checking out tips that were overwhelming police switchboards in all three I-O-N states. An anonymous caller claimed that Pogue's body was bleaching in the sun on a rockslide in the Blue Mountains, twenty-five miles west of Winnemucca. Searchers found the carcass of a cow.

Tim Nettleton spent a second straight day looking for evidence on the killing ground. Late in the morning he arranged for the frozen body of Conley Elms to be airlifted to St. Alphonsus Hospital in Boise. Search warrants finally arrived and he followed the letter of the law by slapping the side of the abandoned tent and calling out, "Anybody in there?" Then he probed the rear wall for boobytraps while Jack Arbaugh, a deputy sheriff from Canyon County, Idaho, waited to enter through the front flap.

Arbaugh inventoried a box and a half of .38 shot-shells, leather work boots, red-trimmed western boots, Mexican spurs with over-size rowels, a pair of waders and a raccoon hide on a stretcher board. On the bed lay an open box of Remington .22 long-rifle shells with two loose rounds alongside. Apparently Dallas had loaded up before firing the final slugs behind the wardens' ears. Nettleton was excited by the discovery; it showed premeditation, a key ingredient of first-degree murder, recently made punishable in Idaho by lethal injection. That needle bullshit's too good for him, the sheriff said to himself, but I don't want to be picky.

Early in the afternoon Jim Stevens was flown into Bull Camp to help out. Nettleton was glad to get another crack at the only living witness. "I don't want to swallow his whole story," he confided to Harry Capaul. "If I do, then I close my mind and I might miss something. I think he's more involved than he's admitting. He's probably scared of Dallas and lying to save his ass. He might even know where Dallas is—and Bill, too."

Capaul agreed. It was true that the potato farmer had a sterling reputation in Humboldt County, but parts of his story didn't make sense and word was out that he'd had problems on the lie box the day before.

The slope-shouldered sheriff watched as Stevens climbed from the helicopter and picked his way through the sage. He walked like a farmer, a strong point in his favor. The two men shook hands and made small talk. He talked like a farmer, too, another good sign, but he also sounded like someone who read a lot of books. The sheriff decided to withhold judgment.

Owyhee County Prosecutor Alan Koffel stepped up and suggested that they stand the witness in front of a video camera and interview him on the spot. Stevens asked, "Why? I've been interviewed already."

Koffel said, "We'll need the tape in case Dallas blows you away."

Stevens's eyes rolled back in his head; the sight put Nettleton in mind of a bull coming out of a chute. Then the potato farmer looked from the sheriff to the prosecutor and said in a strong voice, "I'm not afraid of Claude Dallas no more."

The sheriff felt the hair stand on his neck. The reaction was too intense to be faked. His doubts dissipated in the cold desert wind. He had to believe in the man.

Jim Stevens hadn't been nervous about returning to the scene of the crime, but he'd been nervous about everything else since the incident three days before. Any loud noise or violence was likely to start him trembling. He'd jumped into the air when one character shot another on the TV at home. "God darn!" he'd snapped at his children. "Turn that off!"

Now he stood at the bottom of Bull Basin telling his story for a VCR, using landmarks to make himself clear. He showed where Claude and the wardens had stood, where Pogue and Elms had lain when Claude finished them off, where he and Claude had tried to slide the heavy body onto the mule. He walked through a detailed re-creation of the crime while forensic investigators marked and measured like tailors. For the first time, he felt that he was thoroughly understood.

He'd brought in his metal detector to help find bullets and other evidence, but the gadget went dead as soon as someone tried to use it. He was just as glad. Once he'd considered Bull Basin the apex of his collecting career; now he just wanted to get home. Before boarding the helicopter, he overheard Nettleton saying, "We'll take dynamite and blow up those stone cabins."

He was stunned. What kind of a man would obliterate history? Back home with his box of a thousand arrowheads, he confessed to his wife, "I just about fainted."

In Myrtle Beach, South Carolina, the FBI paid its first visit to the neatly lawned residence of Claude Lafayette Dallas Sr. and his wife, Jennie. The senior Dallas described the meeting later in his stentorian voice: "They sent over the local agent, Don Myers, bet-

132

ter known as Barney Fife. A nice enough fella. We sat in our living room and he tried to work up a profile on Claude—and I didn't have enough sense to know what he was doing. Jennie kept coming to the door and shaking her head at me. Myers asked me how Claude parted his hair, everything—what he liked, what he disliked, where he might hide out. I didn't tell him any more than I wanted to. When he left, I told him, 'Now I don't want you coming around here tomorrow bothering my wife. Don't come back unless I'm here!' "

Tim Nettleton hadn't been serious about destroying the stone cabins. Two days in Bull Basin's cold desolation were enough; he had no intention of returning with dynamite or anything else.

Around 4:00 P.M. the sun fell behind the clouds and emitted only glints, not nearly enough to work by. As his last official act at the scene, he placed a copy of the search warrant and a receipt for the tent contents in a plastic bag under a rock. Then he delicately balanced a couple of tent poles so that any movement would dislodge them. He explained to a puzzled deputy, "If Claude comes back we'll know he's been here. I'll fly down once in a while to check."

The party began boarding the helicopter for the return flight to McDermitt. "I can only take eleven," the pilot warned, but fourteen pushed inside. Nettleton knew it would be a hairy flight, but he dozed off anyway.

When he opened his eyes, the helicopter was slowly descending on its landing lights to a pad just down the street from the Say When Cafe. Back at his room he found a pileup of phone messages. Citizens had been calling all day, their ire aroused by TV pictures of Conley Elms in the river. There were calls from *The New York Times* and other newspapers, calls from the networks and the wire services, calls from police agencies, from old friends, friends of friends, relatives and strangers. Everyone wanted him to call back *right away.* He almost wished he were still at Bull Camp with its radio silence. It had taken till 3:00 A.M. to handle all the bullshit the night before. If he returned all his calls tonight, he'd be on the phone till dawn.

The final blows were several high-priority requests by various coroners and other medical experts to rush to Nevada and postmortem poor Conley Elms. Nettleton had a mental picture of a pack of mad surgeons with scalpels aloft, arguing over who would make the first incisions and the first pronouncements. Well, the case belonged to Owyhee County and he would see that a proper autopsy was conducted just as he'd seen that the evidence had been preserved and everyone's rights protected. He fired a telegram to his dispatcher in Murphy:

> CONLEY ELMS BODY IS AT SAINT ALS AT THIS TIME. I'M PUTTING UP WITH A BUNCH OF BULLSHIT! CONTACT THE CORONER AND EVERYONE ELSE THAT WILL LISTEN AND TELL THEM TO KEEP THEIR HANDS OFF THE BODY UNTIL WE ARE PREPARED TO DO A PROPER AUTOPSY. THANK YOU.

Then he went out for a drink.

29

ON FRIDAY, FOUR days after the killings, Jennie Dallas answered her door in Myrtle Beach and found FBI Agent Donald Myers standing in the morning sun. She told a friend later: "I'd taken a Valium from the doctor the night before and I was pretty well knocked out on it. My husband had told this same FBI man not to come around if I was alone, but there he was, wanting to know the kids' Social Security numbers. I told him, 'Didn't my husband tell you I was on medication?' He said, 'Yes, ma'am.' He told me, 'We could come in your house and take anything we want. We could take the pictures off your wall.'

"I told him, 'I wouldn't advise you to try it.' Then I told him to leave. We had a picture of Claude in there. I took it out of the living room so he couldn't come back and stare at it."

Around noon on that same Friday, FBI Special Weapons and Tactics personnel converged on Winnemucca from San Francisco, Reno and Las Vegas. Special Agent Joe Goss told reporters the twelve men were prepared to search for weeks. They debriefed the locals, donned bulletproof vests, grabbed their artillery, and boarded a blue-and-white Bell UH-1H "Huey" military-type helicopter, coordinating their search with two fixed-wing aircraft and several patrol cars. At the end of the sweep, SWAT leader David Guilland reported that his men had seen "nothing but a lot of animals."

By now the searchers had reached the point where they were accepting help from any source, including a psychic who solemnly reported that the body of Bill Pogue would be found "in water." Someone remembered Jim Stevens's report that Dallas had considered dumping the body in Chimney Rock reservoir. A dive team led by Sheriff's Investigator Stan Rorex made the long bumpy drive. Below a rocky face they found a man-size hole in the reservoir ice. Rorex went down in zero visibility while Winnemucca policeman Brad Valladon held his lifeline and stirred the opening to keep the ice from re-forming.

Rorex recovered nothing but loose wire and trash. A douser walked onto the ice and found two other likely areas, but a half hour of diving produced only blue hands and chattering teeth. A similar routine was tried at another small reservoir with similar results.

On Friday night a cowboy drove to the sheriff's office in Winnemucca to report a campfire a few miles east of Bonita Springs on the Black Rock Desert, fifty miles west of Sand Pass Road. The searchers were already stretched over five thousand square miles, mostly to the north and east, and no one was available to investigate.

Later that night a former Humboldt County deputy sheriff named Noel McElhany made camp in a deserted adobe house a few miles from where the campfire had been spotted. Years before, he'd crossed Dallas's trail twice: when he'd helped arrest the young buckaroo for draft evasion and when he'd provided backup for warden Gene Weller on a poaching matter in the Bloody Run Hills.

Trying to sleep, McElhany counted off the mountain ranges he'd crossed in his pickup to get to this isolated camping spot called Bonita Springs. He'd started in the Bloody Runs, then pushed across the Slumbering Hills, up the eastern slope of the Jackson Mountains and down the other side to this pretty little basin in the Black Rock Desert. The old house had a sod roof and adobe walls so thick that candles kept it warm. Outside were the springs and a grave marked by a piece of tin.

McElhany had always been drawn to places like this. Still in his early thirties, he'd been brought up on a primitive Nevada ranch—no power, no phones, no public water, just shallow windmill wells, manpower, horsepower, and the simplest of tools. He still had no use for motorized farm equipment and not much for civilization either. He lived in Winnemucca but left town every chance he got, collecting remote spots the way others collected stamps and coins. He was fascinated by the surrounding deserts: the Black Rock, the Smoke Creek, the Alvord, the Owyhee. He'd often camped at Bull Basin and Devils Corral.

He was lying half awake when he heard a squeak. Something—more likely some*one,* he decided, judging by the sound—was on the small wooden porch.

He cracked back the hammer on his .357 magnum. It was a reflex, clumsy and loud, and he realized that the intruder couldn't have missed the metallic click.

He lay immobile for twenty or thirty minutes, breathing softly. Maybe the visitor would see his pickup, parked around back, and maybe he wouldn't.

Around 2:00 A.M. he stepped outside. The moon cast an opalescent bluish glow on the grave. In the distance a coyote cut loose with a string of frenzied yipes, and another answered from so close that McElhany figured it must have come in for a drink. Then everything was quiet again.

On the porch he found a clump of fresh mud in a waffle imprint. The mud must have come from the spring; the rest of the ground was frozen. Someone had hiked in for water and rest. He wondered who.

An aircraft crisscrossed the mountains and deserts shooting infrared photographs in the dark. Two "targets" turned up, but their location made it almost certain that they were hunters. No one had time to check.

30

Toward the end of the week the hunters began to lose heart. At the outset they'd felt satisfyingly vengeful, but the monotonous fieldwork had dulled their edge. The daily strategy sessions continued; the FBI conferred with state police who conferred with Fish and Game officials who conferred with Humboldt County sheriff's officers who would have conferred with the Winnemucca police department except that the two agencies were feuding with each other when they weren't feuding with the state police. As for the Owyhee sheriff's department, it kept to itself at McDermitt and Bull Camp, gathering evidence.

For the searchers, most of whom were military veterans, the hunt settled into the familiar pattern of "hurry up and wait," followed by tedious hours of slogging across mud and ice, manning roadblocks, exploring musty cabins and caves, patrolling roads and trails, and listening for the crack of a rifle. There hadn't been a trace of Dallas or Pogue.

Morale wasn't helped by imaginative descriptions of the mighty mountain man by customers of the Paradise Hill Bar and others. A friendly drinker sounded the theme to a newspaper reporter: "Claude knows every gopher hole and cave in the northwest. He's not a big man, but he's healthy and hearty. I'll bet he could go sixty miles on foot in one night."

Some of the volunteers threw up their hands and left. Who could catch a sagebrush Clark Kent with a four-day lead? Journalists exploited the easy phrase "mountain man" and its epic connotations. A Boise newspaper reported that an outdoorsman with Dallas's talents wouldn't merely survive in the desert, he would *thrive:* digging sego lily bulbs, biscuit-root plants and stream-bed plants, putting out night snares for birds, rabbits and deer, drinking water from dew and seeps. If he was living in a cave or a mine shaft, he could make an entrée of pack rats and mice—"high protein and good-tasting meats." A survival expert was quoted as saying that Dallas could last a lifetime on the desert and added, "If he's as good in the outdoors as I've read he is, he's got it made."

Others wove their own ideas into the pattern of myth. Humboldt Sheriff Frank Weston labeled the man who'd never been seen in a fight as "a tough little turkey" and told a TV interviewer that Dallas knew the desert like his own living room. "He loves to live off the land," the sheriff said, apparently unaware of the teams of provisioners. Said Weston: "He can live days without anything other than just a little place to lay down."

Tim Nettleton was quoted as saying, "Claude's in his backyard and he's not going to leave." The backyard, he said, encompassed five thousand square miles and at least seven camps stocked with food, arms and ammunition. Would the mountain man return to town for supplies? "For what?" Nettleton replied. "Not him! He's completely self-sustaining."

Few took the pedestrian approach of men like Idaho C.O. Jerry Lockhart, who insisted that Dallas wasn't a true outdoorsman or mountain man but simply "a renegade that can't live with people." The more popular view was summed up by a TV newsman: "If Dallas is found, it will only be because that's the way he wants it." A dozen years had passed since the brown-eyed kid from Mount Gilead, Ohio, had headed west, and suddenly he'd become the new Butch Cassidy, a cunning but idealistic desperado, the facts of his life distorted and distended to fit. *Claude Dallas, outlaw.* It was what the people seemed to want.

Rancher Benny Damele spoke with his usual bluntness: "I think the son of a bitch just wants to be chased." Duane Michelson agreed. "Claude's acting out something he read in a book," he said. Frank Weston wondered aloud about the eerie trip from Bull Basin to Paradise Hill. "It doesn't compute to bring Bill Pogue's body all that way and take him up on the main highway," the sheriff said.

Gene Weller said it computed perfectly. "He brought it back to show George Nielsen, the same way he used to bring back poached deer and lions," the Sunday School teacher theorized. "Imagine, he drove all that way with a body—*two* bodies is what he wanted. Think about that!"

Paradise Valley mourned. Old Frank Gavica brushed a tear from his lined cheek as he spoke about the young man who'd once insisted on paying him fifty dollars for a small favor. "Claude wouldn't harm anybody unless they approached him wrong. He *couldn't* hurt anybody. He was out there living the life he wanted. Why bother a guy like that? But when you corner somebody, God knows what they'll do."

In the desert saloons, the facts of the case were rearranged nightly like Scrabble chips. Customer Mal Naumann told an investigator: "Pogue was always pushing people around. I think he went looking for trouble and got more than he could handle out of Claude." In this updated version of events, Pogue was responsible for his own death. "He had it in for Claude," Naumann explained. "He was bound and determined to get Claude one way or the other. George Nielsen told me this and other people did, too."

Up at Steens Mountain, rancher Hoyt Wilson said, "Our first reaction was we couldn't hardly believe it. Our second was, Boy, those wardens sure must've done something wrong."

His mother agreed. "The stories that we've heard don't hang together," observed Coco Wilson Ickes, now the wife of an Idaho veterinarian. She made it plain whose side she was on.

Dallas's old friend Irene Fischer was one of the few who resisted mythology. She and her husband Walt had been Claude's close friends, but they'd always regarded him as a little strange. "We didn't hear about the killings for a coupla days and we had no doubt who did it," the former buckaroo and camp cook said in her soft western drawl. "My first thought was I hated those two game wardens for making Claude do that. I set up at night and cried. I went through all our pictures. He was *so* interesting. But then I realized it wouldn't've happened if he hadn't wanted it to. It was hard for me to face."

She paused, as though hesitant to take issue with other citizens of Paradise Valley. "Some folks are trying to blame the wardens. That's how people make a hero out of the wrong man. They want to be able to say, 'I met him, I seen him, I'm a friend of his.' Then their loyalty lays in sticking up for him. They do it for their own ego. And pretty soon a man has an image that's not true."

Mark Crane wrote in the *Idaho Statesman,* "Some of Dallas's acquaintances are openly rooting for him to escape." A few did more than root. Evidence was concealed, "wanted" posters destroyed, false information disseminated. Lawmen became the enemy. Bar owner Jerry Sans proudly told friends, "Claude had drawn me a map how to get right to Bull Camp, because he figured I'd be taking out mail and grub. As soon as I heard what happened, I burnt that damn map. When the feds and all those guys were in and out of my bar, they'd say, 'Whattaya know about Claude Dallas?' I'd say, 'Who's that?' "

Eighteen miles away, George Nielsen announced that he was ordering T-shirts inscribed GO CLAUDE GO! His place was crowded with curiosity seekers and fans of the killer. A rancher from McDermitt said that if Dallas showed up he'd give him "a big meal and my best horse." Friendly residents announced that they were leaving their pickup trucks out every night, keys in the ignition, gas tanks topped, sandwiches and beer in coolers.

"It's the nature and location of their work," explained an embarrassed Winnemuccan who'd been brought up on a local ranch. "In country like this, folks get pretty coyote. They're estranged from the law because they're so much without it. It's almost a tradition that a wanted man isn't gonna be turned in. We're still the Wild West in that respect."

It was a good place to hide.

31

SATURDAY'S SEARCH EFFORT was as conspicuous as a Fourth of July pinwheel and equally substantial. Helicopters from the FBI and Nevada Fish and Game dipped down on nervous Indians at the Duck River Reservation. Sheriff's parties toured Elko and Lander counties looking for Dallas's old camps. Winnemucca policemen set up roadblocks and stopped everyone with a beard or a ponytail. Gene Weller told his wife, "Every hippy's being picked up. There's guys stick out their thumbs for a ride and fifteen policemen surround 'em. It's kinda funny, but kinda sad, too."

Late in the day Frank Weston called his men off. The frustration of chasing a will-o'-the-wisp was causing too much interagency friction. From the first day of the search there'd been criticisms about ego trips and pomposity, the failure to broaden the search to the west, the long skull-sessions and longer lunches of certain officials, and other complaints often heard when killers make fools of police. A weary deputy was asked to sum up the progress that had been made in four days of searching air, water and land. He held thumb and forefinger in a circle.

Zero.

On Saturday night Tim Nettleton hitched a ride back to Murphy. As usual, the world's smallest county seat was dark except for a few rectangles of yellow light from windstruck houses. Party night, the sheriff said to himself. Folks'll stay up till ten.

He walked across the worn two-lane highway in a light snowfall and circled the back of the one-story courthouse toward the sheriff's office and jail, passing his mini–motor pool of jet boats, snowmobile, Jeep, Sno-Cat, and other specialized vehicles necessary for maintenance of law and order in Owyhee County.

His cramped office held stacks of unanswered phone slips. A dispatcher stabbed at the "hold" button and talked on the radio simultaneously. A deputy waited to report on the crime wave that had broken out in his absence: an illegal fire on the Snake, a Durham bull absent without leave, and a no-decision brawl featuring a married couple who'd been trying to revive the Friday-night fights for years.

He took care of the local problems as quickly as his innate courtesy would permit, then riffled through the phone reports. Dallas had been sighted in Alaska, Colorado, Arizona, Georgia, and a dozen other states on foot, in a car, on a bike, on a plane, in a gym, a barbershop, a McDonald's and a Kentucky Fried Chicken, and had also found time to visit Guadalajara and Toronto, all in the last forty-eight hours. The sheriff still believed that his man would be a conspicuous misfit anyplace except the desert area that he knew so well, but it was also possible that he was gone. Given his busy feet and the mobility of the era, he might even be in Toronto or Guada—whatever that other place was. So, Nettleton asked himself, where does that leave the poor jerk that's running the chase?

He fired up a cigarette and called in his dispatcher. "Let's start cataloging these," he said, handing back the phone slips. "If they look good, make sure I see 'em. We'll work 'em one by one, nice and slow." Then he asked her to set up a meeting with the IBI, meaning the moustachioed Harry Capaul, and the FBI, meaning Boise-based Agent George Calley. It was time for a change of pace.

At the strategy session, he offered ritual sips of Black Velvet from the pint in his lower desk drawer and said, "I ain't at all big enough to handle this case like it oughta be done—flying investiga-

143

tors to the scene of every sighting, keeping a watch on everybody, all that bullshit."

"We'll help you," Calley said.

"I'm counting on it. Thing is, there's only seven thousand folks in this county, and that means we run on nickels and dimes." The others nodded; every cop thought he ran on nickels and dimes. "My commissioners are farmers," the sheriff continued, "and farmers don't want to hear about overtime. So it's not a question of what I want to do but what I *got* to do."

"And what's that?" Harry Capaul asked. The veteran IBI agent had been crossing Nettleton's path for years and had a high regard for his talents, rough-hewn though they may have seemed to a few unobservant others.

The sheriff opened a fresh carton of Chesterfields. "I've gotta play the country bumpkin," he said, ripping at a pack. "I've gotta jes' set back and poke and let somebody else do the chasin' for us." He peered through the cracked window at the snow. A mongrel was barking itself into a hernia. There's probably some coyotes around, he thought. Danged things own this place at night. . . .

He went on, "Any police agencies, any reporters, any TV folks that want to help us find Dallas, I'm gonna wine 'em and dine 'em and Charlene's gonna cook 'em steak. I'll be available for interviews *when*ever and *where*ver. I'm gonna send out a ton of bullshit and work the phones and run down every tip." He paused. "We'll put so much heat on Dallas he won't be able to use a public toilet." He broke into one of his tractor-starting laughs. "He'll have to buy his own Porta Potti just to take a leak."

"The press'll milk this dry and then drop it," Capaul said. "How you gonna keep 'em interested?"

The sheriff slumped backward. "I don't know," he said in his soft bass voice. "I'll work on that tomorrow."

The FBI man said it might take a lot of time to flush Dallas out. Nettleton peered through the haze and said, "I got time."

On the other side of the continent, Claude Lafayette Dallas Sr. discussed his latest contact with the FBI. " 'Barney Fife' called again, asking for pictures of Claude," he told a friend. "I said, 'I don't intend to give you any pictures and I don't intend to tell you anything else about Claude. You'd hang my son! You'd put him in the electric chair if you could! I don't want any more to do with you!

"The next day that same FBI agent came to the house again. I said, 'I don't want you in here, Don.' He pushed his foot in the storm door and I pushed it out. I said, 'I haven't got any use for you. I don't wanna hear *anything* from you.'

"The FBI man said, 'I gotta tell you what's gonna happen to you if you cover for Claude.'

"I said, 'I don't wanna hear a damn word you got to say. *Now get the hell out and stay out!*' He got!"

32

"CONLEY DIDN'T BELIEVE in froufrou," Sheri Elms said, outlining her plans. "He believed in basics, and a big funeral is not basic."

Medical examiners had released the body in a sealed container with the recommendation that she not look inside. She took the advice but later wished she hadn't. One last look might have made it easier to accept his death. Instead she took the remains to the city morgue and had them cremated, then spread the ashes in his favorite riffle in the south fork of the Boise River.

Allia, the baby she and Conley had agreed to adopt, would soon be en route from India, and Sheri busied herself with the layette. New life for old, she told herself. There's a plan to all this. She kept remembering what Conley had said when she'd asked him how he would feel about a baby that wasn't biologically his. He'd said, "The minute I put that baby in my arms, she'll be mine." It made her start crying again.

The Pogue family lacked even a sealed container to focus its grief. "Without Bill's body, it just doesn't seem final," Dee tried to explain to a friend. Every morning she was shaken by fresh waves of grief. Little things upset her. She went to a photographer's shop to arrange for a print for the obituary columns and fled when the clerk said, "Oh, was he your husband?" When she wrote a check at the supermarket, the clerk asked if she was *the* Mrs. Bill Pogue, and she broke into tears. She would have given anything to be anonymous.

She thought her job at the bank might prove therapeutic, but she went through the motions like a zombie and wondered why the other workers tolerated her. At night she took comfort from her children, never far. "We'll be strong for each other," she told them. They agreed that their father was beyond suffering; it was just his body that was gone. The more they said it, the more it helped. They tried not to look toward the Owyhee. "We're sure he's out there," Dee explained, "He loved it so much."

Bill's sister Peggy came down from Alaska to help out for a few weeks. "She's my backbone right now," Dee told a cashier at the bank. "She tells me the craziest things about Bill as a child, and we laugh. He had a heart murmur and his mother was worried about it. She'd say to Peggy, 'Don't make Billy cry!' We joke about things like that."

Now and then Sheri Elms paid a visit. The poor woman seemed barely able to function. Her mother had moved in with her, but no other relatives lived nearby. She would listen to the stories about Bill and say, "I don't know how you can laugh." But the way Dee saw it, laughing at the past made the present endurable.

After a month or so, son Steven and the three daughters began joining in the reminiscing—a good sign, Dee realized—and even managed a smile now and then. Kathi told how he would let her comb his hair in different ways, even putting bobby pins in it, and one day he'd rushed off to work in a barrette. Dee reminded them of the hand-rendered cards he'd sent, and told how he'd left her a note, after an argument, showing a man sticking out his tongue; Dee couldn't draw, so she'd saved the card and flashed it back at him on appropriate occasions. When the children laughed, she thought, If only we could have his body, I think we'd start to heal.

Her father began appearing in eighteen-year-old Linda's dreams, telling her where to look. One night his shaky finger pointed to a creek. When she woke up, all she could remember was that the place had been named after an animal or a bird.

The family studied the map and decided that it was Eagle Creek, between McDermitt and Paradise Hill. It was a four-hour drive from Boise, but off they went. After a supplemental dream on the same subject, they narrowed the search to a dirt ledge in the area. Linda found an overhang that looked familiar, but there were no signs of a body. Mother and daughters held and patted each other. And cried.

A hundred game wardens from Idaho and surrounding states joined three hundred other mourners at an outdoor memorial service. Pogue's friend Jerry Thiessen eulogized him as a man who "could disagree without being disagreeable, chuckle without being loud, work with never a cross word, fish and never have to catch a thing to have a good time." From their first day together in training school, he said, he'd seen something special in Pogue—"a diamond, with many facets."

Conley Elms's fishing buddy Jeff Lundy told the crowd, "I can still see Conley in his old flannel shirts with more patches than original fabric, an old pair of Levis big enough for two mortals, and his old beat-up but beautiful felt hat that I stepped on more than once." He said he'd become accustomed to telephone calls at work inviting him to an evening's trout fishing, and he brought tears to the audience when he said haltingly, "Thank God he called as often as he did."

After a closing prayer, two Boy Scouts blew taps on silver trumpets, one echoing the other.

33

A SHERIFF'S DISPATCHER took the message. Claude Dallas was on a northbound bus that had just pulled out of Jordan Valley, Oregon, a little Basque town midway between McDermitt and Boise. In less than an hour he would arrive in the Snake River town of Marsing in Owyhee County. From there the bus would go on to Nampa on Interstate 84, a wave of the thumb from Salt Lake City and points east.

Tim Nettleton alerted his posse members in Marsing. He warned that Dallas would probably come out shooting—"He's got nothing to lose and he's a proven killer." Within minutes, two men were en route to the terminal. On the way they contacted the bus driver by CB radio and spelled out their plan.

The bus eased into the parking bay. The suspect stayed in his seat, his face averted. The men could see his ponytail through the window. They stumbled down the aisle like drunks, arguing about who would sit where. At the height of the diversion, one rammed a gun in the suspect's face and the other grabbed him from behind.

He wasn't Dallas.

The scenario was repeated with a train. Daredevil Harry Capaul raced the Amtrak express sixty miles to Ontario, Oregon, and stopped it short of the station by parking on the tracks. He and Ontario police searched every inch, including the baggage car, but the fugitive wasn't aboard.

Late in January, Idaho deputies and C.O.'s returned to Bull Basin to look for more evidence. Tim Nettleton had flown over the camp several times and noted that the search warrant was intact under its rock. The delegation found traplines stretching nearly thirty miles. A bobcat lay more dead than alive in one trap. Another held only a paw. Two raccoons were dead, their eyes pecked out by birds. A smelly heap of feathers marked an eagle carcass.

It was trash trapping at its worst. Every set held illegal baits. Hardly any had spacers, and none were tagged. Trappers were not known for compassion, but none of the officers could remember one with so little regard for the rules of the game.

Tim Nettleton plugged away on his publicity campaign, but he was running into a shortage of information. "I've been all over northern Nevada trying to find out about Dallas," he told an FBI agent, "and everyplace I go I find guys that worked with him but don't really know him. He rode that whole desert and stayed a week in every small town, set out his traplines so there was a town at both ends and then worked 'em back and forth. A nomad. Folks know him as a hard worker and a quiet drinker and that's about it. Looks like he keeps a lot inside."

The sheriff ran up a big phone bill trying to flesh out the profile. With FBI assistance, he pinpointed the young Ohioan's arrival at the Alvord ranch in 1968, when he'd been hired by Hoyt Wilson as a hand. Over the phone, Wilson said that the name didn't ring a bell. He phoned back to confirm that "Claude L. Dallas" appeared in the Alvord's pay records, but insisted that he still couldn't place the man.

Sometimes alone and sometimes with IBI Agent Harry Capaul, Nettleton yoyoed up and down the countryside, chasing leads. Two other searchers remained active: Ed Pogue, who'd vowed that he wouldn't return to his home in Bakersfield, California, till he found his brother's body and/or killed Claude Dallas, and Stan Rorex, the skinny and saturnine Humboldt investigator who seemed to have taken the case as a personal challenge to him and his Reising submachine gun. Once in a while the searchers found themselves looking for old cabins or line camps on a hot tip, or hanging headfirst down shafts. It was dangerous work, and it produced nothing.

One night Nettleton, Capaul and a polygraph expert named Ed Brake came up with the idea of outdrinking George Nielsen in the interests of truth. They were sure he knew more than he was telling, if not about Dallas's location, then about Pogue's. In his latest lie test, he'd registered "deceptive" on the same old subjects again.

The three men met Nielsen and his wife Liz at the Reckon Bar in Winnemucca, and Nettleton ordered a round of drinks. Capaul and Brake bought refills till the walls began to spin. The sheriff had a mild acquaintanceship with Black Velvet and other liquors, but after a few hours he wobbled away. So did the polygraphist. Capaul lasted a little longer. Later he told the others that when he got up to leave, Liz Nielsen's speech had become a little slurred, but George looked set for the night.

The FBI dogged Dallas's family, to the annoyance of the paterfamilias. Claude Sr. complained, "That Don Myers came back. I laid a .357 out where he could see it, then I run him off again. He went to my daughter Mary's house, tol' her he was satisfied that she knew where Claude was. Said if she didn't tell him, he'd camp on her doorstep. She told him to do as he pleased. He came back the next day and tol' her he was gonna tell all the neighbors. Well, she could care less and neither could I. In fact, I was right proud of Claude, that's how I felt about it."

The killer's abandoned rolling stock was searched—an old yellow school bus with a Minnesota license plate, a gold-and-brown 1950 Chevrolet pickup truck, and a gray twelve-foot travel trailer, all parked behind the Paradise Hill Bar. Deputies found wolf traps, three deer hides and a mountain lion pelt, a box of arrowheads, a lariat, chaps, a Reed cowboy hat, snowshoes, an Aladdin hair massager, maps of Canada, a bulletproof vest, several speedloaders, a package of human-shaped targets, four empty wooden boxes for a 120mm antitank gun, copies of *The American Rifleman, Shotgun News,* and *American Handgunner* magazines, a Confederate flag, five or six knives with extra cases and blades, a field manual for "Submachine Gun Caliber .45, M3 and M3A1," manuals for Ruger Mini 14, Model 71 Winchester, and Colt AR-15 rifles and for Ruger Blackhawk and Super Blackhawk revolvers, catalogues of cartridges and military items, handgrip exercisers, an Israeli army tanker's helmet and a gas mask.

They also found maps of Elko and Mendocino County, California, pamphlets on the Yukon, a Spanish-English dictionary, and a box of books on guns and shooting, including *Firearms Silencers* and *The Machine Gun,* part of a series called "Workshop Guns for Defense and Resistance." *Kill or Get Killed* was described on the flap as "a book which belongs in every institution charged with the training of police officers or soldiers." *No Second Place Winner* included the warning, "Be first or be dead—there is no second place winner in a gun fight," and "Fast gun handling can be a fascinating game as well as the grim difference between living and going down."

The Idaho Fish and Game Department drew its own conclusions. Director Jerry Conley testified before a legislative committee that Dallas "envisioned a shoot-out with lawmen and movement from place to place in a kill-or-be-killed situation." He added, "The killings were not spur-of-the-moment or a fit of passion. It wouldn't have made any difference if it had been our officers or a sheriff's officer or a mailman looking for four cents postage. They would've got killed."

By early February Bill Pogue's body had been missing for a month, and even the placid Tim Nettleton was seething. If George Nielsen had been truthful about the gasoline consumption the night Dallas borrowed his pickup truck, the body couldn't be farther than an hour's drive from Paradise Hill. "Why don't that mountain man send a postcard and tell us where he put Bill?" Nettleton griped to his friend Dee Pogue. "Or make an anonymous call from a pay phone? It's plumb cruel of him to let you and the kids suffer like this."

Together with the sheriff, a search party formed up to make a last attempt at finding the body. On a sleety Friday afternoon, three dozen men and women from three states and six sheriffs' departments assembled at the old BLM station two miles north of the Paradise Hill Bar. Ed Pogue was there along with Stan Rorex, Tim Nettleton, Harry Capaul, Gene Weller, Noel McElhany and other members of the original cast, plus newcomers from the BLM, mountain rescue groups and a bike team from the Twin Falls sheriff's department. A middle-aged couple named Les and Verna

Hardgrave explained that they'd lived next door to the Pogues when Bill had been Winnemucca's police chief, and when Les had gone hunting and spotted a flock of buzzards in the air, "I thought, What if that's him? I just got to thinking, if they could just get the body in the ground with a headstone, I would think the family could get over it a little easier."

This time the hunt was carefully planned. BLM officials drew concentric circles on finely detailed maps showing every road and trail. Nevada wardens provided briefings. Sheriffs' departments loaned cars, digging equipment, scintillators, wet suits, radios and men. For the most part, Humboldt deputies stayed home. "Their feelings are hurt," a Nevada warden explained. "It's like people are coming down here and saying, You didn't do a good job the first time around so now we're gonna do it for you. But it's true; they *didn't* do a good job. They quit way too soon, when the trail was warm. Now it's cold."

Hardly any of the Paradise folks took part in the hunt. When a few of the searchers stopped at the Nielsens' bar, it was closed. Friends said that they were spending the weekend in California.

By Saturday sundown the expanded group of seventy volunteers had worked the perimeter of the Bloody Runs, the south end of the towering Santa Rosa range, parts of Paradise Valley, and the east face of the Slumbering Hills, walking and riding and biking and jeeping while two airplanes provided by Eddie Pogue and Tim Nettleton circled overhead. Nothing showed. Six weeks of snow and rain and wind had leveled the sand like a grounds keeper. A mountain search-and-rescue leader came in from a long day's hike and complained, "It's more boring than the mountains. It's difficult to contend with flat, sagebrush valley because it's hard to hold your attention." Young Steve Pogue was asked if he was bored. "You don't get bored looking for your dad," he said.

Everyone had high hopes for Sunday; warmer weather was forecast and up to a thousand volunteers were expected. But only stragglers arrived, and after another fruitless day the hunt was called off. Someone with accounting skills figured that a total of 110 searchers had worked 4,890 man-hours, walked 1,666 miles, driven 5,000 miles and ridden horseback 128 miles. If the equipment hadn't been provided free and the searchers had drawn the minimum wage, the hunt would have cost twenty-thousand dollars. "All because that son of a bitch doesn't have the decency to go to a phone and make a collect call," Eddie Pogue complained. Tim Nettleton swore there'd be a reckoning.

A South Dakota steelworker named Randall Curry was puzzled. One of his fellow workers at the plant in Sioux Falls seemed annoyed if you even said good morning. The guy had made it plain: all he wanted was to be left alone.

The new man's name was Jack Chappel, and he was about thirty years old, clean-shaven, with small brown eyes, slightly waving brown hair, wire-rimmed glasses and the best work habits that any of the other employees had seen. When he helped lift the heavy steel gates that came along the conveyor belt, he always pulled more than his load. The long-haired young Curry was chagrined one day when he lost control of his end of a gate and the heavy steel edge caught Chappel hard in the chin. Curry rushed over and said, "Hey, man, I'm sorry. I mean, I'm *really* sorry."

Chappel said, "Being sorry don't mean shit," and grabbed the next gate.

A few days later a prankish worker was amusing himself by flicking little steel burrs into the air. Jack Chappel endured the barrage silently, then went over and told the prankster to cut it out. Something in his eyes made the man stop. "That guy's got a quick temper," a worker named Allen Granum confided.

"Tell me about it," Curry said sarcastically.

But he refused to give up on the new man. Apart from his temper and his taciturnity, he seemed like a quiet, peaceful dude. One day Curry tried to start another conversation. "Hey, man," he said, "what'd you do before you came here?"

Chappel frowned. "Me and my brother were peeling bark off trees," he muttered, then turned away. Well, thought Curry, it's a start.

A few afternoons later he was driving home in his Datsun 210 when he spotted Chappel struggling against an icy wind. Sioux Falls was enjoying a typical February day: chill factor forty below zero. The steelworker pulled to the curb and called out, "Hey, Jack!" Chappel didn't break stride. Curry yelled, "Where ya headed?"

"Home."

"Lemme give ya a ride."

"No, no. I'll just walk."

"Come on, man!"

Chappel climbed in, but he turned away Curry's attempts at conversation. For eight blocks they rode in silence. Chappel asked to be let out at the Sunshine food store. Curry wondered if he lived nearby, but he knew better than to ask.

34

As THE MONTHS went by, the FBI continued to watch Dallas's family. Sometimes other agencies helped, staking out on the various residences, making phone checks, tailing one of the brothers. But if he was getting help from relatives, it was being done cleverly. Nothing turned up in a postal watch. A pen register recorded incoming and outgoing telephone numbers, all routine.

Claude Sr. complained about strange noises on his phone in Myrtle Beach. "The FBI won't let us alone!" he told a lawyer. "That FBI bastard traced every call that we made out west for the past three years. He placed a call to my wife's niece. She didn't even know Claude."

For a while he thought he had the agents fooled with a new cordless phone. "Then one day a big tall black man walked in, pretending he was from the phone company. Said he had a report my phone was out of order, and asked me how my new phone worked. I said, 'It works well and I wish you wouldn't bother it.' That cordless befuddled them for some reason."

He griped about other confrontations. Twice agents had approached his son Bob and said, "Hey, Claude!" Son Jim, a schoolteacher, was gassing his car when an FBI man called out, "Claude,

William "Bill" Pogue.

Conley Elms and Blue, his black Labrador retriever.

REWARD
UP TO
$20,000

For information leading to the Arrest and Conviction of
CLAUDE LAFAYETTE DALLAS, JR.
for the Murder of two Idaho Fish and Game Officers on January 5, 1981.

- Date of Birth: 3-11-50
- Height: 5' 10''
- Weight: 180 lbs.
- Brown Hair (may be shoulder length)

- Brown Eyes
- May have full beard
- Wears glasses
- Social Security No. 270-49-0296

Subject is an accomplished trapper and shooter.

SUBJECT IS ARMED AND EXTREMELY DANGEROUS.

CONTACT —
Sheriff Tim Nettleton, Owyhee County, Idaho - Murphy, Idaho 83650 — (208) 495-2441

DALLAS, CLAUDE LAFAYETTE, JR.

Date of Birth: 3-11-50
Place of Birth: Winchester, Virginia
5' 10", 180 lbs.
Brown Hair (long, wears ponytail), Brown Eyes.
Full Beard, Wears Glasses.
N.C.I.C. Entry No. W247288563
S.S. No. 270-49-0296
F.B.I. No. 208406 MI
N.C.I.C. F.P.C. 12AA0807041652061308
No known scars or marks.

Wanted for 1st Degree Murder (2 counts) of two Idaho Fish and Game Enforcement Officers, January 5, 1981. Warrants issued Owyhee Co., Murphy, Idaho 83650

F.B.I. Class - 12 M I A — I I 4
M I R O I I

CONTACT —
Sheriff Tim Nettleton, Owyhee County, Murphy, Idaho 83650 — (208)495-2441

Reward poster issued by Owyhee County Sheriff Tim Nettleton.
(Illustration by Mike Malloy)

The killing ground on the Owyhee River.
(David Brookman)

(Idaho Press-Tribune)

The scene of the crime.

A drawing by Bill Pogue.

Defense attorneys William Mauk (left) and Michael Donnelly.
(Dean Koepfler)

FBI "wanted" poster.

Jurors leave Canyon County Courthouse after the first two days of the longest deliberations in Idaho history. *(Idaho Press-Tribune)*

Claude Dallas (left) and Hoyt Wilson walking to the Canyon County Courthouse the morning of Dallas's sentencing. (Milan Chuckovich)

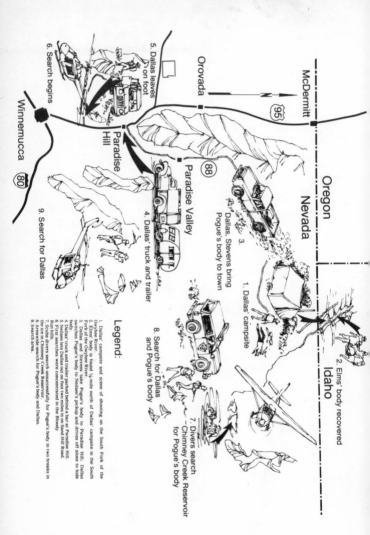

Legend:

1. Dallas' campsite and scene of shooting on the South Fork of the Owyhee River.
2. Elms' body is found ¼-mile north of Dallas campsite in the South Fork of the Owyhee River.
3. Dallas and Stevens take Pogue's body to Paradise Hill; Dallas watches Pogue's body to Neilsen's pickup and drives off alone to hide body.
4. Dallas' truck and trailer parked behind a bar at Paradise Hill.
5. Neilsen lets Dallas out on foot two miles in on Sand Hill Road.
6. First searches were concentrated in the Bloody Run hills.
7. Scuba divers search unsuccessfully for Pogue's body in two breaks in thin ice in Chimney Creek Reservoir.
8. Area-wide search for Pogue's body and Dallas.
9. Search area.

McDermitt

Orovada

Oregon

Nevada

Idaho

(95)

Winnemucca

(80)

Paradise Hill

Paradise Valley

(88)

5. Dallas leaves on foot

6. Search begins

9. Search for Dallas

4. Dallas' truck and trailer

3. Dallas, Stevens bring Pogue's body to town

1. Dallas' campsite

2. Elms' body recovered

8. Search for Dallas and Pogue's body

7. Divers search Chimney Creek Reservoir for Pogue's body

Chronology chart. (Illustration by Grady Myers)

what's your middle name?" Youngest son Stuart claimed he'd spotted agents working near him in the California forests.

"I'll guarantee you one damned thing," the angry father said. "I'll bet my house that the FBI didn't get a true profile on Claude or any of my boys. They might think they did, but they'uz things went on they didn't know about."

Privately, he was disturbed by Claude's failure to call home. "He could call and say, 'Hey, Dad!' He doesn't have to give his name. I could help him. Sometimes I find out where he's hiding, but it's always in a roundabout way, after the fact. Maybe he's afraid of the FBI. *Well, fuck the FBI!*"

He spotted a picture of his son on the local courthouse wall and ripped it down. "They keep putting 'em up," he said, "and I keep takin' 'em down." He was afraid that Jennie would see the picture. "She's near going crazy," he said. "I hear her sobbing at night. She'll come into my bedroom and get in bed with me and she'll be crying. I tell her not to worry."

Other family members tried their best to confuse the authorities. Said oldest brother Will, the charterboat captain, "My brother Bob and I talk. Bob's in Houston, and we know his phone is bugged. So he'll say, 'Jeez, you know, I just took Claude across the border today. By God, I'm sure glad he's down there.' This'll go on three or four times a week. The son of a bitches'll spend a hundred thousand dollars of the taxpayers' money trying to find Claude in Mexico."

35

Tim Nettleton had always been a little like Louis L'Amour's *Bowdrie*: "From boyhood he had slept when there was opportunity." As a young buckaroo riding night herd, he'd perfected the art of the catnap. "I sleep fast," he explained to friends. But now he'd lost the touch, even in his own bed. Claude Dallas troubled his mind, and he missed his friend Bill Pogue and worried about Dee and the kids. He thought, It's like a double loss—first his life, then his body. No wonder they're so upset.

He would fall asleep and wake up minutes later, trying to guess where Dallas had hidden Bill's body and how he'd slipped away. He tried to put himself in the other man's boots, using information from the thickening profile. Let's see, he would say to himself at four in the morning, where would I go if I'd spent most of my childhood in the Upper Peninsula of Michigan? Well, I sure as hell wouldn't go to Mexico. I'd go north.

But north was a big place.

The county seat of Owyhee County was an unlikely command post for a hunt that now reached fifty states. The brown little town of Murphy sat in the middle of rolling sagebrush hills forty miles from the nearest community. It had no mayor, no council, no firemen or policemen, no markets, theaters, churches, schools or newspapers. There was a parking meter in front of the squat courthouse, but a slug from someone's .38 had reduced its earning power. Murphy wasn't big enough to be called a city or town; it wasn't even a crossroads. It was a huddled collection of a dozen or so houses, the county courthouse, two gas pumps, a cafe, a landing strip—and the sheriff.

The Law South of the Snake hadn't been home much lately. He divided his time between directing a nationwide publicity campaign and gumshoeing around northern Nevada. Sometimes he hung out with Dallas's friends and admirers. "I just set around and drink beer with 'em," he explained. "But I never bring up Claude. Drives 'em nuts. They'll say things like, 'How you comin'? You ever gonna find him? What're you hearin'?' I'll say, 'Well, we're workin' on it.' We'll talk about cows and coyotes, and then somebody'll say, 'Well, where ya think he's at?' and I'll say, 'Well, maybe Alaska. Maybe Virginia. We plumb don't know.' We go round and round. It's cat and mouse. Everybody thinks they're the cat."

His overworked dispatchers filled logbooks with tips and leads. Each was checked by phone or in person, usually by the sheriff himself. All collect calls were accepted, even international ones. The office budget for 1981 was overdrawn before the year was three months old.

Assisted by the IBI's Harry Capaul and a few underpaid deputies and unpaid posse members, Nettleton would hit the trail, come back home, catch up on his PR campaign, stuff his suitcase with shorts and socks, and hit the trail again. The odometer on his Chevy patrol car clicked back to zero. "You know, Harry," he confided one night as they sped through a sleet storm at his customary eighty miles an hour, "this is the type of case that a career only needs one of."

Capaul responded with his Don Adams impression. "Would you believe *none?*"

When Charlene suggested that her husband slow down, he replied, "Don't worry, I been chasin' smoke all my life." Of all the lawmen involved in the case, he figured he knew his county best. He'd spent years on the slopes and deserts rounding up strays. "It's not a hard job," he told his wife. "But it takes time. You go where the cow should be and you do a little bit of trackin' and a little bit of lookin'. Sooner or later you'll cut his track."

He'd promised himself that everyone would know Dallas's name and face and the details of his crime. Whenever he passed a police station or a sheriff's office, he dropped in to jawbone and leave posters. Sometimes he planted them in stores, like a schoolboy pushing the senior play. The FBI posted "wanted" notices in public buildings from Bellingham, Washington, to Key West. Sporting goods stores and gun shops ran the picture, and in Boise one turned up in a funeral home.

With literary assistance from Charlene and others, the sheriff composed laborious letters to writers and editors. The Idaho Fish and Game Department backed him with its own media campaign. Articles began appearing in such disparate publications as *Rolling Stone* and *The American Rifleman, Startling Detective* and the *FBI Bulletin, The Washington Post,* and the *Hungry Horse News* in Columbia Falls, Montana. Every Fish and Game bulletin in every state carried something about the case. Nettleton pressed his luck by asking editors to reproduce their stories and "mail 'em around." Fish and Game officials in Virginia, the state of Dallas's birth, distributed hundreds of flyers on the suspicion that he might have come home to roost. At the height of the PR campaign, Nettleton figured there were two hundred thousand pictures of Claude Dallas around. They began to produce results.

Two months after the killings, a packet of leads arrived from the Royal Canadian Mounted Police. Capaul reported to Nettleton, "Mountie Intelligence is going balls to the wall for us." On March 5, a Montana prospector told the RCMP that he believed Dallas was in the Calgary area. He promised to contact Owyhee County officials but disappeared. A Dallas look-alike was stopped and released. Nettleton felt they were getting warm.

A week later another flurry of sightings came in from farther northwest. Dallas had been spotted in Beaver Creek, Yukon Territory. The next day he was seen about eighty miles northwest in the Alaskan town of Tok, and soon afterward at a gas station in Glennallen, midway between Tok and Anchorage. Canadian officials confirmed that the same brown-eyed bearded man had cleared

Customs earlier. All-points bulletins went out, and for a few days Nettleton stayed by his phone.

The man in the high-crowned trapper's hat was just walking out of the Federal Building in Fairbanks, a sheaf of maps in his hand, when the two FBI men spotted him. The suspect backed up when he saw the guns. The agents patted him down, took him inside and checked him against the posters and physical descriptions from Idaho. Everything matched: age, height, weight, eyes, hairstyle and color, beard, glasses, clothing, and features. Still keeping him covered—the flyers had stressed ARMED AND DANGEROUS—the agents began firing questions.

"What's your name?"

"Uh, Charlie Fannon."

"Where'd you grow up?"

"Virginia."

"What do you do for a living?"

"Well, I trap. Things like that."

"Ever been to Alaska before?"

"I've been on the Yukon River."

"Where else have you spent time?"

"In Idaho. Owyhee County."

One of the agents said he knew Owyhee County. "Good," the man said. "Then you can call and check on me."

"I'll do that."

It took several hours to confirm that the man was a former Army survival instructor who'd hitched into Anchorage from Circle, Alaska. He'd grown up around the Snake. The FBI gave him a card confirming his identity, but the resemblance was so complete that they suggested he visit the Alaska state police before he was arrested again. "Tell 'em there's a look-alike problem and to call us," one of the FBI men instructed.

The soft-spoken Fannon had barely stepped inside state police headquarters when a trooper put a hand on his shoulder and said, "Don't move."

Uniforms came out of the walls. He tried to show his ID card, but no one was interested. He was booked and fingerprinted and held for two and a half hours till a technician discovered that his prints didn't match the "wanted" card.

Fannon decided he'd had enough Alaska. He returned to Idaho and was stopped by an FBI man on the street, but this time he was released quickly. He showed up at Tim Nettleton's office and said, "I'm here to tell you there's a serious Claude Dallas look-alike problem, *and I'm it!*"

"I know," Nettleton said. "A game warden just called from out front and told me he was about to take you down."

As he was leaving, the personable Fannon struck up a conversation with one of the dispatchers. "While you're here," she said, "maybe you'd like to fill out an application for a dispatcher's job?" The office was shorthanded as usual.

"Sure," he said. "I'm not working." Claude Dallas's double was hired.

36

SPRING CAME AND went with no progress. The desert flared with color, then dulled to grays and tans. Tim Nettleton worked patiently with his two main tools: time and publicity. Lawmen who'd never previously heard of him or his county now thought of him as good ol' Tim. His calls, checking out tips and asking for help, began to run in a pattern:

"Hello, Chief? This is Tim Nettleton? Owyhee County, Idaho? I'm calling about—"

"—Claude Dallas. Don't you remember? You called me about him last month. And the month before that . . ."

He often exchanged information with big-city newsmen. "They talk real fast," the ex-cowboy told his wife, "but you get used to it."

He'd cut back to about twenty hours a week on the case, leaving time for other pressing problems, such as where to find the money to keep his office open. He had a vision of arresting Dallas and going broke the same day. He figured it was a good trade-off.

The phantom trapper materialized in a place called Hobo Joe's in Westminster, California; at Sambo's restaurant in Carlsbad, New Mexico; playing basketball in a park in West Virginia; at service stations in Houston and Victoria, British Columbia; at a police supply store in Columbia, South Carolina; driving a truck in Carlsbad, New Mexico; fishing in Baldwin, Michigan; walking the railroad tracks in Nitro, West Virginia; singing with the 8th Avenue String Band at the Elks Lodge in Susanville, California; lying frozen to death alongside the Missouri River with $1,372 in his pockets. Dallas was everywhere and nowhere.

A waitress in No Place Like Sam's Restaurant in Auburn, Maine, found a message on a napkin:

> My name is the capitol of Texas. I killed two wardens
> Jan. 3
> Bobcat trap—out of season
> Only one person in this state can catch me
> Vermont a family
> But here I am
> You'll never get me

Some of the printing was slanted like Dallas's signature. The waitress described the customer to the FBI. He'd worn a felt hat, had a beard like Grizzly Adams, and left in a white van with Virginia tags. She looked at Dallas's picture in an outdoors magazine and exclaimed, "That's him!"

Nettleton yawned at the news. By now he and the FBI had compiled a fat personality file. The man they sought was a hard worker, a gun nut, an antisocial loner, a "man's man" with little interest in women, a remorseless killer, a nondrinker, an exile from his roots and family, and perhaps a paranoiac. He was also a listener, and when he talked he usually told the truth. He was neither showboat nor blowhard; he didn't call attention to himself and scorned those who did. He could not have written the note.

Nor had he left a similar message that showed up in Big Piney, Wyoming. "That type of thing," the sheriff informed out-of-town reporters, "just isn't Dallas's style." The incidents stirred up more national interest in the case. Nettleton was pleased. Publicity was begetting publicity. That had been the plan from the beginning.

In mid-July a dispatcher handed him a police report from Sioux Falls, South Dakota. A twenty-one-year-old employee of Sioux Steel Co. had been leafing through the July issue of *Outdoor Life* when he'd spotted a man he'd known as Jack Chappel. The sheriff studied documents forwarded by a diligent Sioux Falls detective:

"Jack J. Chappel" had applied for a job January 27, three weeks after the Idaho killings. He'd listed his Social Security number as 270-48-0476, only a few digits off Dallas's 270-49-0296. Under "work history," he'd printed: "Self employed, Piercy, California, woods work, 5 yrs." He'd listed two former employers, Gary Rose and Bob Wallace, both of Princeton, Oregon, and said he'd done "Farm and ranch work" for each.

Nettleton laughed out loud as he kicked his cowboy boots up on his desk, scattering papers. He leaned back almost flat and said to his paint-flaked ceiling, *Well, howdy, Claude!* Then he jumped up and began digging through a dangerously tall stack of papers on the floor against the wall—his filing cabinet. At last he found the FBI's first comprehensive report on the Dallas family. Under "brothers," he read:

STUART DALLAS, age 22 years, P.O. Box #288, Leggett, California.

His road atlas was over by the glass display case containing confiscated cannabis, hookahs, Thai sticks, pills, and a sign, HELP HANG A HIPPIE WEEK. Piercy, California, where Jack Chappel claimed to have done "woods work," turned out to be a village in Mendocino County, three hundred miles west of Sand Pass Road and twelve miles north of Leggett, where brother Stuart Dallas scraped bark for a living.

Nettleton thought, Was that Claude's first stop? His brother's place? He could have walked there in a week, hitchhiked in a day. The FBI had reported that Stuart and Claude had always been close; it was Stuart who'd shown up in Paradise Hill to retrieve Claude's belongings.

He dialed a friendly deputy in Burns, Oregon. He was sure that the references to "Bob Wallace" and "Gary Rose" were fictitious, but it never hurt to check. The two "former employers" turned out to be highly respected residents of the Steens Mountain country. Both had been buckaroos and top hands on the Alvord and other ranches including their own.

Rose didn't answer his listed phone number, but Bob Wallace said that he'd known Claude Dallas years ago as a good man and a

165

hard worker. He said he hadn't seen him in years. "Why would he use your name on a job application?" Nettleton asked.

Wallace said he didn't know.

"Well, if that steel company asked you for a reference, what would you've said?"

"I don't know," Wallace said.

Nettleton wondered why the most-wanted man in the West would apply for a job under a fake name and use accurate information on the application. He decided that the answer was in the killer's profile. Dallas was known to be truthful—"honest and direct," as his old friend Lloyd Gibbons had reported. On his Sioux Falls application he'd even written "Enjoy heavy physical work" and "experience with equipment, tractors etc., chainsaws, livestock." Every Dallas article in the national press had emphasized the same qualifications.

The sheriff picked up the Sioux Falls report again. The new steelworker's landlord was quoted as saying that he was "under the impression that Chappel was going to Houston, Texas." The night foreman at Sioux Steel had heard the same. On April Fool's Day, Chappel had left his neat apartment for good.

Nettleton thought, There isn't a killer alive dumb enough to announce his travel plans to a couple of people he hardly knows, except to throw them off. Texas is the *last* place he'll be. On a hunch he took another look at the FBI rundown under "brothers" and found:

JOHN FRANKLIN DALLAS, age 27 years, DOB 8/1/53, single, residing Bermuda Wood Apartments, Suite #103, 1500 Witte Road, Houston, Texas.

ROBERT HAMILTON DALLAS, age 26 years, DOB 12/26/54, residing same Houston address as JOHN FRANKLIN DALLAS.

He asked the FBI to run a check on the brothers in Houston. A few days later he was advised that several members of the Dallas clan had been sighted at the Houston address, but not Claude. The sheriff shook out a new Chesterfield and turned to other matters. He had time.

A few weeks later a man told a truck driver who told his daughter who told police who told the Idaho Bureau of Investigation that he'd seen "the guy who killed the wardens." It would have been just another sighting report—checked, filed, and forgotten—if it hadn't been for the location: Mendocino County, California.

The overworked Harry Capaul contacted the Mendocino sheriff's office and learned that the informant was an elderly logger widely known for hundred-proof blends of fact and hallucination. A few weeks passed before an FBI agent caught up with the old man. Where had he seen Claude Dallas? "In the woods with his brothers."

What made him so sure it was Claude? "I know his face. He worked out here a coupla years ago." The agent nodded; for a few weeks in 1980, Claude had peeled bark with his brother Stuart.

Was Claude working now? "No. He's mostly wandering around in the brush trying to hide."

How long had he been around? "Since June." The agent nodded again. The information squared with the fugitive's other movements.

One of the FBI's most squirrelly-looking operatives had been working in the Mendocino woods for months, and now a few more agents arrived in their bandanas and caulks. They hung on till late August. Dallas didn't show.

37

JUST BEFORE THANKSGIVING, Hoyt Wilson was reading in an upstairs room of his Steens Mountain ranch house when he heard a knock on the back door. He tiptoed down the stairs. A man in camouflage fatigues stood on the porch, a short-barreled shotgun in his arms. "Howdy, Hoyt," he said in a familiar voice. "It's me."

"Who?" Wilson said.

"Claude."

He didn't seem to want to come in, and Wilson was relieved. He considered Claude a friend, but the situation was discomfiting. It was dangerous business to harbor fugitives, especially those who'd killed law officers. He'd already fobbed off police calls about Dallas, and he didn't want to get in any deeper. For months he'd advised friends and employees not to fly over the upper cabin—"If there's anybody there I don't want to know about it."

The dogs barked as the two men shook hands. Claude said that someone would be around to pick him up later. Wilson didn't ask who. "I need a favor, Hoyt," Dallas said in his usual diffident tone. One of his brothers would arrive in a few days with guns and other items. "Just hide 'em for me for a while, okay? I'll come for 'em later."

"Sure," Wilson answered. He didn't know what else to say. After a ten-minute talk, the two men shook again and Dallas melted into the shadows.

Not long afterward, Wilson was relieved to hear that the clandestine drop had been canceled. By telephone, Dallas explained that his brother had slipped back into Bull Camp to recover some of the equipment, "but the cops took it all." He'd never sounded more bitter.

38

WITH THE FIRST anniversary of the killings at hand, Tim Nettleton's cowboy instincts told him that something was up. Dallas's friends and fans continued to feign friendliness, but now, as he told Harry Capaul, "They're jabbing me a little. It's—I don't know. Something's changed."

On a frosty December night at the Say When Cafe in McDermitt, he overheard a couple of buckaroos. "Claude's smarter," one said.

The other said, "No way a rube like him'll ever catch Claude." It almost seemed as though the two men wanted him to hear. The sheriff had spent so much of his life on horseback that he swore he'd never ride again except on pain of death; he understood cowboys and even admired them. But a few were a little too coyote for his taste.

He left the Say When and drove south toward Winnemucca. The new Owyhee County prosecutor, a fiery young lawyer named Clayton Andersen, had ordered him to keep away from George Nielsen —"We don't want to aggravate him"—so instead of stopping at Paradise Hill he drove eighteen miles across the valley to Jerry Sans's JS Bar.

The elfin middle-aged proprietor was polite and friendly, as always, and the talk in the homey saloon with the comfortable arm-chairs turned to the search. A gaunt young man in a black cowboy hat said Claude was in Alaska. Another said, "Naw. He went south." A third said he was sure Dallas was in northern Michigan.

Nettleton wondered why they were suddenly so positive after a year of "Who knows?" and "Don't ask me." He decided they were giving him the old Indian bullshit: He went thisaway, he went thataway. But why were they trying so hard to convince him?

He picked up a few reports on Danny Martinez, the rangy Winnemucca cowboy and trader who affected black hats and black pickup trucks. The earlier word had been that Martinez was like a son to the Nielsens and a brother to Dallas. "Up to now, Danny's been pretty quiet," an informant told the sheriff, "but he's popping off every chance he gets. Says you couldn't find your dick in the dark with two hands."

A spud trucker provided another tidbit. He'd stopped at the Paradise Hill Bar and heard Nielsen and Martinez and the other regulars discussing the case. "They say you done gave up," the driver said. "They say Claude's too slick for ya."

"That's right," Nettleton said. "I done gave up. Be sure to tell 'em."

The first anniversary of the murders brought media recaps and more sighting reports. Dallas had been spotted at a rod-and-gun show in Boise. He'd attended a Seattle SuperSonics home game, rooting for Portland. He'd dyed his hair black and was dealing 21 in Jackpot, Nevada. He was starring in a TV soap opposite Morgan Fairchild.

Several reports from northern Nevada caught Nettleton's eye. A Paradise Hill resident had told an off-duty cop, "A lot of good people are hiding Claude out down here," but refused to name names. A Humboldt County trapper found crosshatch footprints in a desolate area behind the Bloody Runs. An anonymous caller told of a peculiar conversation with a miner who invited her to his camp on the southeastern slope of Pahute Peak. "It's a great place," the woman quoted him. "We're even hiding a murderer."

"You mean Claude Dallas?" she'd retorted. The miner had changed the subject.

The sheriff recalled an earlier mention of the 8,500-foot Pahute Peak. Sixty miles west of Sand Pass Road, it was the largest mountain in a minor range between the Black Rock and Alvord deserts. The area was so open that locals claimed you could see an intruder for three days. Nettleton went to his sagging files and found a sighting report dated September 24, 1981. A ranch foreman who'd known Dallas for years had been driving on the Indian reservation near Pahute Butte when he stopped for a disabled pickup truck. An Indian climbed out and talked, but a white man stayed in the cab, averting his eyes. The rancher recognized Dallas.

As usual, the information had reached Owyhee County in a roundabout way—from a ranch foreman to a buckaroo to the Oregon state police in Bend, two hundred miles away, and thence to Nettleton's dispatcher several weeks later. The same problem had come up again and again. There were so few roads and so few phones. The sheriff asked Nevada deputies to investigate, without result.

He was more convinced than ever that Dallas had gone to ground in his own back yard, if not around Pahute Peak, then somewhere else in northern Nevada. Maybe he was trapping again. How else could he make a living in a world wallpapered with his pictures and fingerprint charts? His friends are helping out, the sheriff decided. They seem to think it's a game. With a little help, Dallas could move from the Black Rock Mountains to the Fox range to the Snowstorms to the Stillwaters and back to the Black Rocks with very little chance of getting caught. And keep it up for years.

At Nettleton's suggestion, the FBI flew more surveillance missions, looking for campfires or other signs of life, but there was still too much countryside to cover. New sighting reports came in, though none as intriguing as the ones at Pahute Peak. "He's around," Nettleton told Harry Capaul. "There's too much bullshit goin' on."

Noel McElhany was brought back into the picture. The wiry young lawman who'd helped arrest Dallas on draft evasion charges was considered one of the best trackers in the West. On a recent trip to the Owyhee Desert, he'd camped at Devils Corral and found a fresh-skinned coyote and a magazine containing a story about "the mountain man, Claude Dallas."

Hearing of the find, the FBI made McElhany a proposition: Return to the desert and find Dallas. The reward money had reached $20,500 and there would be a generous stipend besides. "We're not hiring you to apprehend him," an agent explained. "Find him and back off. We'll do the rest."

"I want one thing understood right out front," McElhany insisted. "If I get in a situation where my life's in jeopardy, I'm gonna smoke his ass." The agent said that was fine.

Another FBI man was assigned to second the tracker. McElhany said he would rather go alone. A few days later the plan was scrapped on orders from above. "Too damned dangerous," one of the agents told him. Dallas was free to roam.

39

By the spring of 1982, Tim Nettleton was willing to bet his .556 Ruger submachine gun that Claude Dallas was in or near the Paradise Valley. He wondered what the FBI knew. The agents were friendly, but they had the old J. Edgar Hoover habit of sitting on information. Every week for a year Special Agent Frank Nenzel had been driving to Humboldt County from his office in Reno to test the air. Nettleton had a deep respect for the tall middle-aged agent. "Frank Nenzel's the only FBI man I know that could go undercover with a bunch of farmers," he told Harry Capaul. "He don't look right without a little bullshit on his boots." It was intended as praise.

The sheriff also had a high regard for George Calley, the short intense Irishman who worked out of Boise. But he was concerned that Nenzel and Calley knew a few things that he didn't, and perhaps vice versa. In the interests of catching Dallas, it was time for a meet.

The agents were amenable. On the surface, the case appeared stagnant. Dallas was in his sixteenth month on the run. No one had a clue about Bill Pogue's body. *Startling Detective* was on the newsstands with an article about the case, but media interest was slipping. At the conference in Winnemucca's Thunderbird Motel, the sheriff went straight to the point: "Frank, I think Claude's come back."

The FBI man's eyes narrowed. "Oh? What makes you think so?"

"Nothing," Nettleton said, feeling a little foolish. How to explain a conclusion based on a bunch of bullshit from barstool cowboys? "Just—a few little things."

"Well," said Nenzel, taking a deep breath, "you're right." He swore the sheriff and Harry Capaul to secrecy and brought them up-to-date:

Dallas had been slipping in and out of Paradise for months, using his many friends. Two weeks earlier he'd celebrated his thirty-second birthday in the area. Then he'd gone off to trap in the mountains to the east—the nearby Snowstorms or the Tuscaroras, where his poaching had got him in trouble years before. A full-scale assault might flush him out, but it wasn't considered man-power-effective. In a wilderness firefight the hunted man would have the advantage, and he'd already shown that he would shoot to kill. There was also the risk that he might spot the searchers and fade away for another fifteen months. The FBI position was that it made better sense to wait a little longer, then nail him good when he returned to Paradise.

"What if he doesn't come back?" Capaul asked.

Nenzel smiled. "You know Claude," he said. "What can he do without his friends?"

He briefed the others on Dallas's most likely contacts in the Paradise Valley. Nielsen's place would have to be watched, although there was no sign that Dallas had touched base with the loquacious barman. Danny Martinez had boasted that he'd be proud to help Claude, and so had a dozen other stockmen and buckaroos. The best bet was a fence-builder named Craig Carver, a loner who lived in a trailer on a mud-and-dust lot in Paradise Flats, nicknamed "Poverty Flats," just east of the bar and the highway. Dallas had been seen at Carver's a week or so earlier and was expected to return. The two men were tight; ex-Marine Carver had been in the original caravan that hauled Dallas and his mules to Bull Camp. It might not be simple to take the two of them down, Nenzel concluded, but it made more sense than a highly exposed assault in the mountains.

"How can Harry and I help?" Nettleton asked.

"Go home and wait."

*　*　*

Later that week, FBI agents from the Portland bureau called on Dallas's old employer Hoyt Wilson at his Steens Mountain ranch. Afterward the ranch operator told a friend, "Those FBI men acted so dumb. They wanted to know dumb things like, 'Did you know Claude? When did he work here?'" Wilson indicated that he didn't tell them much.

As the weekend approached, Nettleton killed time by preparing maps showing the homes of Dallas's closest friends in the Paradise Valley and the nearest high ground, low ground and exit routes. He made discreet checks on other residents, trying to determine who could be trusted. When he ran out of busy seat-work, he studied the available reports on Craig Carver: "Tall, thin, ramrod-straight. Crewcut. Military boots. 175 pounds, not an inch of fat. A Marine lance corporal in Nam, 18 mos. in combat. Four firefight commendations and other citations. When a shot is fired he still flops down in military prone position. Calls men 'sir.' Top secret clearance on a missile base in Nevada when discharged."

A confidant described his work habits: "He does everything by hand—he won't use power posthole diggers or power saws. He'll run a corral line so precise that you can put a straight-edge on the fence rails. His gate is wired so tight he's the only one can open it. Insists on working alone. He was building corrals for a rancher, and the rancher said, 'Craig, we can get you two or three men to help and you can supervise.' Carver said, 'I build 'em alone or I don't build 'em.' If you walk up, he stops working till you leave."

So this is Claude's asshole buddy, Nettleton said to himself. In a lot of ways they're alike. Another report said: "He has long arms from loading hay. A smile like a toothpaste model. He's 36, originally from L.A., been here eight or ten years. Lives a simple life with his dog, has an outhouse, heats his trailer with wood. Drinks a little beer. If you spend five bucks on him he'll spend five bucks on you. Compulsive about keeping it even. But he might be going a little downhill. He's nervous as hell. His place is a shambles, inside and out—all those junked cars and trash. He doesn't always shave or wash. He still has the bearing and haircut of a Marine, but it looks like he's lost some pride. He likes guns."

Nettleton thought, Doesn't that sound familiar?

176

40

THE RINGING WOKE him out of a dream. He grabbed the phone in the darkness and said his customary "Yello."

George Calley sounded even more intense than usual. "Claude's at Carver's trailer," the Boise FBI man said. "He's getting ready to take off again. Meet us at the Thunderbird Motel in Winnemucca."

"When?"

"As soon as you can get there."

Still in his pajamas, the sheriff dialed his overnight dispatcher and ordered her to round up his team. It was a few minutes before 5:00 A.M., Sunday, April 18, four days after the Winnemucca meeting with the FBI. He was wide awake. In his mind's eye he saw Claude Dallas coming out of the trailer in his pigeon-toed walk, hands in the air. Fifteen and a half months was a long time.

The county's official patrol cruiser was a white Chevy sedan that he'd bought cheap from a car-rental agency in an effort to stay within his ruined budget. The car was a rolling collection of wreckage with only one attractive feature: a high-speed gearbox. Stuffed inside when it headed south at dawn were four veterans of the case: Nettleton, State Trooper Rich Wills, Deputy Sheriff Gary Olsen and Allen Bidwell, chief of police of Homedale. The trunk overflowed with armament including the sheriff's personal submachine gun.

Nettleton stomped the accelerator with his cowboy boot. Maybe the car could take the strain and maybe it couldn't, but he and his friends weren't going to miss the final act even if it meant crawling the rest of the way. Whipsawing the Chevy along a twisting drop-off a thousand feet above Squaw Creek Canyon, he heard a small voice from the back. "Tim, nothing personal, okay? But I'd really appreciate it if you'd slow down to sixty-five on these curves marked thirty-five."

He slowed a little, then resumed speed. "Sheriff," Gary Olsen said in the middle of a flat stretch, "I just thought I should tell ya. We're doing a hundred and twenty."

"The gauge says eighty," Nettleton said. Eighty was the highest number.

"I timed it with the markers."

They barely slowed down for the little town of Jordan Valley, Oregon, where a sign said, TOUGH TIMES DON'T LAST FOREVER. TOUGH PEOPLE DO. Nettleton's riders hoped it was true. They ended up driving just under two hundred miles in two and a half hours. "How'd you get here so fast?" Frank Nenzel asked when they knocked at his door at 9:30 A.M.

Allen Bidwell answered, "We flew."

Two other FBI men had driven up from Reno with Nenzel. Bureau aircraft and additional agents were due in from San Francisco. The Butte Division SWAT team was expected momentarily and the Las Vegas team was on the road. All were graduates of the FBI's special school at Quantico, Virginia, but the separate teams had never worked together as a unit. Briefings would have to be held before they could make their move.

A small delegation led by Nevada State Trooper Jim Bagwell was detailed to watch Craig Carver's trailer from a distant bluff. They found a remote parking place north of Paradise Hill and walked nearly three miles along the foothills to avoid being seen from Poverty Flats. With them they carried a 25X spotting scope, binoculars and portable two-way radios. Their instructions were to maintain radio silence except in emergencies.

The temperature was above freezing, but there was a cold wind from the north. When they arrived on station, Craig Carver's old Ford pickup was gone and everything was quiet below.

At Nenzel's request, Nettleton and Rich Wills borrowed a Cessna and took Polaroid shots from high up. No one was in sight around noon as they sortied high above the tin-roofed trailer surrounded by junked cars and trucks. When they returned to the motel, SWAT members were assembling in ceramic bulletproof vests, military boots and olive-drab camouflage coveralls. Following bureau niceties, their M-16's were locked on semiautomatic. Nettleton realized that he would be the only lawman at the scene with an automatic weapon. Then he remembered Stan Rorex, the Humboldt sheriff's investigator whose Reising submachine gun had been conspicuous in the earlier investigations. He started to ask why Rorex and Sheriff Frank Weston weren't present but decided it was none of his business.

Stan Rorex was working a burglary case on his day off when the dispatcher reached him by radio. "What's your twenty?" he was asked.

"Shelton antelope range."

"We need you back in Winnemucca."

"It'll be a few more hours anyway. I gotta take a report."

Five minutes later his radio crackled again and he recognized the voice of Sheriff Frank Weston. "Stan? You got an hour and a half to get back."

"I'm a hundred and forty miles out."

"Get back here!"

"Sheriff, I'm driving my new four-wheel-drive Jimmy. I don't want to burn it up."

"I don't care if you *blow* it up. Get back!"

Rorex wondered what was up. If it was a homicide, Weston would have said so. Then he remembered that his wife and children had planned to spend the day patching the roof. Maybe someone had fallen.

"Frank," he said, "can you tell me what it is?"

"I can't now. *Just get in here!*"

He'd never heard such urgency in Weston's voice. He thought, It has to be something personal. Something I've done, maybe. He wants to tell me in my face. God, I hope it isn't the family. . . .

He reached the office at 2:30 P.M. and found the sheriff pacing the floor of his office. As usual, every blow-dried gray hair was firmly in place, but he was wearing boots instead of his customary highly shined street shoes. "Come on," he said, grabbing his hat. "We got an FBI briefing at three."

En route Rorex learned that Weston had dropped into the building on this quiet Sunday and spotted an FBI man on his way to the city police department. "They were going to leave us out," the sheriff complained. Rorex knew that certain cops had been spreading the rumor that Weston was incompetent and Rorex trigger-happy. They'd probably brainwashed the FBI. He couldn't think of another explanation.

On the bluff, the spotting team watched impatiently and maintained radio silence. In this fourth hour of their vigil, the wind had become a factor. Alkali caked their mouths and noses, and there was no place to shelter. "I'd rather be getting shot at," Bagwell complained.

Something moved below, and he grabbed the scope. Craig Carver's pickup truck, white with a black top, was moving along the dirt road so slowly that it wasn't even raising dust. Five miles an hour, the state trooper figured, and wondered why.

The pickup stopped outside the trailer and a man climbed out. After a while he began tinkering with the truck, driving it a few feet, going under the hood again, then retesting. He loaded something on the homemade flatbed. It looked as though he was preparing to leave.

Frank Weston and Stan Rorex listened and watched as a SWAT member outlined the plan of attack. A Cessna 206 would fly cover. A Huey would deposit the Butte SWAT team in the desert behind Carver's place, and the Las Vegas teams would take up positions on both sides. On signal, the units would pinch in and make the arrest. To the eager Rorex, it sounded like a fine plan, except that it was all FBI.

He had to admit that the agents seemed professional. He watched as a spindly young SWATman changed from a business suit into fatigues: Clark Kent in the phone booth. Someone else was issuing .223 ammunition by the box. Over in a corner a leader was warning the helicopter pilots to land at least five hundred yards from the trailer; Dallas had been seen practicing marksmanship on his back. The same agent walked up to Rorex. "How well do you know the area?"

"Real well."

"We'd like you to set up here." The FBI man pointed on a map to a spot between the trailer and the Little Humboldt River, hundreds of yards from the action. "You'll serve as a roadblock, and you'll also keep observers away from the fire zone."

Rorex said to himself, A *roadblock?* Why, if Claude can get hold of some wheels, that's exactly where he'll head. He'll try to reach the willows along the river and then he'll be gone. "I need a man," he said. "Gimme a marksman or something."

"We don't have one to spare. Our Vegas team isn't here and everyone else is assigned."

Rorex got the feeling that he was being discounted, but he pressed his demand until Idaho Trooper Rich Wills was assigned to work with him.

Before leaving the motel, Rorex whispered to his boss, "Frank, do you see what could happen?"

"Yeah," Weston replied. "Claude'll try to get to the river."

"Straight over me."

"Well, I know you'll take care of it if he does."

Driving away from the motel, Rorex asked Rich Wills, "Whatcha got for a weapon?"

"I don't," the Idaho trooper said. "I'm assigned to take pictures."

Rorex handed over his new .44 magnum revolver. They stopped at a general store and bought film and extra shells, then doubled back to the sheriff's office for an M-1 Garand rifle. His Reising submachine gun was already in the truck along with another pistol. They were ready.

The two sheriffs, Nettleton and Weston, gravitated together in the Thunderbird briefing room. Target time was 4:00 P.M., but the SWAT team from Las Vegas still hadn't arrived and the operation was on hold. An FBI agent assigned them to perimeter patrol, a sort of free-safety position in football parlance. He asked Nettleton, "How bad do you want Dallas alive?"

The sheriff had to think before answering. "I don't want him to get away from the flat," he said slowly. "It's his choice whether he's alive or in a box. But I *would* like to have Bill Pogue's body, and who can tell us but Claude?"

By 5:00 P.M. Stan Rorex and Rich Wills had been at their assigned post on 101 Ranch Road for over an hour. Wills watched the trailer through binoculars. Craig Carver had been joined by another man, shorter and stubbier. If FBI information was correct, it was the fugitive. An observation plane was a dot high above and every few minutes the voice of the pilot or Harry Capaul came over the radio. Eight miles to the south, a helicopter carrying the Butte SWAT team held a circular pattern over Dutch Flat Road. "What the hell are they waiting for?" Rorex said.

"They must be on the way," Wills said.

"FBI," Rorex said. "You know what that stands for? 'Fuckin' Buncha Idiots.' " He looked west. The sun glowed red atop the Bloody Runs. "They got an hour," he observed. "After that we can forget it."

It was almost dark by the time the convoy of lawmen sped past George Nielsen's bar and turned northeast on the two-lane Highway 8A toward Paradise Flats. On a signal the cars pulled off the road a mile from the trailer to let the long-delayed Las Vegas personnel catch up, necessitating another short briefing. The assault force was now at strength.

The experienced SWAT units from Vegas moved up first, flanking Carver's trailer on the potholed dirt road. Nettleton and Weston stayed a half mile behind at a trailer owned by an elderly couple. Weston was still complaining about the FBI's high-handedness. "Relax, Frank," Nettleton said. "We got box seats at the greatest sight anybody can ever see."

At ten minutes before six, a big black Huey topped a nearby ridge and came out of the sun at a hundred and fifty knots. It cleared the trailer and butterflied down in the desert so briefly that the last member of the Butte team had to jump about six feet. Then it lifted up and reversed direction. Less than a quarter mile from the trailer the pilot spun tight high-speed circles and hit the siren. His amplified voice announced, "This is the FBI. Claude Dallas, come out with your hands up!"

Dallas burst through the trailer's window in a shower of glass.

At the far end of the lot, Craig Carver flopped on his face, his arms and legs spread.

The ground parties moved up from opposite directions, some of the SWAT members trotting behind the open doors of their cars for cover. An agent shouted, "This is the FBI. Put your hands over your heads and don't move. Do . . . not . . . move!"

Carver slipped between junked trucks and disappeared. Dallas grabbed a rifle, jumped into the pickup truck and drove down the driveway toward the potholed access road. As FBI cars cut him off from both directions, he spun the truck and aimed for the back fence, his tires throwing sawdust and debris and light blue smoke.

He narrowly missed the trailer, careened past the outhouse and burst through Carver's tight barbed fence onto an alkali flat dotted with hummocks of sand and rabbitbrush and greasewood two or three feet tall. From the rear the truck looked like a hydroplane in lumpy seas, bouncing in the air, flopping hard, then bouncing again, leaving a wake. As the lawmen raced up the access road to head him off, Dallas steered toward the farms along the river. It was almost dark.

The two sheriffs saw the truck break out and moved in to back up the operation. As they approached the trailer they noticed Carver on foot. "Isn't anybody gonna do anything with him?" the Humboldt sheriff asked.

"I think we better pick him up," Nettleton said. By now Dallas's truck was slaloming under the power lines to hold off the pursuing helicopter, while FBI vehicles continued to give chase. Nettleton thought, It's like watching sheep being worked by a dog, except that this time there's a whole flock of dogs and only one sheep. The image was reassuring.

He held his submachine gun on Carver while Weston applied the cuffs. Then they deposited the fence-maker in the back of a wrecked car while they secured the area around the trailer. As they were finishing up, gunfire resounded across the flats. A boy of eight or ten appeared on a bike. "What's going on?" he asked.

"Kid," Nettleton said, "you better get back."

The boy rode to a bush and stared at the cars whirling around the desert like waterbugs. Nettleton shouted, *"Kid! Get the hell outa here!"* The boy didn't budge.

The radio was cluttered with traffic. Pilot Norman Smith, "Hawkeye" to his crewmates on three hundred missions in Vietnam, reported that Dallas had fired on his Cessna; he'd seen the telltale "blue winks." The Huey tried to herd the fleeing truck toward FBI positions. Smith saw more muzzle flashes. He asked the helicopter if it had been hit. "No," the pilot radioed back, but a few seconds later he reported that he'd taken two hits in the fuselage.

SWAT leader Guilland broke in. "Green light," he said calmly. "Green light." It was the clearance to open fire.

Dallas had bounced and jounced nearly a mile in the general direction of the river when Stan Rorex and Rich Wills broke from their fixed post and helped to head him off. The fleeing Ford turned sharply, went through another fence, and stopped. A line of barbed wire trailed across its tailgate. The light was going and the fox was at bay. The radio crackled: "Take him out."

Rorex heard a shot and saw something shiny poking from the truck window. He'd been shot at before, but he'd never returned fire. He grabbed his Reising and hosed off the magazine in one long burst. He tried to keep his pattern low, but the range was too long for accuracy. He threw the submachine gun in the car and grabbed his M-1 Garand, knelt and began to fire. SWAT teams were shooting from the opposite side, and the Cessna added to the confusion by raising great clouds of dust.

After eleven rounds from the World War II rifle, Rorex noticed that Dallas's silhouette was gone. My God, he thought, I've killed him. The radio called for a cease-fire.

High on the bluff, Nevada State Trooper Jim Bagwell and his fellow observers watched as Dallas dived from the truck, crawled about a hundred yards, then flattened out in brush. The SWAT members were too distant to see where he'd gone. The helicopter doubled back toward Carver's trailer, picked up the farthest team and dropped it two hundred yards from the truck. As the agents closed the perimeter, Bagwell swept the range with his spotting scope and realized that they might overshoot their target.

"Isn't that a sight!" Frank Weston said. The SWAT teams were leapfrogging toward the truck, using dips and brush for cover. One man bobbed up at a time as the unit advanced in rhythm.

Nettleton said to himself, Those boys are heading straight into Dallas's guns. It's dark and there's dust all over the goddamn place and they won't see him till they're in his face. And then they'll be dead. I wonder whose widow we'll have to call tonight. He was filled with awe and fear and wonder.

The new silence was broken only by the twitterings of night birds settling back down. SWAT leader Guilland moved ahead on hands and knees. When he was about sixty yards past the truck, a meek voice said, "Don't shoot. I'm over here."

Off to one side, a man lay on his back, his elbows on the ground and his arms and hands in the air. Guilland raised the snout of his M-16 and called out, "Keep your hands where they are. *Don't move!*"

The man said, "I'm not gonna do anything."

The others came running when they saw their leader stand up and point toward the spot where Dallas lay next to his rifle. There was blood on his heel and his forehead, but he insisted that he wasn't hit. The SWAT leader kept him covered while another agent picked up the loaded .30-.30. It was eight minutes after six. The operation had taken twenty-two minutes.

Guilland called in the black Huey and ordered Dallas to stand. The "mountain man" was wearing Levi pants, sneakers and a multicolored shirt. His trapper's hat was missing. He appeared to have a small wound in the right ankle, just below the calf muscle.

Agents pushed in. One read the wounded man his rights and another said, "Move, you son of a bitch!" Frank Nenzel patted him down and found a speedloader in his pocket. They handcuffed him and put him aboard the helicopter for the ride to Winnemucca and the hospital.

An inspection of the truck showed why he'd stopped. A strand of barbed wire had ripped off a battery cable. There were nine bullet holes in the doors. Two revolvers lay on the front seat: a .22 and a .357, both loaded. Stan Rorex snapped pictures, including one of SWAT members standing behind the truck with their rifles. In their coveralls and grins, they looked like a party of slightly drunken hunters.

On the way back to Winnemucca, the last car to pass the Paradise Hill Bar gave a long blast on its siren. It was a little message for George.

* * *

Dallas's wound was treated at the Humboldt General Hospital. Dr. Michael Stafford said it was "a mass of shot around the ankle. The largest fragment was about a quarter inch. It was almost like birdshot . . . quite superficial really." Apparently a bullet had shattered a metal part and turned it into a light spray of shrapnel.

The doctor said he was impressed by Dallas's attitude. "He was very relaxed. I can understand now why people who knew him talked about how much they liked him back when it happened. He was very cordial."

On this quiet Sunday evening, head nurse Liz Nielsen was off duty. Other nurses took care of the celebrity, and when Stan Rorex arrived to help with security, he heard Dallas telling one of them, "Be sure to say hello to your dad." Another attendant was consoling the wounded man. "It's really too bad," she said. Rorex turned away so she wouldn't see the look on his face.

Later that night, lawmen met briefly with reporters. FBI Agent George Calley was asked what had brought Dallas back to Humboldt County. "I believe with the exposure in the media, everywhere you looked," he said, "maybe that drove him back."

Tim Nettleton said, "It's just like a dog that you kick in the side. He runs in a big circle and then comes back home." Had they expected to take the fugitive alive? "I figured he'd be tougher than that," the sheriff said. "But he didn't walk on water or anything. He's just a man. Our boys outmanned, outgunned and outmaneuvered him. It was surrender or die."

Humboldt County Undersheriff Steve Bishop said, "We knew what his potentials were. Some of it was potential and the rest of it you might call a myth. You can get anything out of a myth. You can make a myth as big as you want."

41

ON MONDAY, APRIL 19, the day after the arrest, Craig Carver was interviewed in his cell in Winnemucca. He said that Dallas had arrived unexpectedly at 2:00 A.M. on Friday with a rifle, a handgun, a backpack, some duffel and books, and asked if he could stay for a while. Carver prepared breakfast and the two men talked about mutual friends: the Nielsens, Dean Taylor, Lloyd Gibbons, a few others.

FBI information was that Dallas had been at the trailer much earlier and had been in touch with Carver during his fifteen months at large. Harry Capaul, an expert interrogator, took a crack at the quiet fence-maker and recounted the conversation later:

"Didn't you know Dallas was wanted?"

"Yes. But he needed a place to stay."

"What'd he tell you?"

"Nothing."

"Did he say where he'd been?"

"No."

"Who brought him to your place?"

"I don't know."

"Did you ask him?"

"No."

"What kind of car left him off?"

"I don't know. All I saw was taillights."

"One or two? How far apart were they? Were they big or little?"

"It was dusty. I couldn't tell."

"What'd you guys do while he was here?"

"We target-practiced out the back door with Claude's guns."

"Where'd he sleep?"

"On my couch."

"What'd you talk about?"

"Guns, mostly."

Carver was freed. A lawman explained, "The only way we can prove he's lying is to burn our informants. We can't do that. Two men are dead already."

Everyone had a comment on Dallas's boomerang return to the Paradise Valley. A longtime Humboldt County resident recited folklore: "Once you get Paradise dust on your boots, you always come back."

Noel McElhany had a simpler explanation. "Dallas made a big thing out of being a loner," the expert tracker observed, "but he wasn't capable of making it on his own. He had to have Liz's cakes."

At the bar, Liz Nielsen's husband continued to preach the legend of the indomitable mountain man. "Claude realized there was no place to get lost when you're really being hunted," George Nielsen said of his old partner in the fur trade. "So he came back and made himself available."

Dallas's real father sounded disgusted. "It shocked us that Claude was in Paradise Hill," said Dallas Sr. "He oughta have better sense'n that. He's not stupid. For a twenty-thousand-dollar reward I couldn't trust my mother. I hoped he'd come here to South Carolina. To me there was no reason for him to go back to northern Nevada. Why, there's people'll kill ya for five dollars! Twenty thousand bounty on your head and you come back to a place where everybody knows ya? *Shit!*"

A more detached student of Dallas's behavior seemed almost amused at his return. "If you watch John Wayne often enough," warden Gene Weller observed, "you get to thinking you're indestructible. But when the bullets start flying, the hands go up in the air. Claude was always concerned about his persona, so he busted out the front window instead of going through the door. I guess he saw John Wayne do it once."

Potato farmer Jim Stevens didn't join in the commentaries; the subject of Claude Dallas was still too painful. On the afternoon of the capture, he'd been walking the banks of the Little Humboldt, searching for arrowheads. "Do you realize," he told his wife, "if Claude had kept on going in the same direction, he'd've passed me?"

Sandra said she'd rather not think about it.

Twenty-four hours after the capture, Tim Nettleton and Stan Rorex, accompanied by the freed Craig Carver, returned to Paradise Flats with a search warrant. The inside of the forty- by eight-foot trailer looked fresh-fragged. A breeze poured through the window where Dallas had executed his swan dive, adding fresh dust to the fillets in the corners. Weapons were everywhere, most of them identified by Carver as Dallas's: five handguns ranging from a small .22 trap pistol to a pair of heavy .44's, plus a .22 rifle, a .30-.30 rifle, and a 12-gauge pump shotgun. Rorex commented, "All of the weapons are good, expensive guns. You're not looking at some cheapies." Apparently Dallas had built up a whole new armory after Bull Camp.

The searchers also confiscated a survival knife, four holsters, reloading equipment, boxes of ammunition, a cartridge belt stuffed with .30-.30 shells, four gunnysacks full of traps, and several wooden drying racks, as well as personal items like a portable radio, a sleeping bag, cooking gear, toiletries, and two short books: *The Criminal Use of False Identification* and *The Paper Trip: A New You Through New I.D.* Nettleton pointed to the stack of gear and said, "There's no way Claude brought that in on his back. It would have taken two or three trips. He had plenty of help."

When he returned to Murphy, he heard from an anonymous caller: "Did you know that Claude and Danny Martinez drove through the county last November on a business trip? It was their way of taunting you. Danny brought a load of horses to some gyppers over near Caldwell and took back a load of fence posts. They thought it was funny as hell." Nettleton remembered it was

189

just about then that he'd begun to suspect Dallas had returned. There seemed no end to what the man's friends would do for him.

By now insiders had a pretty good idea of how Dallas had escaped after the killings. All the original theories were wrong. Despite the overblown rhetoric of the time, he hadn't lived off bugs and roots, outhiking and outthinking the poor dumb lawmen with his mountain man skills. Hours before the search had effectively begun, he'd hiked to the home of a friend. He laid low for a few days till the evening TV news programs showed that the heat was off, then headed north, stopping to bury the incriminating evidence —the guns and Fish and Game insignia and other equipment— with the help of another friend. Next stop was South Dakota, then successively Texas, Mendocino County, the Alvord, and finally the friendly environs of northern Nevada and the shoot-out at Poverty Flats.

FBI officials kept a tight lid on the identity of their informant(s). "I don't know who it is myself," Tim Nettleton told reporters. "Claude had friends that would've snitched him off for a dollar ninety-eight and a used rubber."

Frank Weston said he'd heard that the tip had been anonymous, suggesting that even the FBI didn't know the party's identity. A justice of the peace in Paradise Valley said it was just as well because most residents believed that "whoever turned Claude in should be hanged." Folks at Poverty Flats eyed one another warily. By the end of the week, no one had claimed the $20,211 reward.

Dallas's wounds were treated daily, and for his own protection he was held in protective custody in the big Washoe County jail in Reno. Michael Donnelly, the lawyer who'd been retained a year earlier by Claude Dallas Sr., flew down from Boise. Requests for the location of Bill Pogue's body drew blanks; Donnelly claimed that Dallas wouldn't discuss the subject. Dee Pogue broke into tears at the news. She'd refused to believe a rumor that her husband's mutilated body had been scattered across the desert. Now she had to wonder.

Dallas's old friends lined up behind him. Hadn't he murdered two game wardens in cold blood? No, said his backers. He must have been defending himself, which made it involuntary manslaughter at worst. But hadn't Jim Stevens seen him draw and fire? No. Jim Stevens was lying. Claude was a gentleman, a hard worker, a good man who loved fresh air and animals. A man like that would *never* kill unprovoked. A few denizens of the Paradise Hill Bar, including the proprietor, suggested that Pogue and Elms got what they deserved.

Outside of Humboldt County, sentiment ran the other way. Bill Pogue's brother Ed told reporters, "Let's knock off the mountain music. He's a goddamn murderer as far as I'm concerned."

Toward the end of the week Dallas was ordered to Murphy for arraignment and trial, and the security headache reverted to Tim Nettleton. A slight infection had developed in the prisoner's wound, and he had to be handled with care. The sheriff considered borrowing a twin-engined aircraft and then rejected the idea. "There's always a chance that a fan would quit over the desert," he explained. "This isn't the kind of guy you'd want that to happen with." He considered using an ambulance or an aid car, but they were inherently insecure. He needed something big enough for a reclining Dallas and three or four guards. "We're not gonna have another Jack Ruby," he promised.

He grabbed his favorite law enforcement device, the telephone, and began scrounging up equipment. A posse member offered his twenty-six-foot air-conditioned Winnebago. The sheriff of adjoining Canyon County promised M-16 automatic rifles and flak jackets for all. Nettleton alerted his staff: "Stand by your phone. Claude's coming home."

The drive to Reno took nine hours. After a skimpy night's sleep in a motel, Nettleton and Idaho State Trooper Rich Wills entered the Washoe County jail to pick up their man. The sheriff was resolved to be polite, just as he'd always been with prisoners. As he explained to Wills, "When the runner's picked off second base, the second baseman shouldn't say *yah yah yah yah.*"

Three other Owyhee lawmen stayed with the RV, their semiautomatic rifles drawn and cocked. It was sun-up on a Saturday, six days after the capture. "You're Claude Dallas?" the sheriff asked the short man in the wheelchair.

The man didn't respond. Nettleton extended his hand and spoke the lines that had run through his head for nearly sixteen months: "I'm Sheriff Tim Nettleton, Owyhee County. I'm here to take you

191

back to Idaho and I'm gonna prosecute you to the fullest extent of the law for killing my friend Bill Pogue." Dallas hesitated, then shook hands and explained that he'd been instructed by his lawyer not to talk.

He was snapped into handcuffs and shackled to a belly chain and Peerless leg-irons. Clinking and clanking with every move, he stretched out on a hideaway bed below the RV's window, his back against a cupboard and his swollen ankle sticking out. He's hurting, Nettleton said to himself, but I don't expect he'll show it. He asked the question that he customarily asked returning fugitives: "Are you gonna give us any trouble on the way?"

Dallas said, "Let's go." He sounded impatient.

Two posse members followed in the white Chevy and two deputies stood guard inside the Winnebago as the sheriff steered onto Interstate 80 for the first leg of the four-hundred-mile trip. An hour out of Reno, they stopped for gas and breakfast. Dallas was asked, "Do you want milk?" He didn't answer. "Apple juice?" He turned away. "Orange juice?" Silence. "Well," Nettleton persisted, "what *do* you want to drink? We're buying." Dallas stared at the wall. Apparently he intended to take his lawyer's advice literally.

A deputy went inside while the others stood guard. The roadside store was in a low-risk area—they were still a hundred miles southwest of Winnemucca—but the sheriff was taking no chances. At the sight of the drawn guns, Dallas's narrow-eyed look turned to a smile. Nettleton thought, We're making him into a big man, a regular desperado. He probably had that same face when he saw the smoke from Bill's chest. . . .

The caravan bypassed downtown Winnemucca and turned north on Highway 95 toward Paradise Hill and Murphy. As the dunes came into sight near Sand Pass Road, Nettleton revved up the Chrysler engine and the big RV jumped to eighty-five. He radioed the chase car to move in tight. Dallas propped himself up and stared out the window as they flew past the bar at ninety. It was ten in the morning and no one was around.

The two vehicles drove flat out to McDermitt, sixty miles away, then halted again for a snack. Rich Wills loosened Dallas's chains and handed him a bologna and lettuce sandwich and some juice. This time he accepted.

At the first mountain pass, fifteen miles north, Nettleton tilted his mirror to look at Dallas's face and said, "Claude, this is where we quit worrying about your friends and start worrying about mine."

Dallas frowned. Nettleton thought, He must've thought all this security was to protect us, not him. It probably never occurred to him that some of *my* friends would like to shoot *him.* There'd been plenty of threats. Someone in Boise was already peddling T-shirts with a hangman's noose and the words, WELCOME HOME, CLAUDE! The sheriff was glad to see Idaho state police cruisers waiting at Jordan Valley to lead them home.

In the country town of Marsing, thirty miles from Murphy, he alerted his office by radio. Every Owyhee County deputy was on duty along with every posse member. "Your cousin Paul's here," the dispatcher radioed back. "He got a flat tire passing through."

"Give him a pistol and a badge," Nettleton ordered.

When the convoy pulled into the gravel parking lot at 3:10 P.M., the one-story courthouse looked like a besieged fort. Six men armed with automatic rifles stood in a semicircle at the back door. On the roof, a deputy surveyed the scene through the sight on his rifle. Other lawmen guarded each entrance with drawn guns.

Nettleton adjusted his shades and SWAT-type cap and directed the transfer of the prisoner to a wheelchair for the thirty-foot procession to jail. At one point Dallas grimaced, but he didn't complain. Bound in irons, stripped of his guns and knives and mountain man hat, with one bare foot on the metal rest and the other in a jogging shoe, he looked about as murderous as a young priest. When a camera clicked, he squinted, then stared silently ahead as the wheelchair scraped through the narrow doors and into the whitewashed jail.

He was booked and locked in a corner isolation cell that had been made available by transferring a convicted murderer to Canyon County. The door was a solid metal slab with a few small holes for air and a slit for food trays. When Nettleton turned the key and heard the tumblers click, he sucked in a breath of air and said to himself, Well, that's it for me. The job's done.

A reporter asked him what he intended to do tomorrow. "Probably sober up," he answered.

That night he invited newsmen to his split-level home and broke out his personal stock of Black Velvet and other essentials of life.

Ed Pogue showed up and said, "God, I'd like to get a look at that Dallas." Barbara Wright, one of the dispatchers, was throwing a housewarming party just down the blacktop from the courthouse, and the whole population of Murphy turned up. Around ten o'clock, dispatcher Charlie Fannon asked if it would be okay to go back and check on his look-alike in the isolation cell. Nettleton said, "Why not, Charlie? Just be sure to tell him you're not a mirror." They all laughed at his little joke.

The office was empty except for the regular night dispatcher and a Fish and Game agent standing voluntary guard. A steel plate had been installed across the dispatch room window to discourage snipers, but otherwise nothing was changed. Inside the adjoining jail, Dallas and two fellow prisoners had been quiet all evening. In the small operation, inmates cooked for themselves and scuttled around the eight-bunk jail in orange coveralls. They'd been instructed to prepare an extra plate.

It was just after 10:00 P.M. when Fannon quietly let himself into the cellblock. He walked to the rear and looked through the slit. "Claude," he said in his soft voice, "my name is Charlie Fannon and I wanted to meet you. I wanted to see if you need anything."

Fannon had heard about Dallas's sullenness, and he was surprised when the prisoner hobbled to the door. "No," he said in a voice as soft as Fannon's. "I don't need anything."

"You know," the dispatcher said quickly, "I kinda owe you my job. I would've never come to this place except for getting picked up a coupla times 'cause I looked like you." Dallas tilted his head. He seemed interested.

After Fannon detailed some of his adventures as a Dallas double in Alaska, the prisoner said, "What part of Alaska?" When he learned that Fannon had trapped and worked as a survival instructor, he acted as though he wanted to hear more. Fannon thought, He seems lonely; I guess nobody else wanted to talk to him as a human being. He felt obliged to say, "Claude, if you talk about your case, I have to read you your rights."

"I'm not gonna talk about that," Dallas said politely. He told about canoeing a river in the Northwest Territories and inquired about cold-weather survival techniques. The look-alikes discussed Alaska and the Yukon for an hour. Fannon asked, "How's it feel to be back in Owyhee County?"

Dallas said he liked the isolation, the countryside, the animals.

"I like doing for myself," he added. He spoke about his family, how much he loved them, how close they were, how his brothers were exactly like him.

It was close to midnight when the words ran out. As the dispatcher turned to walk away, Dallas called through the slit, "You know, I tried the best I could."

Fannon said, "I don't understand."

The response was barely above a whisper. "I tried the very best I could to keep everything right, and to be straight and . . . all that."

Fannon tried to think of a reasonable comment. The poor man seemed so open and vulnerable. "Claude," he said, "the truth will usually come out in court."

"Yeah. I guess I'll have to live with it."

The dispatcher left. It was a biting cold night with thousands of stars. He took a stroll to collect his thoughts. He asked himself, How could a gentle guy like that commit murder? And yet he had. *Hadn't he?*

Later he told a friend, "Claude's such a likable guy. He's respectful. He doesn't intrude on your person. He keeps his voice down. He's level-headed, nice-looking, has a lot of sense. You take an immediate liking to him. A jury would, too."

Down the road at the housewarming, the sheriff of Owyhee County was thinking that it didn't take much 86-proof liquid these days to make him feel warm and sociable. He wondered if he was getting old at forty-two. Eddie Pogue walked across the room in his California cowboy outfit with the polished black boots and black five-gallon hat with white band and cock-pheasant feather. He'd rushed up from Bakersfield to be in on the action just as he'd rushed back and forth to Nevada for fifteen months trying to find Bill's body. He told Nettleton that he couldn't believe that Dallas was still keeping the secret. "What the hell's the difference now?" he asked. "Doesn't he know what he's doing to Dee and the kids? What kind of a goddamn animal is he?"

"Can't tell you, Ed," Nettleton replied. "There's ladies around."

"Listen, Tim," Pogue asked, grabbing him by the elbow, "can't I just take one look at him?"

The sheriff stopped to think. It wasn't Pogue's first such request that evening, but it was the first time that the idea seemed reasonable. There was no chance that Eddie would do anything out of line; he'd worked as a jailer and a reserve officer and he'd been a lawman for fifteen years. Most important of all—or so it seemed to Nettleton at the moment—he was Bill Pogue's little brother. Who else had a better right to see the killer's face? If it wasn't a part of the common law, it ought to be. He said, "No, you can't take one look, Ed. But . . . maybe you could inspect my jail."

There was one problem: Eddie Pogue always carried, and Nettleton would not allow weapons in his jail, least of all when a notorious cop-killer was in residence. He called Deputy Gary Amon over. "Take this guy inside the jail and let him inspect it. And be sure to follow procedure." That meant a good frisk for weapons.

"What?"

"I said, Be sure to follow procedure. And no bullshit!"

Pogue overheard. "Here," he said, reaching for his belt. He handed over his Chiefs Model 36, the five-shot revolver made by Smith & Wesson. It was loaded.

Just before the two men left, Nettleton whispered to his deputy, "Pat him good." Then he relaxed. Even if Pogue lost control of himself, he couldn't force solid steel with his bare hands.

Pogue walked up to the isolation cell and looked inside. Dallas sat up on the single bunk and said, "Who are you?"

"Asshole," Pogue said evenly, "you're goddamn lucky they got to you before I did."

Dallas asked a little more shrilly, "Who are *you?*"

Bill Pogue's brother walked away.

42

DALLAS'S ATTORNEY PLAYED tough. Michael Donnelly was thirty-six, a graduate of the University of Missouri Law School, a former Legal Aid lawyer who'd headed the Canyon County office before joining a respected Boise firm. A short man with finely textured curly hair and a shy smile behind aviator glasses, he was known for his thorough and aggressive representation.

When court convened after the weekend, he testily insisted that his client's life was in danger in Tim Nettleton's jail. By order of the court, the prisoner was transferred sixty miles north to the modern jail in Caldwell, an agriculture center of some 18,000 inhabitants not far from the Oregon border. Nettleton sounded almost wistful about the change: "I only had Claude forty-eight hours. We just took his tray back and handed it to him, and he never even smiled or said thank you. He wasn't being smart-aleck or sullen; he was just being Claude. I'll miss him between now and the execution."

Donnelly demanded and won the disqualification of a lay magistrate, invoked an ancient statute to close preliminary proceedings to the public, insisted on other concessions for his client. After Dallas pleaded innocent to seven counts ranging from first-degree murder to concealing evidence, his lawyer told the press that the

197

affair was "a simple case of justifiable homicide." Dallas, he said, had killed in self-defense.

At the first meeting of opposing counsel, tempers flew. Thirty-two-year-old Clayton Andersen had just convicted his first murderer, a man who'd stabbed a Job Corps volunteer in the little Owyhee town of Marsing. Before taking office in 1981, Andersen had helped his predecessor collect evidence at Bull Camp. A graduate of the University of Idaho College of Law, descendant of a distinguished line of Idaho physicians, the young prosecutor with the intense Van Gogh eyes and reddish-blond Viking beard was as formidable in his own way as Donnelly. If he had a professional weakness, it was that his intensity was sometimes mistaken for ferocity, not always an asset in trial. With his secretary-wife and a clerk, he worked out of an old green house in Murphy, where some of the case files were stored in rafters and bathtub. He enjoyed the part-time job. When he was elected, he'd said, "I reached my dream at an early age and I'm content with it."

Now Mike Donnelly and his partner William Mauk were giving him all the legal misery he could handle. The two sides clashed immediately on the subject of Bill Pogue's body. The prosecutor recounted the argument later:

"I came right out and said, 'Where's the body?'

"Donnelly said, 'Are you insinuating that our client is aware of where it is?'

"I said, 'You can cut the crap. I know and you know that your client knows where Bill Pogue's body is. I'd like to have him think about the Pogue family.'

"They said they didn't know anything about it. I pointed out that they had an ethical duty. Under the law, they're not allowed to be a repository of evidence. They said, 'Are you threatening to arrest us?'

"I said, 'If I find out that you were aware of where that body was located and you withheld it from us, I would do everything in my power to have you arrested.'

"They got all puffed up about that. Bill Mauk yelled at me, 'By God, we've got to protect our client!'

"I said, 'There's got to be some way you can let the Pogues know where that body's located, even if you have to do it confidentially, through a third party. But if you don't have that much ingenuity, then I'm not gonna suggest it.' "

The erudite young Mauk, a graduate of Georgetown University who prided himself on good manners and the correct pronunciation of such phrases as "voir dire," admitted later that the body presented a problem. "We grappled with it and so did Claude. Andersen had told us we were committing an unlawful act and that he could get to us. To me, that's a threat. At that point Mike and I made a decision that we didn't want to know where Bill Pogue was. We didn't want to risk our practice or somebody suing us or filing criminal charges. If Andersen wanted the body so badly, he didn't have to take that posture about it. He left us with no alternative."

Both defense lawyers denied a claim that they'd agreed to reveal the location if the charges were reduced to voluntary manslaughter. Said Andersen, "No way I'm ever going to let the body of a murdered man be used as a bargaining chip." There the matter rested, along with Pogue.

The prosecutor wasn't pleased at his first sight of the man he intended to execute. "I was looking for a typical killer, and what I saw was a gentle-looking guy with an expressive, intelligent face. You wanted to pat him on the head and tell him that everything would be okay." He had an idea how the cute little man with the cute little walk would look to a certain type of female juror. The media might think that the state had a lock on two first-degree murder convictions, but Andersen couldn't stop dwelling on the oldest precept of law: you *never* know what a jury will do.

When he and his aides learned that the defense intended to characterize Bill Pogue as a bully with a long record of intimidating citizens, they made thirty recording tapes of typical game violators stating that Pogue had cited them without being quarrelsome, dangerous, violent or troublesome. Under pretrial discovery rules, they turned the tapes over to the defense.

Donnelly and Mauk looked for the opposite point of view and had no trouble finding volunteers. In fifteen years as an Idaho game warden and a lifetime in law enforcement, Bill Pogue had made enemies. Even gentle Conley Elms had made a few.

* * *

The defense was helped in its task by an unlikely pair of secret agents. Herb Holman was vice-president of a Reno bank and looked the part: small, quiet, middle-aged, an ardent hunter, a thoroughgoing conservative. His wife Geneva was a handsome buxom woman with a big frizzy hairdo, brown Basque eyes and a laugh that shook the thickly textured blue walls in her living room. To her friends, this descendant of an old Basque family successfully combined at least two personalities: the dignified Nevada Bell executive in the silver Mercedes coupe and the natural actress playing against the overweight female stereotype with the energy of a schoolgirl ingenue. She thought nothing of driving her "Swinger" motor home three hundred miles to a chili cook-off. She used her gift for mimicry as a stiletto, and she had a short tolerance for fools. In her opinion, these included Bill Pogue and Conley Elms for intruding in the good life of her friend Claude Dallas, and Tim Nettleton and anyone else who persisted in harassing an innocent man for winning an old-time shoot-out fair and square.

The Holmans had met Claude at George Nielsen's bar six or seven years earlier. "We'd been going to Paradise Hill for years to go chukar hunting," Herb recalled. "One night after we'd known him a couple years, we were sitting at the bar when I mentioned to George that we'd sure like to have some potatoes. Claude got up and left. About an hour later he came back and he'd brought a hundred-pound sack and put 'em in my truck."

The transaction was vintage Dallas: a good deed performed for a couple old enough to be his parents, followed by multiple reciprocations by the recipients. "After that we had him over to our trailer a half-dozen times," Herb Holman said. "He had long hair is the only thing, but I discount that because of his personality." Like the Nielsens, Frank Gavica, Jerry Sans, Everett Miles and so many other citizens of the Paradise Valley, the Holmans could sit and talk to Dallas for hours and never be bored. "That man listened better than anybody I ever met," said Geneva. "You just had to love him."

On a morning in chukar season the Holmans were having breakfast at George Nielsen's when the host mentioned that it was going to cost a ton to defend Claude; the lawyers had mentioned a preliminary figure of fifteen to twenty thousand dollars. Tom Pedroli, a stockman in his sixties and a Dallas admirer, stuffed a hundred-dollar bill into an empty jug. With her customary ebullience, Geneva Holman said, "We'll solve *this* problem quick as the mop flops. Herb and I'll put up a thousand." She looked at her husband and added, "Each."

Soon a flyer went out on plain paper all over northern Nevada:

> We are assisting in the Defense of Claude Dallas.
> We understand you are willing to help us.
> We need character witnesses that would be willing to appear in court and testify to his good character. If you cannot appear, we would appreciate a letter of good character be written.
> In addition we are seeking funds to help with his defense. If you are able to make a contribution make your check payable to Claude Dallas Defense Fund. We have established a checking account. If you are able to make a contribution you will receive a receipt by return mail. Save your receipt so you will have it for contributions.
> We hope you will be able to help us.
> Thanks again.

It was signed "Geneva."

The solicitation was followed by one from Myrtle Beach, South Carolina, bearing the words "Contributions for the Defense Fund for Claude L. Dallas, Jr.," and instructing donors to send money to Dallas in care of his lawyers. That letter was signed "Jennie and Claude."

Funds poured in along with personal attacks on the dead wardens. An unemployed truck driver said, "Pogue had an attitude problem. In his usual district around Idaho City he was generally hated. There was laughter in Calamity Jane's cafe the morning the paper came out saying that he'd been killed. They were glad to be rid of him. Bill Pogue was a master at antagonizing people. He'd stop you to check your license and leave you so mad you couldn't see straight. He had a special dislike of trappers and spoke ill of them. I know a trapper, Buzz, at Oriente—Pogue went out of his usual area and pulled this guy's traps to check 'em. Three days work for a trapper. It was a nasty thing to do. . . . He treated everybody like a crook."

A whispering campaign began in Nevada. A Winnemuccan named Carl Garrett said, "Pogue's reputation was bad in this area. He was ruthless, overbearing, but not to me. . . . I know one time he hit Bill Abel with a billy club. Lost his temper at old Irene's whorehouse in Winnemucca when he was on duty as a policeman, and hit Bill on the head."

Danny Martinez, former Golden Gloves boxer, rodeo rider and protégé of George Nielsen, pitched in with scathing attacks on the dead wardens. "Pogue would never win Mr. Congeniality around here," Martinez told an interviewer. "The things I heard, I couldn't believe the man would be allowed to pack a badge. One of his very best friends got drunk one night and told me that when he was going through his training his police instructor made the comment that if that man didn't kill somebody he'd be killed himself and shouldn't be allowed to pack a gun. . . . This same man said he asked Pogue one time, 'How come you quit hunting?' Pogue answered, 'Well, there's no challenge there. I'd rather hunt a man.' " At the end of the interview, Martinez admitted that he hadn't met Pogue.

Frank Gavica said, "Pogue was a good lawman, but he really threw his badge around a lot of times. I don't know anybody he did it to, but I've heard stories."

Gavica's Paradise Valley neighbor, gray-haired Jerry Sans, reported that "Pogue once drew a gun on a minister and a priest when they were trout fishing and asked to see their licenses." The minister turned out to be the Reverend LaVerne Inzer, a colorful Baptist circuit rider who said the twenty-year-old story was true and furthermore Sans hadn't told the half of it.

Hoyt Wilson threw in a comment from Steens Mountain. "The biggest problem was sticking a badge on a turkey like Pogue," said the ranch operator. "They ran him out of Winnemucca, you know. Either that or he was gonna get buried someplace." City officials and Dee Pogue swore that Bill had agreed to work a year, had kept his word and then gone on to a better job as an Idaho C.O. But the report took strong root.

One believer was Wilson's mother. "You hear all these stories," said Constance "Coco" Ickes. "There's got to be some truth to them." She sent a TV to Dallas's cell and made plans to visit.

A few declined the invitation to speak ill of the dead wardens and well of the defendant. "They asked us to come up and be friendly witnesses," Irene Fischer told a friend, "but we refused. There was too many things we'd seen in Claude, things we'd seen him do."

Old target-shooting companion Duane Michelson was telephoned in Winnemucca by Mike Donnelly's wife, assisting with trial prep. The Nevada state policeman said flatly that neither he nor his wife would testify. Mrs. Donnelly asked him to call if he changed his mind, and passed along a message from Claude: "You and Jackie are my best friends."

Threats were heard from both sides. An Idaho police official warned Donnelly and Mauk that Dallas would be killed if he made one false move in jail. "And if you get in the way," the lawman added, "you'll go too." Geneva Holman reported that Dallas had been handcuffed and shackled and led to the roof of the jail by three deputies with machine guns. "Now just who the hell who do we have here?" she asked in her ebullient manner. "Al Capone?"

Canyon County Sheriff John Prescott flatly denied the report. He said that Dallas had been treated exactly like his other seventy-two prisoners and hadn't made any special demands. He was a model prisoner.

43

A MONTH OR so after the arrest, Mr. and Mrs. Claude Lafayette Dallas Sr. motored west to visit their son. They'd intended to drive the family sedan straight from Myrtle Beach to Caldwell, but it was decided that the South Carolina license plates might expose them to Idaho hotheads. They left their car in Reno and headed north in the Holmans' motor home with Geneva at the wheel.

They were greeted warmly in the Paradise Valley, where they engaged in long heart-to-heart talks about the situation. Jennie struck everyone as honest and direct. She repeated an earlier statement that Claude Sr. had put the blame for the shootings on her, not on his son. "But he really didn't mean it," she told Walt and Irene Fischer. "He just had to have somebody to blame it on. I think it's guilt." Then she changed the subject.

At first the Fischers and others had trouble discerning the son in the father. Claude Jr. had always been quiet, a good listener, but Sr. held the floor nonstop with his penetrating voice, barely brooking interruptions. His mood seemed to range from boisterous to humorous to bellicose as he discussed his favorite subjects—guns, knives, pickup trucks, horses, cows, hunting dogs and the sons of bitches who enforced the law. Colorful phrases from his native Tennessee spiced his tales:

"That gun'd knock the soda out of a biscuit."

"I'm the wayward son with the rambling feet that was never meant for a steady beat."

"It was dark as four foot up a bull's ass."

"I'll play any man from any land any game that he can name for any amount that he can count."

His speech blended sophisticated and rustic phrases that seemed to reflect both his Tennessee hill country origins and a higher education. To Nevada ears it sounded as though he were saying "Ah won't" when he meant "I want" and "Ah cain't" when he meant "I can't." He said he prayed that his son wouldn't get "the electric cheer." He called his second son "Clode" and spoke of him often. "I have one son that I coulda possibly expected something like this. He's got a short fuse. But all my boys looked up to Clode. This thing—it's completely out of character." No one disagreed in Paradise.

Dallas Sr. appeared to be in his late sixties, a man of almost three hundred pounds with thinning gray hair, a prominent nose, a reddish complexion and a kettledrum under his belt. He'd suffered a stroke—"I was out dodging the law that night," he explained— and he'd been placed on a strict diet that he refused to follow. "You should've seen him twenty years ago," said his petite wife. "He had a thirty-two-inch waist, weighed a hundred and seventy-five, stood five eleven. Looked a lot like Claude Jr. He 'uz a strong man with a barrel chest. Now look at him."

His Nevada hosts noticed that the father breathed heavily, even at rest. He complained of gout and dwelled a lot on his heart and other organs. But his colorful style distinguished him from the classic geriatric bore. "May you live to be a thousand and I come to your funeral," he told his new friends, offering his meaty hand. He was manly with the men and courtly with the women, laughingly insisting to Danny Martinez's wife that he had fallen in love with her instantly. Everyone enjoyed him, though no one claimed to see him clearly. Said Jennie, "I've lived with Claude thirty-eight years and I can't describe him. He's one of a kind."

Later she said, "I've never really known how he feels about anything. I don't know whether you'd call him a loving man or not. He's a big mystery and he'll probably die one. But life with him is never dull. I've learned a lot from him. He always tells me, 'If I'd had the money, I'd've been essentric.'"

"It wouldn't do for me to be a rich man," her husband confessed. "I get terribly arrogant when I get money. That's why the Lord kept me poor."

"And gave you all those kids," Jennie added.

Some of Claude Jr.'s more observant friends began to pick out the threads connecting father and son. Like Dallas Jr., Dallas Sr. was direct, as ingenuous and devoid of cant as the typical dairy farmer he'd once been. Like his son, he'd consecrated his life to work, mostly outdoors. He was openly contemptuous of authority and almost apoplectic about game wardens. "I give those bastards fits," he said, "and always have." He blamed Bill Pogue for his son's plight. "If the truth was known," he added, "Pogue's wife is glad the bastard's gone. I mean, she didn't lose much."

After meeting the senior Dallas, Coco Ickes commented, "I can see why Claude turned out the way he did, especially about guns and hunting and the law."

Some professed to see strong similarities between Dallas Sr. and George Nielsen, but the biological father was not pleased by comparisons to the surrogate. Claude Sr. was still annoyed that Nielsen hadn't telephoned him the night of the killings. He claimed that the bar owner had once mailed him a rubber check "and I had to send it in for collection." He hinted darkly that Nielsen was the FBI's informer: "He had to bargain off that accessory charge."

Before leaving Paradise, the father groused to the mother, "Those damned Nielsens didn't invite us in for breakfast or say good-bye or kiss my ass or what." He had kinder words for Nielsen's neighbor and protégé Danny Martinez. "Danny runs a little bidness," he explained, "but he's really a bill collector. He tol' me, 'Claude, if you find out who turned Claude in, let me know and I'll break both his knees. He'll be in a wheelchair from now on.' He said, 'I generally get a thousand dollars and expenses for a collection job, but if you'll just pay for the transportation . . .'"

Sr. said he was tickled that his son had friends like that.

Cruising northward in the Holmans' "Swinger," the old man told jokes till he gasped for breath. When he stopped, Geneva took center stage. Jennie Dallas sat quietly and listened. "Claude remembers dirty jokes so well," she explained. "He never misses *Playboy.*"

"Yeah," said her husband, "and they're still using jokes I heard when I was a kid around the livery stable." He raised his iced bourbon and proclaimed a toast: "Here's to the four links of friendship: swearing, lying, stealing and drinking. When you swear, swear by your country. When you lie, lie for a beautiful woman. When you steal, steal away from dull company. And when you drink"—he finished in a stage whisper—"drink only with me."

Jennie looked as enthralled as a bride, her unlined face beaming in a first-lady tilt toward her husband's as the long Happy Hour rolled north on Highway 95. It was the same route their son had taken in chains a month before.

Occasionally the old man turned autobiographical, with bursts of fire and smoke. To hear him tell it, his life had been one long feud—with public officials, lawmen, the "Fish and Game," anyone in a position to pass judgment on him or criticize his actions. Businessmen who owned the farms he'd operated were "egotistical, overbearing bastards." In northern Michigan, where Claude Jr. had spent most of his early childhood, there'd been fights over dairy-code violations. In Ohio the trouble was over a small oil well that spudded in on the family property and made the townsfolk jealous. In Myrtle Beach the battle started after the father fired his shotgun in the general direction of a night visitor, resulting in police charges that were later dropped for lack of evidence.

"I never in all of my life had a good experience with a cop or a lawyer, and I'll be sixty-seven this year," Sr. complained. He remembered undeserved traffic tickets three decades old. "I've never known an honest cop. I had a buddy in the Navy that was an ex-cop and he was one of the lowdownest sons of bitches I ever knew. And we got 'em back home in Myrtle Beach, too, just as bad. The chief of police won't even talk to me, and that's the way I like it."

Every transaction with his fellow man seemed to have ended with an exclamation point: "You have it built in a month or the deal's off!" "I wouldn't feed that goddamn slop to mah pigs!" "I want those stones on that plot by next week!"

He said he'd told his twenty-year-old son Frank, "You know the rule, buddy. You can't stay out all night. I'll give you one more chance." Frank transgressed again and was ordered away for good. "I felt bad about that," the father confessed. "I wanted to buy Frank a nice present, a thirty-thirty. Whenever I want to buy my boys something nice, I buy 'em a gun. Give a boy a gun and you're makin' a man." He seemed nettled that all his sons had moved far away.

Jennie confided, "It hurts him that he hasn't been able to hold the family together." She described how they'd moved from state to state when the children were young. "He'd always say, 'We're leaving, we're moving!' Our son Jim would've been valedictorian in Mount Gilead, but we had to move. My husband would tell people, 'I moved this woman twenty-seven times!' Finally I told him, 'Don't tell people how many times you've moved this woman. It sounds terrible!' " Later she said, "He worked so hard all his life. And so little to show for it."

When the big RV crossed the border into Idaho, Geneva Holman suggested that Sr. stop flashing his credit card—"There's a lot of bad feeling around here about Claude." But the father said he was proud of his name and had nothing to hide.

The jailhouse reunion was a disappointment. Over the father's objections, Attorney Donnelly had preregistered the Dallases in a motel under a false name, but when youngest son Stuart phoned and asked for "Mr. and Mrs. Dallas," he was put right through. An hour or so later, a delegation from the hated Fish and Game pulled into the motel parking lot and stared up at their window. "That's goddamn childish," the father complained.

After the Canyon County sheriff refused to permit a private meeting, the parents faced their son through a thick glass panel and talked on a telephone shared with the chatty Geneva. The children of jailed migrant workers roughhoused in a corner and made it hard for Sr. to hear.

He came away in a rage. He said, "We come three thousand miles to see Claude and the goddamn sheriff gives us thirty goddamn minutes. And that Holman woman butts right in. She just took over! That burnt the hell outa me. She's so pushy."

The return trip to Reno was uneventful, but Sr. continued to stew on the drive to Myrtle Beach at the wheel of the black Chrysler. "It bothers me the way those Holmans act about Claude," he told his wife. "It's one thing to be solicitous towards a man when he's troubled, but it's something else to go the second mile for nothing. What the hell, *you* wouldn't do that, *I* wouldn't do that. These people don't know Claude. *What's behind all this help?*"

Jennie theorized, "Claude's their idea of an ideal son. They really like Claude."

"There's more to it than that " he said. The miles passed slowly, without jokes.

44

WITH THE DALLASES back in South Carolina, Geneva Arribalsaga Holman set out on her mission to save their son from the executioner's hot needle. The Basques had a reputation for going their own way, independent and tough. Geneva's maiden name meant "big rock" in the mother tongue, and the personalized license plate on her silver Mercedes coupe was BASCO2.

"They never intended for Claude to live through this thing on the desert," she explained as she went around soliciting money for the defense. "Claude was to have been killed." She believed that with all her heart.

While Dallas awaited trial she enlisted the aid of his Basco admirers Frank Gavica and John Zabala, borrowed Claude's old school bus and a four-wheel-drive vehicle, and led an expedition across the Owyhee Desert with surveying instruments and a sheaf of maps. Object: to prove that Bull Camp was in Nevada, thus depriving the vindictive Idaho authorities of jurisdiction. But no matter how long the survey party sighted and measured and paced, the location turned out to be at least two and a half miles north of the Nevada line.

Undaunted, Geneva drove back to Reno and her job at the

phone company, and turned her attention to the next item on her list: Who had turned Claude in?

The subject of the informant's identity had been little publicized but widely discussed, especially at the Paradise Hill Bar. "We got a lotta cowboys around here that know how to castrate," George Nielsen was quoted. "They'll feed his nuts to the coyotes." As always, the FBI was keeping a tight lid on the subject.

Idaho Fish and Game officials met secretly and voted to release the reward. Early on the morning of June 1, six weeks after the capture, C.O. Gary Loveland, FBI Agent George Calley and other officials drove to the Idaho First National Bank and cashed a check for $20,500. The payoff was made the next day by Reno FBI man Frank Nenzel, the informant's sole contact. At the payee's request, the attaché case full of bills changed hands in California. Nenzel asked the man if he could recall whether Dallas had ever dropped any hints about the location of Bill Pogue's body. Riffling through the stacks of cash, the man said no.

The payoff remained a secret for a month before the *Idaho Press-Tribune* ran a story by Wayne Cornell under the headline REWARD PAID IN F&G MURDER CASE. The next day the *Idaho Statesman* quoted Tim Nettleton: "I don't know the informant personally. But [his] life may be in danger. We've got to protect him."

Geneva Holman took the payoff as a personal challenge. The payee, she insisted, was a "Judas" who'd taken "blood money." And he wasn't an informant, he was a plain old-fashioned snitch. Once again she hit the trail, starting at the Paradise Hill Bar. "George," she told the proprietor, "I'm gonna track him down. And when I do, you're gonna be the first person I tell."

It didn't take long. Within a few weeks she'd narrowed the field to four or five, then two, and finally settled on a single Dallas friend. "I wish we could get something on that asshole," she told her husband.

She let out a big Basque whoop when she learned that bank records showed that her suspect had recently made a big cash deposit. Phone records completed her bill of particulars. "In the week before the arrest this guy phoned the FBI eighteen times," she reported gleefully. "He called the FBI about five minutes after he saw Claude Friday night, and seven times the night before the

211

capture. They had a plan to trap Claude when he came over from around Elko, where he was trapping. Somebody over there got some reward money, too, but I can't find out who he is. I checked and checked and checked."

For a while, the news was kept from Nielsen. "We'd have another shooting if he found out who snitched on Claude," Geneva explained. "George would shoot him. So it's best to leave it lie."

She gave the name to Dallas on one of her seven-hundred-mile round trips to the Canyon County jail. "I want the world to know who he is," she told him. "He's a sidewinding rattlesnake."

"I'll get outa here sometime," Dallas said quietly. "You just be polite and nice to him."

She said, "Everytime I see that asshole I'm gonna go out and flatten his tires."

Dallas told her to stay away from the man. "I don't want anything to happen to you. Let him live with it."

The putative "snitch" began hearing threats from Dallas's friends. When the pressure became intolerable, he drove to the Paradise Hill Bar and told George Nielsen in the presence of witnesses, "I don't know what type of dangerous game you're playing, but I'll tell you right now: if you jack at me and I have to go, you can dismiss the rest of these witnesses 'cause you won't need 'em. I *always* carry a gun." Things settled down after that.

Late in August, a few weeks before the trial was to begin, Tim Nettleton and Harry Capaul and others called on Claude Dallas and Mike Donnelly to show them the physical evidence in the case under pretrial discovery rules. Dallas identified books, guns and other equipment and thanked the sheriff for taking care of his guns. "I'd appreciate it if you'd keep 'em oiled," he said. There were seventeen by now.

Toward the end of the session, he turned uncharacteristically jovial. Shown a picture of the hides found in his camp, he cracked to Donnelly, "Here's a coupla cat hides I'll sell ya."

Nettleton displayed a photograph of Dallas standing beside a rare bighorn sheep that had been poached in Canada. "Oh, yeah," Dallas said with a smile. "There's a sheep that got out of someone's pasture."

* * *

Soon afterward, Claude Dallas Sr. received a message from his son: "Dad, if you come to my trial, I'm gonna plead guilty and fire the lawyer."

The father explained to friends, "He'd be too embarrassed if we came out."

45

As trial approached, defense attorney Mike Donnelly continued to fight like a hyped-up overmatched boxer, never giving his opponent a second's rest, shedding punches and moving forward with his gloves a blur. He and co-counsel Bill Mauk were handling their first murder case in the tradition of F. Lee Bailey and Louis Nizer—give no quarter, seek every advantage for the client, delay and twist and fight till something gives.

Five days before jury selection was scheduled, Donnelly won another postponement and a critical change of venue from remote Murphy to the Canyon County courthouse in Caldwell. His warnings about pretrial publicity made the judge issue a gag order. His complaints about security made the judge seal off a hallway in the courthouse and cover the windows with black plastic. It seemed to the prosecutors that he was getting his way on the basis of sheer energy, wearing down the judge and his opponents. It was a bravura performance by the young defense attorney who'd been hired sight unseen by Dallas's parents.

The State of Idaho had assigned a veteran deputy attorney general, thirty-four-year-old Michael Kennedy, to assist the inexperienced Owyhee County prosecutor, Clayton Andersen. The two prosecutors were behind on points when the trial opened on September 15, 1982, but no one doubted that the main question was still whether the sentence would be life or death. Outside the courtroom, Tim Nettleton repeated his old Wild West rallying cry: "Let's give the son of a bitch a fair trial and hang him."

From the outset Andersen and Kennedy had sensed that Dallas's persona might be their biggest problem. He looked like everybody's favorite son, the kind who sent money home each week. But they noticed that once in a while he broke into a nervous, inappropriate grin. The air-conditioned courtroom was laid out in arcs and circles, and they arranged to slide Dallas and his lawyers a few feet farther around one of the arcs so that he would sit closer to the jury box. "We want to expose that smirky grin," Andersen explained. "It's an unappealing look. The jurors'll see it and say, 'Look at that son of a bitch!' "

To negate any romantic or maternal appeal, Andersen and Kennedy planned to shape a male jury with a well-developed (preferably overdeveloped) sense of order and justice. The venire had been drawn by chance, and the prosecutors got a bad roll of the dice: it was predominantly female. "They were not only female," Andersen complained, "but females of Dallas's age. So their sympathy and empathy were at a maximum."

The prosecutors spent hours puzzling over the very first candidate: Jimmie Gayle Hurley, forty-two years old, a comely rodeo official who occasionally wrote free-lance articles. On a scale of one to five, they rated her a one on the grounds that writers were often radical antiestablishment types with a liberal bias toward loners and underdogs. They elevated her to a three and a half after questioning revealed that she was the wife of a retired Air Force master sergeant, mother of three teenagers, and, like most native southerners, held strong views on law and order. After she was accepted by both sides, the prosecutors were unhappy to hear that she'd complained to the court clerk about another potential juror. "That woman's prejudiced against Claude," Jimmie Hurley had said in her soft Mississippi accent. "Her daddy was Fish and Game for twenty years." It was a bad sign.

As the selection process wore on, it became clear that the obligation to give Dallas a fair trial was producing a specific type of jury. Candidates who believed in gun control were excused for cause, as were those who questioned the absolute right to keep and bear arms and those who were prejudiced against hunters or trappers or the leghold trap. A semiretired farmer named Bill Lewis came under typical questioning by the judge: "Is there anything [about serving on the jury] that would cause a hardship on you?"

"Just so you let me go moose-hunting on the twentieth of October," Lewis answered. He explained that he'd hunted all his life. "I've killed several elk and several deer and bear and pheasant." As a boy he'd trapped muskrats. His piercing voice carried through the small courtroom as he described his guns: "a thirty ought six, a field rifle, a twenty-two, a Browning shotgun and an eighteen sixty-four Springfield that my great-granddad carried."

The defense happily accepted the sixty-seven-year-old outdoorsman. Prosecutor Kennedy asked, "Mr. Lewis, can you think of any reason at all why you could not sit on the jury in this case and be entirely fair and impartial?"

The voice rang out, "No!" Plainly, Bill Lewis was up to the challenge. He was selected.

The second male on the jury turned out to be Milo M. Moore, a secondhand store owner who testified that he liked to hunt, fish, read, watch TV football games and lift weights. He'd spent six and a half years in the Army as a supply sergeant, owned a handgun, had an in-law who trapped, and used to hunt but stopped "because I figured my time is coming close and I had better give it up for a while." He was forty-five.

As brothers Frank and Stuart Dallas looked on in the audience, Donnelly and co-counsel Bill Mauk foreshadowed their strategy by asking prospective jurors if they believed that private citizens had a right to use deadly force against lawmen who "acted beyond their authority." The two lawyers examined prospective jurors so slowly and carefully that the judge urged them to pick up the pace "or we could go on forever." Once he told Donnelly, "We're looking for an impartial jury, not a sympathetic one."

The final twelve ranged in age from Bill Lewis and Wanda Pence, both sixty-seven, to Norma Schafer, a twenty-five-year-old schoolteacher. Ten were women.

Shielda Talich, a thirty-four-year-old teaching assistant, peered out of the semicircular box that made the jurors seem to huddle around the man whose life they held in their hands. She was surprised at how gentle he looked.

A J. C. Penney clerk, Donna Deihl, not quite thirty years old, thought he looked so healthy and clean in his freshly laundered shirt that she began thinking of him as "Mr. Organic." He didn't look like a macho or biker type, just a gentle, natural human being. He wore a beard, she told herself, because God put it there to grow. He looked like someone who probably ate health food, didn't smoke, didn't drink. Her impression was wholly favorable, but she knew it might change after she heard the evidence.

An alternate juror, a widowed junior high teacher named Joyce Blanksma, told herself, I've seen boys like him in school—ordinary, small, withdrawn, quiet. They're very shy, very kind, till they're crossed—and then they explode.

Marlys Blickenstaff, plainspoken thirty-five-year-old housewife, couldn't believe her eyes. "I expected Grizzly Adams," she said, "and in comes this little tiny guy with little hands and little feet and little eyes, and I thought, 'Is this the one who did all this stuff?' " She said she was impressed by the way the defense had arranged the seating "so that Claude looked straight at us. You could see they'd rehearsed. . . ."

Jimmie Hurley thought Dallas was one of the nicest-looking people she'd ever seen. Look at him sitting there all spruced up, she said to herself. His hair's cut, his beard and moustache are trimmed so nice. He looks honest, hardworking, like he should be reading books and chasing butterflies—a regular little professor. She decided it would be hard to find him guilty of anything.

Bill Pogue's old friend, Fish and Game executive Jerry Thiessen, wandered into the courtroom wondering what he would think when he laid eyes on the man who'd killed the best game warden he'd ever known. The act had been unthinkable. But he didn't feel the anger he'd expected. He was surprised.

Michael Kennedy, a former county prosecutor destined for an eastern Idaho judgeship, opened with a methodical description of the crimes. Dallas smiled often during the presentation, especially

217

when Kennedy told how he'd dived through the window of Craig Carver's trailer. It was the smirky look that the prosecution had hoped to exploit, but the jurors didn't seem to be picking up on it.

The co-prosecutor tried to dispense early with the notion of self-defense. "Mr. Elms was shot in the back," he said, and added that both wardens were shot in the head while lying on the ground. He quoted Dallas's comment about quartering the body. He cited Dallas's contempt for the game laws and disregard for life. He quoted the remarks about justifiable homicide and the comment, "This is murder one," and Dallas's statement to George Nielsen that Pogue and Elms "had it coming." He showed pictures of the two wardens. Their killings, he told the jury, were "an execution."

Mike Donnelly insisted that the shootings were in self-defense. "Our contention is that there is justification for an individual's action—in this case, justifiable homicide. He was placed in the situation by the provocative, aggressive, life-threatening conduct of Pogue and Elms. He acted only in reasonable and rational response to the officers who confronted him."

The curly-haired defense attorney strode in front of the box as he asked the jurors to withhold judgment till the evidence was in. "When the time comes," he said, beckoning toward his client, "listen to Claude Dallas. We'll dispel the portrait of evil. The facts of this case do not support a conviction of first-degree murder."

46

Testimony began on a mild Monday in mid-September in the most bucolic of settings. The Canyon County courthouse was only ten years old, a sand-colored three-story building on a back street of the quiet market town of Caldwell. Big-city residents wouldn't have recognized the interior as a courthouse. There were no crowds, no trash on the floor, no stench of smoke and fear and deals made in corners. On most days the corridors were empty, and visitors were lucky to find a maintenance worker or a stray official to provide directions. The town of Caldwell was equally uncrowded and serene, with wide streets and old maples shading the sidewalks. When the wind was right, the smell of sugar drifted down from a beet refinery, and a grazing horse or pony was never far away.

The prosecution was still beset with problems when Third District Judge Edward J. Lodge, a bespectacled gentleman farmer with a cherubic face and handsome gray wavy hair, rapped the gavel. There'd been threats against witnesses on both sides, but prosecutor Clayton Andersen was especially annoyed at a Winnemucca man who kept sidling up and whispering remarks like, "Don't your kids go to Parsons grade school?" There were rumors that Dallas's father and five brothers would break him out of jail; presumably his mother, sister and two half sisters would help with the getaway cars. Eight armed deputies were assigned to the courtroom, five near the defendant.

The first witnesses were Dee Pogue and Sheri Elms, describing the phone calls that had summoned their husbands to the killing ground. After their brief testimony, they took seats in the audience under severe constraints. Mike Donnelly had wanted them excluded as spectators on the grounds that the appearance of two mourning widows would inflame the jury. But both women had strong feelings about attending. "There was a lot of information we didn't have," Dee Pogue explained, "such as where Bill's body was."

A compromise had been reached in the judge's chambers: the two women couldn't sit with each other or the delegation from Idaho Fish and Game; they couldn't show emotion and they couldn't talk to the press. Violations would result in instant ouster. "It was very hard not to cry," Dee Pogue said later. "A few times I just bent my head down and didn't let it show. I sat in the back row so nobody could see."

After the widows' testimony before a hushed courtroom, the tempo picked up. Don and Eddy Carlin described the wardens' dawn arrival at the 45. Criminalists and lawmen testified about the crime scene. Over animated objections by Donnelly, the prosecution displayed pictures of the remains of Conley Elms. "They are not out of *Better Home and Gardens,*" Mike Kennedy apologized to the jury, "but this is a murder case." The judge admitted all the pictures except the one showing the bullet wound behind Elms's ear.

On the fourth day George Nielsen took the stand for the prosecution. It was a heavy risk. For a week he and his wife Liz had been guests of Owyhee County at the Shiloh Motel in nearby Nampa, where their afternoon guest was usually Craig Carver. Tim Nettleton stayed at the same motel and each morning handed an empty bottle of Black Velvet to a chambermaid who collected them. One morning the woman pointed to the Nielsens' room and told the sheriff, "You know, I got a bonanza down the hall there. They're good for five bottles a day."

Right up until the bar owner began answering Clayton Andersen's questions, no one knew whether he would stick by his earlier statements, blurt out an alibi for his surrogate son, or simply dissolve in an alcoholic stupor. The prosecutors had known for months that the Nielsens and Holmans had sparked the campaign to raise money for the defense and that Nielsen was mainly responsible for disseminating the myths about the "mountain man." Andersen took a deep breath and asked, "Would you please state your full name and spell your last name for the clerk, please?"

"George J. Nielsen. N-i-e-l-s-e-n."

His voice was gravelly but he sounded sober. Andersen asked him about the day of the shootings. "When you opened your bar, did you have occasion to have anything to drink?"

"Oh, yeah," Nielsen answered.

"What was that?"

"Early Times and Seven."

"Would you describe that as a stiff drink or a mild drink . . . ?"

"Probably like a kid drinking milkshakes. I like them." The audience tittered at this first of many exchanges about drinking. The witness estimated that he'd consumed about fifteen Early Times and Sevens and two martinis on the day in question, but he certainly hadn't been drunk. It was just an average drinking day.

That night, he testified, he'd just gone to sleep when Dallas arrived at the door and said, "We have a body to cache" and "I just dusted two guys." He described the post-midnight hours as he'd described them earlier—burning the clothes, gassing the truck and lending it to Claude, dropping Claude off later on Sand Pass Road with food and money, and going to the authorities in the morning.

The crucial part of his testimony passed almost unnoticed. Over and over Andersen gave him the opportunity to alibi Dallas, to quote his friend as saying in the middle of the night on Paradise Hill that he'd fired in self-defense or that one of the wardens had drawn on him or even pegged a shot, and over and over Nielsen refused to take advantage of the opportunity. He insisted that all Dallas had said on the subject was, "I did a sloppy job, but they deserved it. They had it coming."

Andersen drove the point home a final time: "Do you recall the defendant, Claude Dallas, during this evening ever telling you anything else than what you have testified here today?"

221

"No," said Nielsen. "I don't." Nor, he said, had he laid eyes on Dallas since dropping him off.

On cross-examination Mike Donnelly asked Nielsen to characterize his friend. The bar owner seemed glad to oblige. "The most honest, industrious man that a person could find," he answered.

"How was your relationship with Mr. Dallas?" Donnelly asked.

"A thousand and one percent."

"Did you consider yourself to have a father-son relationship with him?"

"No. . . . He knew more than a father could teach a son."

Nielsen added that Dallas didn't drink or smoke, never brawled, threatened anyone or drew a weapon.

Once again the bar owner was led through the events drink by drink. Donnelly asked, "Is it safe to say, Mr. Nielsen, at the time you arose [to answer Dallas's knock] the alcohol was still affecting you?"

"Well, I'm not an alcoholic."

"Is it safe to say that the alcohol you had consumed earlier that day was still affecting you?"

"Very possibly."

"You were disoriented at the time, were you not?"

"Disoriented or shocked being awakened out of a—every morning when I get up without a shower, I'm still asleep."

They started back over the conversations, and Nielsen held the line. Claude had said little or nothing about why he killed the wardens. He'd tended to business and disappeared into the night. Unable to shake the story, Donnelly returned to impeaching the witness's sobriety:

Q: Do you have any concept at this time, Mr. Nielsen, as to the number of drinks you consumed during this period of time.

A: Enough.

Q: Enough?

A: Yes.

Q: Enough to disorient you?

A: Well, I'm pretty hard to disorient.

Q: . . . Is it safe to say, Mr. Nielsen, you were in fact drunk at this time?"

The judge sustained Andersen's objection and Donnelly bore in from another direction.

Q: Mr. Nielsen, during the period of time that you were traveling with Mr. Dallas in the pickup that you described, you indicated there were basically one or two statements made during that period of time. One was, "I did a sloppy job and they had it coming."

A: Yes.

Q: Did Mr. Dallas explain to you at that time?

A: No. We had very little conversation. He said they deserved it.

Q: And you don't know why?

A: No.

Q: Now, Mr. Nielsen, also at this time you indicated that you were going to wear a lot of heat. Is that correct?

A: Yes.

Q: Do you recall Mr. Dallas ever stating to you that evening, "I had to do it"?

A: No.

Q: You're sure about that?

A: Yes.

Q: Is it possible that he could have made a statement like that?

The judge sustained another Andersen objection, and the line of questioning was closed. Bibulous or not, George Nielsen had been an impressive prosecution witness. He ended his testimony on a playful note:

Q: How would you describe the lighting in the bar?

A: Dark enough so you could touch the girl alongside of you and not be noticed.

Liz Nielsen's testimony was consistent with her husband's. Claude, she testified, was as much a son to her as her own son. She seemed shaky and on the verge of tears.

47

On the fifth day of the trial Jim Stevens stepped forward to begin the testimony that everyone knew could make or break the case. He was shaking under his fresh-pressed business suit and his neatly combed black hair. Twenty months had passed since Bull Camp, and as he walked toward the witness stand he smelled the sage-scented air all over again. He'd hoped the trauma was gone. God dang, he said to himself, there's not a bit of good can come of this. . . .

He'd been waiting around Caldwell since Monday, collecting nine dollars a day witness fee, a free motel room and a meal ticket for all he could eat at Vip's fast-food restaurant, while back home another farmer was charging a thousand dollars to harvest his potatoes. As he took his seat he saw good old Claude staring down at the table. Maybe he doesn't want to look at me, Jim thought. Maybe I'm the enemy now. Dang, he said to himself, I *like* Claude. What the hell am I doing here?

On direct examination, he told the same story that he'd told at least twenty times with occasional slight variations. He'd told it twice on the lie box—once when he'd been up for two days without sleep and had been so frazzled that he'd registered as deceptive,

224

and later when he was well rested and the FBI polygraphist had given him a clean bill of health on every answer. He'd told the story to a tape recorder in Bull Basin and in front of a video camera on the rim. He'd told it in a preliminary hearing where he was so nervous that he'd referred to his son Darren as "Dick" and talked about attending night school when he'd actually gone to college. There were at least six transcriptions of his version of the events and all were consistent except for minor details. But almost two years had gone by and now he was being questioned in front of an unsmiling judge and jury under an American flag and the great seal of Idaho about details that had become hazy and things that had never been clear in the first place.

He'd spent nearly an hour relating the details of the shootings when Mike Kennedy asked him, "After you asked the defendant, 'Why?,' did he say anything?"

"He said something like, 'I swore I would never be arrested again, and they had handcuffs on.' . . ."

Later that answer would come back to haunt him, the jury, the judge, everyone involved in the case.

Bill Mauk conducted a courteously grueling cross-examination that went on for hours (130 pages in the official transcript) and left the potato farmer and some of the jurors in a muddle. The bearded defense lawyer opened by commenting, "It appears from your testimony, and correct me if I'm wrong, there are a number of things you don't recall about what happened on January fifth?"

Stevens said, "If you could give me a for instance."

"Is your recollection clear in *every* respect to everything that happened on that day?"

"Well, it's been two years ago. I'm sure that I've forgotten some things."

It turned out that he had, and the defense co-counsel revived them in detail, using quotes from earlier statements. In addition to memory lapses, Stevens couldn't be positive about the sequence of events; his diagrams were slightly inconsistent; he couldn't always match up Dallas's quotes—"This is murder one," "This is justifiable homicide"—with exact times and locations. And he couldn't remember some of the details that seemed important to this young wavy-haired lawyer questioning him so intently:

Q: You had to untie the [tent] flap to go in?
A: Yes. . . . I untied this side right here.

Q: Do they tie together in a seam?

A: Well, the flap ties together, yes, on the seam in the middle.

Q: Do the flaps overlap or do they come together?

A: I'm not sure.

Mauk kept throwing his earlier statements back at him. He would approach the witness box waving a sheaf of papers and say, "Does this appear to you to be a true and correct copy of a statement you previously have given?"

Stevens would have to answer yes and admit that he'd been inconsistent, and each time he made the admission he realized that he was looking worse and worse to the jury. Well, there was nothing he could do about it. Memory wasn't an exact science, especially when the event you were trying to recall was the scariest thing that ever happened. He hadn't gone to Bull Basin to take notes and draw up timetables; he'd gone to visit a friend, and suddenly the friend had whipped out a pistol and shot two innocent game wardens. Nothing beyond those facts had ever seemed of much importance to him; much beyond those facts was murky and dark, and some was completely forgotten. Had Claude called it "justifiable homicide" while they were down below or up above? Halfway up? On the first trip or the second? Did the tent flap come together in a seam? His mind moved from blank to blank, and he was amazed that he could answer at all.

After a weekend with his family, he returned for more cross-examination. He found himself adding details that he hadn't mentioned before or had skipped past—later he wasn't sure if he'd remembered the details accurately on the witness stand Friday or been swept along by the intensity of the interrogation. Mauk had been asking him about the events just before the first shots, when Stevens was standing to one side of the tent feeling embarrassed. He'd testified that he looked back toward the circle of three men because he heard a shot and Bill Pogue saying, "Oh, no." Now he couldn't be a hundred percent sure which had come first, the comment or the shot, or whether it was Pogue or Dallas who'd said, "Oh, no." Through all his previous interrogations, he'd never made such an admission. Mauk pressed on:

Q: Are you sure there was not something else, some unusual movement, that drew your attention back to the circle?

A: Well, you know, it's possible. Like I say, I don't know what happened. Everything happened so simultaneously within tenths of a second and—

Q: This is very important, Jim.

A: I'm not sure if it was a movement, and I think I stated before there was possibly a movement, or possibly, 'Oh, no,' or possibly a gunshot. I don't know what drew attention.

Q: Do you recall testifying at the preliminary hearing that perhaps it was a movement that drew your attention back?

A: Well, I said that before. I recall saying that, but I think I also recall saying, I'm not sure what drew my attention.

Q: Could it have been Mr. Pogue going for his gun at that point, Jim?

A: Well, I don't know. I still can't answer your question.

Q: Out of the corner of your eye, you did see Mr. Pogue—his arm—drop down to his gun. Is that not correct?

A: I do recall seeing Mr. Pogue in not a standing position. I do recall, in my mind, seeing Mr. Pogue's gun dropping—not his gun, but his arm or his elbow dropping. I can recall seeing that.

Q: The sequence here is somewhat important here, Jim, so I'm going to ask you—

Kennedy: Your Honor, I'm going to object to counsel keep characterizing his questions. The jury knows that they're important. He doesn't have to keep reminding people how important his line of questioning is.

Mauk apologized, asked a few more questions, then returned to the point:

Q: Now, as far as Mr. Pogue reaching for his gun, you definitely saw his arm drop?

A: During that deal, I did. I saw his arm in an unusual position. I assume he was going for his gun when I saw his elbow kind of cocked.

Mike Kennedy tried to repair some of the damage on re-cross as Stevens's ordeal entered its eighth hour. The special prosecutor elicited testimony that at least one of the earlier statements had been made after two nights without sleep. When he read an earlier Stevens quote that he'd heard "everything" that had been said at Bull Camp and contrasted it with his testimony in court that he might have missed a few things, Mauk jumped up and said, "Your Honor, Mr. Kennedy is impeaching his own witness."

The judge sustained the objection. The potato farmer was the state's witness, and if his story was shaky, the state was stuck with it. Kennedy asked Stevens to explain the discrepancies between his various statements about the motion of Pogue's arm at the time of the shooting. "Well," said the farmer, "I don't know how you can say three things happened all at the same time. I stated everything was simultaneous. I don't know what come first. When you tell people something, you've got to tell them one at a time, you know. And I'm sure sometimes I said I heard a 'No, no,' and then I heard a shot. I saw movement. I might have turned it around again. But bear in mind, all of this happened so fast that I don't know what happened first."

It seemed a reasonable explanation. "Under stress, honest people always have trouble with their memories," Clayton Andersen said later. "It's the liars who talk fast."

In the jury box, Marlys Blickenstaff was thinking: there's something fishy about this Stevens. Claude and all the other witnesses made good eye contact, but Claude never looked at Stevens; he looked down. *Why is their rapport so poor?* Stevens says he wandered off and was looking away when everything happened. Well, if I was with a friend and my friend was being confronted maliciously or aggressively, I wouldn't be wandering off and not paying attention. So either he lied or he didn't tell all the truth or he left something out. Or the words were put in his mouth or he was such a babbling idiot when he got out of Bull Camp that he couldn't remember who said what to who or who did what. Anyway, I sure have trouble believing him.

Donna Deihl, the Penney's clerk, was thinking that Jim Stevens had said "I dunno," "Maybe," "I'm not sure," too many times to be convincing. She remembered something Mike Donnelly had said: "When the time comes, listen to Claude Dallas." She hoped he would clear things up, because they certainly weren't clear right now.

As the prosecution continued its case through the rest of the week, Dee Pogue and Sheri Elms adjusted to conditions. Ordered to sit apart and not show emotion, they cast quick reassuring smiles at each other and hugged in the corridor. Dee was pleased that her teenage daughter Kathi accompanied her each day. Of all the children, she'd had the most trouble adjusting to the loss, con-

228

sistently refusing to discuss the trial or read about it in the newspapers. But now she was accepting reality.

Mother and daughter tried not to react to the comments that reached their ears in the courtroom. "What a nice guy Dallas is!" they heard more than once. And: "How could so many people lie about a guy like that!" And in various forms: "Pogue got what he deserved. It's a wonder it didn't happen years ago."

An old man from Winnemucca sat in front of them one day and chattered about a run-in with Bill that went back to the 1960s. "Just imagine," Dee said to Tim Nettleton. "He carried his grudge all these years. And I don't think Bill even cited him."

Sheri Elms had no one to accompany her to court, but she made up her mind to absorb every detail about the killing of her husband. She told Dee, "When Jim Stevens testified about the things they did to Conley, I kept telling myself, 'This does *not* hurt me! It does *not* hurt Conley!' I kept saying, 'He's dead and gone already.' "

But when Conley's belt buckle and new rubber boots were introduced as evidence, she followed her tears down the hall to the bathroom. She'd never expected to see those things again. After a few more days she learned to save her crying for nighttime, when she was alone with Allia. The little brown baby was a solace.

A club of Dallas supporters formed spontaneously in the courthouse. "We were talking in the hall one day," said Jennie Shipley, a slender forty-three-year-old housewife with curly auburn hair and big brown eyes, "and somebody said, 'I guess you could call us the Dallas Cheerleaders.' The newspapers picked up on that. It makes us sound like a bunch of dumb, kooky women."

Eventually there were about fifteen of them, ranging in age from early twenties to mid-sixties. They were a constant presence, sitting together in court, huddling outside during recess, being interviewed, passing notes to Dallas and his lawyers. Said leader Shipley, "A little gal named Claudia, she even done a live TV interview for Claude. Well, there's something about him. I think some of the women in our group might be in love with him, emotionally involved—not really love, but infatuation. He emits a charisma. He's the type of man that most women would admire—his life-style, the fact that he's his own person, his reputation and all. He's a survivalist, a man's man, and yet when it come right down

229

to the nitty-gritty he's not a wishy-washy. He's not gonna get down on his hands and knees and scrape and bow." She added, "The only other man I know like that is my husband."

Madaline Meeks, a painfully arthritic woman of middle years, didn't want her fealty to be misunderstood. Her husband was already having problems at the plant; one of his fellow workers had said, "My wife saw your wife on TV and she said to tell your wife she's fulla shit." Others had spread the word that Dallas and his Cheerleaders winked and smiled at each other.

"Not true," the Texas-born Meeks insisted. "He always walks into the room with his back to us and sits the same way. Why, I'm a mother of four, grandmom of seven! We're not a bunch of dingbats the way the papers try to make us out. It's not that we're ready to go over and jump Claude's bones. We want the truth to come out, that's all."

The truth, as the Cheerleaders kept insisting to reporters, was that no one with Dallas's charisma, honesty and hardworking ways could possibly have killed two of his fellow men in cold blood. Any fool could see that. Those who disagreed were either honestly or dishonestly mistaken, including Mrs. Pogue and Mrs. Elms. "Those two women and their kids are up and down in that courtroom all the time," Madaline Meeks complained. "They're just trying to disrupt everything." She noticed that the deputies were getting a little sloppy about frisking the widows each time they entered the courtroom. "If anybody should be searched," she told one of the officers, "it's them."

48

TWO WEEKS INTO the testimony, the defense opened its case with a surprise move: a string of character witnesses, a tactic usually reserved for the end. It was as though Donnelly and Mauk had decided that the courtroom needed a change of air. Now the man who'd been pictured as a renegade killer, a "maggot" in one warden's word, was presented to the jury as a sort of free-lance demigod.

Constance "Coco" Ickes led off, her upper Fifth Avenue accent still perceptible, and described her former employee as "quiet and polite, someone you could trust. Claude never made any trouble with anybody."

Banker Herb Holman said that he and his wife had known Dallas for eight years and always found him "peaceful and a hard worker" with an excellent reputation in Paradise Hill. On cross-examination, Mike Kennedy asked Holman if the peaceful reputation "also applied to game wardens." Holman said he didn't think the subject ever came up.

During a short recess, Herb and Geneva drew a few hostile stares in the hall. "Get a load of that woman," Geneva whispered. "She thinks she's gonna whip me by eye contact. If she comes over,

I'm gonna plant one on her." After a short staredown, the woman moved away. It was Conley Elms's wife.

Sheri hadn't been paying much attention to the character witnesses—their opinions seemed unconnected to the murders—but as another one approached the stand she noticed a stir. He was dressed in his Sunday-best buckaroo outfit: lace-up cowboy boots, high-domed wide-brimmed cowboy hat with leather chin strap, crisp new jeans rolled up at the bottom, black polyester shirt with white cuffs and collar, and a bright scarf. All that was missing was the horse. He slumped in the witness chair, tweaked his handlebar moustache and drawled that he was Bruce Waddy Mitchell, thirty-two years old, a Nevada rancher and friend of the defendant's.

He was asked, "How did you become acquainted with Mr. Dallas?"

Mitchell said he'd buckarooed with Dallas for two years, living in the same tent. "I think it was around sixty-nine," he said. He leaned toward the defendant's table and asked in his friendly voice, "Is that right, Claude?"

Dallas blushed and Sheri joined the rest of the audience in a brief therapeutic giggle. Waddy Mitchell seemed innocent and real, a throwback to the Old West, as evil and conniving as Hopalong Cassidy or Marshal Dillon. Even the judge seemed bemused as he said gently, "Just testify as best you recall it." Sophisticated onlookers recognized the scene as a high point in the defense's effort to equate Dallas with the company he kept. How could a vicious murderer have a friend like this?

After Mitchell had made the usual statements about Dallas ("He's really something. . . . He's one of those fellers that just come along very seldom"), he asked the judge if he could remain in the courtroom. To Sheri's alarm, he headed straight for her row. As the lawyers huddled around the bench for a conference, he sat down and whispered, "You been here every day?"

"Yes," she answered.

"Well, how *come?*" He sounded a little like Gomer Pyle.

"My husband was one of the men who were murdered."

He looked startled. "Oh, my gosh!" he said. "You must be Mrs. Elms!" He began a prolonged apologia. He did everything but apologize for being Dallas's friend. He said, "I'm *so* sorry this had to happen."

"Well, thank you," Sheri said. "I am too."

After a few minutes, he leaned over again and asked, "How's your baby? You did get her, didn't you?"

"Yes, I did." She pulled out a picture and showed him.

He seemed moved. Sheri felt good about him, even though he'd testified for Dallas. He came across as a genuine dressed-for-church cowboy, not the Paradise Hill version. He whispered, "She looks like a beautiful little girl."

She said it was nice of him to say so.

Danny Martinez smiled and winked at Dallas, then climbed on the stand and canceled all of Waddy Mitchell's goodwill. Even bareheaded, the rawboned ex-fighter and Nielsen protégé seemed to wear his black hat. His answers were brisk and businesslike as he described Dallas as "peaceful and quiet," a man who "never got in trouble." Mike Donnelly asked if he'd been personally acquainted with Bill Pogue.

"No," Martinez answered. "But I heard him discussed by about thirty different people at one time or another." Donnelly went on:

Q: . . . Do you know if Mr. Pogue enjoyed a reputation in the community for dangerousness, violence, turbulence or aggression?

A: Every one of them, but those weren't the exact words.

Q: . . . What was that reputation?

A: Well, everybody said he was an asshole.

Mike Kennedy jumped up and insisted that the statement was unresponsive. Behind his objection was a larger question: to what extent would the court continue to allow Pogue to be put on trial? Judge Lodge ordered Martinez's remark stricken. Witnesses would be permitted to testify about their general perceptions of the victims, he ruled, but not about specific incidents unless the details had been known to the defendant at the time of the killings.

The deputy attorney general was still steaming at Martinez when he took over the cross-examination. "How do you know about it?" he asked. "You don't know what happened at Bull Camp, do you?"

"I might," Martinez replied.

Geneva Holman was ecstatic when the early newspapers arrived. "They're printing what Danny said about Pogue," she told Herb excitedly. "It'll come out everywhere. 'Bill Pogue is an asshole.' I love it. Everybody loves it!"

More witnesses took the stand to attack Pogue within the limits of the court's ruling. A state health department administrator described him as "quarrelsome, aggressive and authoritative—someone who pushed his weight around." A Nevada roofing contractor and longtime Dallas friend testified that Pogue had been known as a "tough cop" during his year as Winnemucca chief. The Reverend LaVerne Inzer, the colorful circuit rider whose beat included Paradise Valley, said that twenty years back Pogue had had a reputation as a "hard-nosed so-and-so." When Inzer added, "It's not often I get a gun pulled on me," the prosecutors arose in tandem and the judge ordered the jury to disregard the statement.

In the jury box, store clerk Donna Deihl wondered how anyone could disregard such a bombshell. Pogue pulled a gun on a *minister?* Dallas hadn't even testified and she already had strong doubts about his guilt. She thought about the Carlins, father and son. They were as much at fault as Dallas. They hadn't wanted competitors trapping in their area. First they'd set up the Oregon trappers and then Dallas. They should be on trial.

But she made up her mind to reserve judgment. Claude would take the stand in the morning.

49

HE STRODE TO the witness stand in his duckfooted walk, popped a cough drop in his mouth, glanced at the jurors and said, "Excuse me, I'm trying to catch a cold." It was as skilled a touch of theater as Waddy Mitchell's entrance or Herb Holman's tale about the hundred pounds of potatoes. Heartless monsters and unfeeling robots didn't do favors and catch colds; only warm-blooded human beings chewed throat lozenges. Every lawyer yearned for a client who could send such messages without sounding rehearsed.

By now the defense strategy had come clear. It was to turn back the courtroom clock to a time when trials were unnecessary, when real men never backed down, when honest disagreements were settled with honest gunfights and a tenderfoot wasn't considered a man till he'd "made his meat" by killing another—justifiably, of course. In the civilized Idaho of 1982, such a strategy couldn't be implemented openly or it would offend judge, jury, press and public. The key strokes had to be subtle, veiled, almost subliminal: enigmatic smiles by the mountain man as he took notes at the table, twinkling eye contact with the jurors, strong suggestions by credible witnesses that the dead men had been up to no good, and an alibi that made a little sense.

At the prosecutors' table, there was no doubt about Dallas's strategy on the stand. Clayton Andersen told friends that the defense had rehearsed for days—"the most intensive trial prep I've ever heard of"—though he didn't say how he knew. Clearly, Mike Donnelly and Bill Mauk had no intention of losing their biggest case. The main questions remained: how would Dallas lay out his tale of self-defense? And would it fly with the jury?

The weather had turned hot; the courthouse's air conditioner struggled to stay even. A fan or two fluttered in the predominantly female audience. Alone of the major participants, Dallas seemed cool. His ponytail was gone, his beard and moustache neatly sculpted, his western shirt cleaned and ironed. He looked like an overage freshman calling on the dean of a cow college. Coco Ickes said later that from the minute he took the stand a change came over the packed courtroom. His speech was direct, his words simple. "What is buckarooing?" he was asked.

"Well, it's just—buckarooing is just a man doing his job, working with livestock on horseback, doing whatever work that has to be done on horseback regarding livestock and cattle, you know."

Why had he quit?

"Cow outfits were going to hell. I was interested in the old cow outfits and they had changed a lot in the last few years." The jurors leaned forward at this hint of idealism.

The man from Ohio spoke all day in an antique idiom that hadn't been heard around Idaho for almost a century. He told of his life "ahorseback." He didn't arrive at towns; he "rode into" them. He "wintered" here and there. He didn't slaughter deer out of season; he "hung up camp meat." At plowing time, he "ripped a little ground." Sometimes he sounded as though he'd walked off the pages of Mark Twain's *Roughing It.* To those who'd met his parents, he seemed to blend his mother's charm with his father's affability. He glanced at judge and jurors but didn't overdo it. He smiled often enough to confirm that he had a good sense of humor but not so often as to appear disrespectful. Andersen said later, "Mike Donnelly did an excellent job of preparing him for trial." Old friends credited Dallas, not Donnelly. Making a good impression had long been his stock in trade.

Only a stubborn few were unimpressed. When he testified about hanging up three hundred pounds of illegal venison, Tim Nettleton nudged a companion and whispered, "Was he gonna eat three hundred pounds of meat?"

Sheri Elms found him a sociopathic manipulator. "You could just feel the calculating vibrations coming from him," she said. "I was actually afraid."

But she was in the minority. The jurors listened expectantly as Dallas approached the hot core of the case. Donnelly was examining:

Q: As you got to the rim, what did you see?

A: Well, just as I got over the rim, there was two men approaching me. . . . They looked like Fish and Game. I noticed they were wearing—well, I noticed they had patches on. . . .

Q: Claude, as these officers approached you, what was the first thing that happened?

A: . . . I walked up on them. They stopped and the one that told me his name was Pogue, told me they were Fish and Game. And he said he was Bill Pogue, and that was Conley Elms, and I told them my name was Claude Dallas. And he immediately told me that he had been told I had some cats in camp, and that he was there to check on them.

Q: Did you make any reply to that?

A: I told him I had some meat hung up. I said I have to eat. And he said they come out to check on them. . . . The only man that did any talking at that point was Bill Pogue. I told him that he was welcome in my camp, and that my camp was open. And I told him, I said, if you guys come out here a hundred and fifty miles just to give me a citation for meat, I can't see it. And Pogue flew hot at that time. He seemed to be on the fight.

Q: What do you mean by those statements?

A: Well, he seemed like he was on the fight when he got out of the rig, as if he was primed. He read me the riot act right there. You know, he started off, he said, "I'm going to tell you something right now, Dallas, if you want to get along with me." And then he went on into something. I don't recall the rest of it.

Q: Did you make any response to him in reference to that statement?

A: At that time, I told him I had to hang meat up, you know, for subsistence, and this and that. And I wasn't getting anywhere with him. He seemed to be getting hotter. . . .

Q: Mr. Dallas, what did you notice about these officers?

A: At that time, I noticed that Pogue's hand, every time I moved or said something, Pogue's hand kept going to his gun.

Unimpeded by objections, Dallas built the case against Bill Pogue. He spoke in a level voice, more like an unconcerned observer than the central character. Idaho C.O.'s who'd known Pogue for years sat helpless in the courtroom, frustrated by the testimony. Not one of them would have described their fallen colleague as a wimp, but the behavior attributed to him by Dallas was unthinkable. Wardens worked in a fishbowl, and one who "flew hot" and was "on the fight" would have been eased out in a matter of days.

The jurors stared hard as Dallas went on: "They acted as if I had just robbed a bank. . . . Conley Elms' jacket was fully unzipped at that time, and I saw Elms reach inside of his jacket and do something. And I noticed then that he was wearing a shoulder rig and a gun."

He said that Pogue had released the security strap on his revolver and placed his hand on the gun. Then he walked to the Fish and Game truck and took out a small backpack. "And he also removed a pair of handcuffs from behind the seat or between the seat somewhere. But he seemed to make sure that I saw him. And I just told him right then, you know, this thing had been—he'd been fairly hot with me and I just told him I thought he was a little bit out of line. . . . Then he told me, I could go easy or I could go hard. Didn't make any difference to him."

Harry Capaul listened and thought about all the times he'd told offenders that they could go easy or they could go hard. He doubted that Pogue had uttered the line; it was more of a cop's approach than a game warden's. But even if he had, it wouldn't have been unusual. It was a useful expression, especially with hard cases. He'd often added an intimidating remark like, "Hey, this warrant just commands me to take a body before the judge. It doesn't specify dead or alive. So it's up to you." And no one had ever shot him.

238

* * *

Dallas's description of the walk from the rim to the camp sounded like a tense scene from a Wild West movie:

Q: Who went down the trail first?

A: Well, I did, and they followed me. . . . Elms stayed behind me and Pogue moved out on the side flanking me. . . . There wasn't much said until we were probably halfway to camp, and I stopped for a breather. . . .

Q: Where was Officer Pogue's hand at that time?

A: Well, I noticed, as I said from the start, anytime I spoke to him or anytime I moved, he had his hand on the butt of his gun. . . .

Q: When you stopped, was there any conversation?

A: Just short, and not all that sweet. I just told Pogue, I said, "You'll find traveling a lot easier on the trail." And he just snapped something back to me about not to worry about them. . . . And that was the last I said to them.

Nearing the tent, he said, Pogue asked for the .22 trap pistol in his shoulder holster, removed the bullets and dropped the gun in his own pocket. Dallas testified that he wasn't asked for the hip gun underneath his fireman's turnout coat, even though "I made no attempt to hide it. It made quite a bulge under my coat with the pack on."

Stevens arrived and was disarmed, but this time the warden returned the empty weapon. Dallas positioned the men—"I was probably six feet in front of my tent. Conley Elms was on my left and a little in front of me, and Bill Pogue was in front of me." Like a movie director prolonging the moment of high suspense, Mike Donnelly asked for a recess. The SRO crowd refused to leave the courtroom.

In the hallway, Tim Nettleton spoke to Dee Pogue. "He's trying to make it look like Bill was looking for a gunfight," he said.

"That's crazy," Dee said. "Will they believe him?"

Nettleton had been watching the jurors closely. They seemed more attentive to Dallas's testimony than to Jim Stevens's or any other. But they also seemed intelligent. "Never," he answered.

Dallas tossed down another cough drop and resumed. Pogue, he said, had become angered all over again when he saw the venison "hanging in plain sight." They discussed the matter for five or ten

239

minutes. "Anytime I said anything, anytime I moved, Pogue's hand was always in the vicinity of his gun or his gun belt. Anytime I said anything or moved, his hand went to the butt of his gun."

When the warden said he was going to search the tent and didn't need a warrant, "I told Pogue that the tent was my home and . . . I believed that he needed a search warrant. . . . He said he could search the tent, and that he *would* search it."

"What happened at the point?" Donnelly asked.

"Again, that went back and forth a little, and Pogue was getting loud and hot and he told me that I could go easy. He said you can go easy or you can go hard, Dallas. It doesn't make any difference to me."

"What did you understand him to mean by that?"

"Like I say, I was growing increasingly apprehensive. I didn't know where this guy was coming from. I was a little worried about the gun deal at that time. It looked to me like he was itching to use it."

The story continued with Elms untying the flap and going inside. When he came out with two hides, Pogue said, "We're going to confiscate those cats, Dallas."

Dallas said he told the warden, "Now wait a minute. You don't know that I didn't get those cats in Nevada. I showed you my license. I have a resident license in Nevada. I have a nonresident license in Idaho. I'm running traplines here with some mules. I'm not even sure where the line is."

Pogue countered that interstate hides must be tagged. Dallas testified, "I told Pogue I was a hundred miles from town. I didn't have any transportation, that this was my home, this was where I lived, and any fur that I got in the area had to come back here. I said I didn't even know where the line was. And I asked him what was I supposed to do with any fur I got from Nevada. Leave it hang on a bush down there?"

Q: What did he say to that?

A: He came back and said something, you know, I don't know, maybe, well—I was trying to stay under control. But maybe I raised my voice or something. But he said something about he was warning me. . . . He told me they were going to take the cats. And I asked Pogue then if he would just cite me for the cats and cite me for the venison. . . .

Q: Were you willing to accept a citation at that point?

A: I would have taken one, you bet.

Q: After that discussion about the citations, how did this conversation continue?

A: Well, Pogue was growing increasingly belligerent again and on the fight. And he told me that I can go easy or I can go hard. It didn't make any difference to him.

Juror Jimmie Hurley, the free-lance writer and rodeo secretary, said to herself, That's the third or fourth time he's quoted Pogue as saying you can go easy or you can go hard. It's beginning to sound memorized, as though someone told him, Be sure to get that in! Then she thought, If an armed officer of the law says you can go easy or you can go hard, *why not just go easy?*

Dallas continued. "And he told me that he was going to take me and the cats. And at that point I told Pogue that I couldn't go. I said I've got my livestock. I've got my mules here, and I've got all my equipment here. And that I can't leave them."

Q: What did he say?

A: He said that you can go hard.

Q: What did you understand him to mean by that?

A: Well, hard, that's only one way. That's dead.

Q: At that point in time, what happened?

A: Well, after that was said, you know, he said to me, he said that to me, and he said he could carry me out. And that's when Pogue, he was drawing his gun.

Q: He said he could carry you out?

A: That's what he said.

Q: Did he go for his gun at that point?

A: He did.

Q: Then what happened?

A: Well, I just reacted to it. I went for mine.

Q: Then what happened?

A: Well, we fired.

Q: Did he fire at all at you?

A: He fired one round. I fired. His gun went off, you know. And I fired again. And I spun Conley Elms. He was going for his gun. I fired one round at Elms, and Pogue was going down and bringing the gun to bear on me. It was up over the lower part of my body. I just threw two more shots at Pogue. And Elms was crouched and I threw one at Elms. And I just ran back and into my tent and grabbed my twenty-two and shot

241

both men in the head. They were on the ground. Elms was facedown and Pogue was on his back.

Q: Were they alive?

A: I don't think so. They weren't moving, they were just—

Q: Why did you shoot them in the head?

A: Well, I was a little bit out of my head at that stage. I was afraid. I was wound up.

He said that Jim Stevens ran about forty yards to the river and then returned, "babbling something, almost incoherent when he came to me. . . . I asked him why he'd run off. . . . He said because I was afraid you were going to shoot me. . . . I said, 'Jim, you should know better than that. I'd shoot myself first. . . .' "

Q: What did he say then?

A: He asked me, "Why? Why?" You know, he was, I mean, just babbling that over and over.

Q: Did you tell him why?

A: I said, "Didn't you see what happened? Didn't you hear what those men said to me?" And he was just babbling on and he said he hadn't been paying any attention, that he overheard bits of the conversation but that he wasn't taking any part in it. And he said the next thing he knew, sparks were flying.

Q: After you said that, what happened then?

A: Well, you know, I was just standing there, and Stevens was standing there. And like I say, Jim was almost in a state of shock. And I told Jim at that point, I just said, ". . . I'm sorry I got you into this, Jim. I said the best thing you can do is go to your rig and head back to Winnemucca and turn this deal in. The only thing I'll ask is that you take your time getting there."

Q: Did Jim say anything to that comment?

A: He said, "I don't want to do that, Claude. I'll help you in any way I can."

For the rest of the morning, Dallas's testimony followed that of Stevens and Nielsen closely, except for the absence of such incriminating remarks as "This is murder one" and "I coulda took 'em on the rim." After the lunch recess he told about taking the body to Sand Pass Road by a circuitous route. "I turned down the fence to the north and I drove up there a ways and out in the brush. And that's where I buried Bill Pogue."

* * *

Tim Nettleton had been waiting for the word on Bill's body. It was late in the trial, but a corpus delicti might help the prosecution as well as end the family's concern. Important evidence was missing—the murder weapon, a mini–tape recorder that Pogue had been using to record confrontations, Pogue's and Elms's own guns, other items—and maybe they were with the body. Why else had Dallas kept the secret till now?

He remembered Sand Pass Road and the trail that ran along the fence. But that area had been searched dozens of times, even with dogs. It was close to the spot where Nielsen said he'd dropped Dallas off. He decided to wait till Clayton Andersen picked up better directions on cross-examination.

Dallas and Donnelly finished with a reprise of earlier testimony:

Q: Claude, you told Jim Stevens at Bull Camp that this was justifiable homicide. And you told George Nielsen at Paradise Hill you had to do it. Why, Claude, do you feel this was justifiable homicide?

A: Because those men were going to kill me. The whole thing started right on the rim with the initial approach. The first belligerence. And, I thought, the gun threats. The first words out of Pogue's mouth were threats. They were that he could take me easy or he could take me hard, it didn't matter which. Every time I moved the hand was on the gun. They were flanking me and Pogue and Elms cleared their guns. There was no reason for that. I gave them no reason to approach me in that manner. And when we left the rim, it was the way they flanked me all the way to the camp, the whole thing was unreasonable. There was a lot of belligerence and hostility there, especially on Pogue's part. . . . I was trying to get along with those men to keep that situation in hand. . . . Anything I said to Pogue was—he got hostile, he got hot. I couldn't talk to him about citations. Anytime I moved again, the hand was always on the gun. I had a very strong feeling that that man was itching to use that gun. And again, I'd given him no reason for this. There had been nothing said on my part or nothing done."

Clayton Andersen had heard enough. There were advertising precepts about pounding points home by repetition, and he was afraid he was in the presence of a skilled practitioner. "Your

Honor," he said, "I hate to interrupt, but I believe he has engaged in more than a response to the question."

Donnelly said, "I think he is giving a narrative response."

Judge Lodge overruled the objection, and Dallas forged ahead. "It was everything leading up to that. It was the threats he made to me in front of my own tent. It was his insistence on searching my home and the threats that he made to me in front of my tent where at least twice Pogue told me that he could take me easy or he could take me hard, it didn't make any difference to him. And when Pogue told me that he was going to take me out of there and he was going to take those cats, I told him I couldn't leave. I said, 'I've got my livestock here, I've got those mules, and I've got my gear.' And it was just—Christ, it was all that. When I told Pogue that, his immediate response was, 'You can go hard.' And I told Pogue right then, I said, 'You're out of line, Pogue. You're crazy. You can't shoot a man over a game violation.' And Pogue said, 'I'll carry you out,' and that's when he went for his gun. And I just—I did the only thing I felt that I could've done to save my own life."

Donnelly said, "No further questions." The direct examination was over.

Juror Donna Deihl was thinking, He's *completely* believable. Everything he says matches the rest of his life. Other than the fact that he has something to lose, there's no reason for us not to believe him. Lying doesn't fit him. If I'd been in his shoes, I'd have shot, too.

Juror Shielda Talich, mother of four, a teaching aide, was thinking, He's a very gentle man. No one who's testified has changed that image. He's on trial for murder, and yet if he walked up to my door tonight it wouldn't upset me in the least to have him come in and visit with my family.

50

CLAYTON ANDERSEN'S CROSS-EXAMINATION strategy called for heavy concentration on the shootings and the rough handling of the bodies. He intended to leave no doubt that the killings had been wanton murder and that Dallas had compounded his crimes by treating his victims like stockyard meat. But first he tried to feel out his opponent. He asked why it had been necessary to kill deer out of season. Why not pack in food like anyone else?

"Not anyone else that I know lives like I do or under the conditions that I do," Dallas answered without hesitation. "It's not practical to carry in the kind of meat you need to carry you through the winter. You can't bring in cut meat and frozen meat. Meat has to be hung in carcass form to keep."

"You could have made arrangements," Andersen said.

"I could have made arrangements, but even if I'd have wanted to I couldn't have afforded it." He admitted that he'd intentionally violated game regulations.

Andersen intended to introduce the confiscated books *No Second Place Winner* and *Kill or Get Killed* to show that Dallas had intended to violate far more sacred laws. But Mike Donnelly beat him to the punch. In the middle of a question, Donnelly said,

"Your Honor, before this I think we need to take up a matter outside of the presence of the jury."

When the jurors had filed out, Donnelly said, "Your Honor, counsel for the State has premarked for purposes of some sort two books reportedly taken from the residence of Mr. Dallas in Paradise Hill. These items are wholly irrelevant to any issue in this case and are only intended to inflame and prejudice the jury."

Andersen argued that the books showed Dallas's state of mind at the time of the killings. The defense, he said, "has put at issue the defendant's character through testimony that he is peaceable and quiet, and his own testimony that he was not the aggressor." The fact that he studied books on quick-draw gunfighting seemed to suggest otherwise.

The judge examined the texts and ruled: "They appear to be legitimate books for legitimate purposes, and to have the jury speculate that they were read for other purposes I believe is too dangerous. And the court is going to sustain the objection."

Andersen was forbidden even to display the jackets of the gunfighting manuals to the jury. The ruling was a heavy blow to the first-degree murder counts. The only other way to demonstrate Dallas's preoccupation with pistol combat appeared to be to subpoena his old shooting partner Duane Michelson, but the Nevada truck cop was on a long vacation, incommunicado.

Slightly shaken, Andersen asked about the gun that had killed the two wardens:

Q: And that is the Ruger Six that you talked about earlier?

A: Yes. On my right hip.

Q: That's the .357?

A: Yes, it is.

Q: Had you had occasion to practice with this pistol at Paradise Hill?

A: Yes, I have. . . .

Q: Officer Pogue had taken your .22 from your shoulder holster?

A: Yes.

Q: And you had not told him about the .357 magnum sitting at your hip?

A: No.

Q: Where did you learn to outdraw an individual?

Donnelly objected. The question, he said, was "speculative and argumentative."

Once again the judge ruled for the defense. "Assumes facts not in evidence," he said. Andersen thought, He's sure right about that. He just excluded the evidence himself.

He tried again. "Where did you learn to outdraw an individual who is drawing his gun?"

"Same objection," said Donnelly.

"Sustain the objection," said the judge.

Andersen tried still another approach. "Did the pistol that you have have combat grips?"

"It had *custom* grips," Dallas answered smoothly. "I had made them."

Andersen abandoned the dry hole and took Dallas back over the sequence of shots. "Do you recall when Jim Stevens testified concerning the way and the manner in which you were positioned when you were shooting?" Stevens had testified that he'd been crouched—the classic stance of the combat shootist.

"Yes," Dallas said. "I do. I recall that."

"Was Jim correct?"

"No, he was not."

Donnelly objected to the references to Stevens's testimony, and the judge said, "The witness should testify to what he knows, not what somebody else knows or testified to. That's invading the province of the jury."

The legal bickering continued through the afternoon, and there was no doubt who was winning. Dallas had mastered the art of turning tough questions to his own advantage. Asked if he left his mules and possessions behind at Bull Camp when he fled, he said, "Yes, and I lost them all, also," depicting a man made destitute by events. When he needed to recall details, he was precise. When haziness seemed advantageous, he was disarmingly hazy. On the potentially damaging subject of the coups de grace, he answered, "All I know is that I fired a round into each man's head. Now I can't tell you exactly how I did that. I was somewhat out of my head myself."

He even scored points off Bill Pogue's missing body. When Andersen asked if he could mark the grave site on a map, he smiled and said, "I would be happy to." For twenty-one months he'd kept the location a secret, resisting all pleas, but the jury now saw a cooperative man who was happy to help.

247

While Dee Pogue and the rest of the audience watched attentively, he stepped to a large map and X'd a spot just off Sand Pass Road. Several onlookers rushed from the courtroom as Andersen was asking, "Did you bury anything with Bill Pogue's body?"

"No, just the body."

"What did you do with the officers' personal effects you put in the pack sack?"

"I buried those."

". . . In a different location?"

"Yes, I did."

". . . When and where did you bury these other items?"

Dallas paused. "I couldn't tell you within four or five miles. I was heading across one of the flats and valleys when I buried it. It was at night."

"Mr. Dallas," Andersen asked, "what did you do with the .357 Ruger Security Six that you shot Bill and Conley with . . . and the .22 Marlin rifle that you shot Conley and Bill in the head with?"

When Dallas answered that he'd buried them also, the experienced Mike Kennedy nudged his co-prosecutor. "Clayton," he whispered, "you'd better sit down. The jury's sympathetic towards him."

Andersen riffled through his notes. Nine pages of questions were left on the yellow notepad. He felt frustrated and confused. He wanted to ask Dallas about his arrest for draft evasion and whether it had given him a permanent grudge against the law enforcement community, but the rules of evidence forbade any mention of a previous record. The jurors had heard Jim Stevens quote Dallas: "I swore I would never be arrested again, and they had handcuffs on." But Dallas couldn't be examined on the subject.

The part-time prosecutor remembered a complaint by Dee Pogue during a recess: "Why shouldn't the jury know what kind of man he was before this happened? A person doesn't just drop down off a cloud and suddenly commit this act. There were things that led up to this that the jurors should know. But every time something like that comes up, they're led out of the room." The reason was simple: it was the rules.

And there were other problems. From the beginning it had seemed to Andersen that the venerable Judge Lodge was guiding the jury toward a second-degree murder conviction. The prosecutor had been told that in two decades on the bench, His Honor had never sentenced a man to death. If the jury returned first-degree, he would have little choice this time.

Something else about the judge bothered the young prosecutor. There'd been loud complaints that the trial was too expensive for little Owyhee County; under the circumstances a retrial could be a political embarrassment. Since the doctrine of double jeopardy gave the prosecution only one shot and the defense as many as it could win on appeal, the judge was bound to lean toward the defendant. It was nothing new; it was a routine fact of American courtroom life.

Andersen said, "No further questions."

In the jury box, Marlys Blickenstaff was thinking, The defense tried to show us what a doll Claude is, how nice and kind and considerate and mild-mannered and meek. The prosecution tried to prove there was something wrong with him—and they couldn't.

She looked around. Sheri Elms was staring hard at Dallas. It was obvious that she hated him. Dee Pogue was calm and reserved. Marlys admired that.

Mike Donnelly asked a few questions on re-direct and then Andersen took the witness for the final time:

Q: Did you not think it would have been easier if both you and Jim had gone to the authorities and told them what happened?

A: At that time, no. And I still don't think so. I think I made a big mistake in touching those bodies from what I seen, and the attitude, and the lynch mob attitude, that the state tried to cultivate. I think it would have been suicide if I had been picked up then. And I believed it then and I believe it now even more so.

The question might better have gone unasked; now Dallas had been handed another chance to justify his flight as the pathetic act of a man fighting for his life instead of the desperate act of an escaping murderer. Andersen provided one more opening by asking why Dallas had bothered to haul Pogue's body away.

"I felt I had to get the body out to buy me a little time," Dallas explained in his methodical style. "And once I took the body out of there, you know, if I had left the body anywhere along the way, well, you know, it would have fouled up Jim Stevens' story. . . . If they found the body they would be right on me. And I felt that

249

my life might depend upon whatever I could get by removing that body. . . ."

He was trying to protect a friend, and he was trying to stay alive. My God, Andersen thought, he's projecting as Saint Francis of Assisi. The young prosecutor took his seat. He'd fought toe to toe with the mountain man and lost.

On re-redirect examination, Donnelly moved to fill the last remaining gap. Dallas had testified for nearly five hours; it was time for a word or two of remorse, largely absent from the virtuoso performance. The courtroom was silent as the curly-haired lawyer asked, "Did you want or intend to kill Bill Pogue or Conley Elms?"

For the first time, Dallas looked moved. "All I wanted to do was keep those men from killing me," he said. "I responded in the only way I could have, to have prevented those men from killing me." Everyone waited for him to take the final step, to say that he was sorry, to offer the solace of apology to Dee Pogue and Sheri Elms and the wardens' old friends in the audience, but he couldn't seem to do it.

Donnelly said he was finished, and the judge said, "You may step down, sir."

51

FRANK WESTON YELLED, "Stop!" and Stan Rorex hit the brakes. The pickup slid to a halt along the fence off Sand Pass Road. The sheriff pointed to a dull green splotch in a patch of thigh-high rabbit brush. It looked like a weatherworn pair of pants. They'd found Bill Pogue.

Not two hours had passed since Tim Nettleton had relayed Dallas's instructions from the pay phone up at the courthouse in Idaho. Rorex had alerted his Search and Rescue team and headed for the site. It was late in the afternoon. Darkness mantled the Bloody Runs and there was a threat of rain.

Weston clomped into the brush. Sixty paces from the fence line he stopped and said, "It's a thighbone." The trousers were Fish and Game green. Nearby were more dirty bones and rags. Rorex thought, A hundred people must've searched this place the first time around, but mostly on the other side of the wire. You could be ten feet away and miss something in this valley. Still, he wished he could get his hands on the tracking dogs.

About fifty feet from the pants the two men found a rocky place where someone had started to dig and quit. They pulled aside the Russian thistle and found a few splinters of bone. "Ribs," Weston said. Then it was night.

At daybreak Thursday the sheriff's office was filled with reporters and cameramen. Rorex and two Nevada state investigators slipped out a side door and sped to the burial site in a crime-scene van. A cold north wind lifted their collars. They started digging up an old coyote den a hundred feet from the femur that Weston had spotted the day before. Rain had fallen and the sand was moist and soft. Two or three feet down, the tip of a laced boot came into sight, then another. The lower leg bones were crossed and disappeared into the boots.

It was an unsettling sight, but Rorex felt almost happy. "We looked for this for over a year," he said as he reached for a screening frame. "God, I must've been down every mine shaft in Humboldt County. Now we can go home."

The skull appeared, a small hole behind the left ear. The diggers lifted out another few sacks of sandy dirt, but the bones of the torso were gone. Rorex said, "Dallas must've known that coyotes would scatter the body. The ground was frozen that night and the den made easier digging. He knew every inch out here." The sheriff's investigator pointed across the dirt road to Nate Smith's potato farm, where Dallas had worked off and on.

The exhumation party found a penny and fragment from a .38 or .357, then fanned out to look for more remains. The wind was blowing; the wind was always blowing. Clothing and bones were found as far away as three hundred feet. The searchers marked each remnant with numbered survey sticks and orange-pink engineering tape. From a distance, they looked like California poppies.

Dee Pogue saw the bone garden on the TV news. For months she'd refused to tell her children about a rumor that Dallas had mutilated Bill's body. Now she realized that the rumor was true, but the work had been done by coyotes.

Regardless, she felt better. Eddie Pogue called, and he felt the same. "It really helps," Dee told Sheri Elms. "Now we can accept everything and make our lives go on." She made a mental note to ask if the diggers had found any signs of Bill's good watch and the star sapphire ring she'd given him. They meant so much to her.

Jurors had been puzzled by the testimony about the grave site and at least one had been bemused. Marlys Blickenstaff said, "It was really hilarious. Claude drew on this map and everybody was buzz-buzz-buzzing. The judge recesses and we're marched off and nobody says boo to us. So we figure we're gonna come back in the morning and hear all about the body. We never heard one thing!"

Instead they heard increasingly bitter attacks on Bill Pogue. The judge had reversed an earlier ruling, explaining, "I think now that the defendant has testified and put into evidence the issue of self-defense, the victim's prior conduct as to aggressive and violent behavior is now an issue."

Mike Kennedy argued that the ruling would create "a series of trials on a series of incidents. This could go on forever." The judge conceded that anti-Pogue testimony might prejudice the jury, but he said that a defendant facing the death penalty should be "given the benefit of the doubt."

While the warden's calcified bones headed home in a box, the trial wound down with a succession of attacks on his personality and his methods. A man named Larry Morris testified that Pogue was "awfully aggressive" in citing him twice for fishing without a license. Under cross-examination, Morris admitted that Pogue hadn't threatened him but had kept his hand on his gun.

Art Castagnola of Boise told the jury that Pogue had been "extremely hostile and extremely belligerent" while discussing violations near Juniper Creek three years back. "I got the impression he was trying to provoke me," the electrician testified. "His attitude was rude and abusive. He acted like we had committed a major crime." C.O. Gary Loveland reported that he, not Pogue, had talked to Castagnola that day; Pogue was elsewhere.

Thomas Derr of Boise testified that he'd been "startled" by Pogue on the Snake in 1977. Derr said he put his hand in his pocket to pull out his fishing license and the warden reacted by reaching for his gun. He admitted that he might have done the same thing himself.

Buford Lee of nearby Nampa told the jury that Pogue elbowed and shoved him at a check station in 1977. Said Lee, "He just had more badge and more gun than he could handle."

Bill Lewis listened with interest from his lime-green-cushioned chair in the jury box. He knew about game wardens. One had given him a hard time and he'd remembered it for forty years. As he'd told a friend, "I was caught by a federal game warden by name of Bock. He later got killed, he was so damn mean here in Idaho. He arrested everybody and they sent him to the Everglades in Florida and them niggers got him down there.

"He stopped me and said, 'You'uz shooting after hours.' I said, 'You never seen me.' He said, 'I did too. I had my glasses on ya.' I said, 'Well, why don't you try to prove it then?'

"About that time somebody started shooting down on the Snake River, and he and the other warden just let us go. I didn't like this Bock. Nobody did." The old farmer added, "I'd probably never been on this jury if they'd asked me about that." In a way, they had. Mike Kennedy had asked if there was any reason he couldn't be entirely fair and impartial. He'd answered, "No."

Over the Columbus Day weekend, Claude Dallas wrote a rare letter to his father. He confided that he felt good about the trial. "Have caught a wink or two from the jury so we'll see," he wrote. He hinted about future plans: "Also, Dad, I haven't resigned myself from the family. I intend to get out of this one way or another. Family at the wrong time could screw up some plans of mine." He noted that security seemed to get tighter when the family was around. "Stuart and Frank had a tail put on them the last time they were up."

He ended on the subject of guns, apparently a mutual interest, and suggested that Sr. read a book called *The American Shotgun*. He said he suspected that some of his father's gun collection had been sold to raise money for the trial and "I'll try to get it back as soon as I can. It's going to take me a while to get rolling again even if I beat this as I'll have to move out of this area or else I'll have to pop another one of these bastards."

The letter closed, "Take care. Claude."

The last two of the trial's eighty witnesses were a pair of angry brothers, Horace and Earl Chapman. "Bill Pogue was a bully," Horace said by way of preamble, and then told of a time when Pogue had questioned him about illegal traps he'd found on the family farm. "I invited him in for a cup of coffee, and he kept questioning me about these traps. . . . And I kept telling him, 'No, we are not in the trapping business. We are in the *farming* business.'

"And in the course of sitting there, Mr. Pogue had a sidearm that he was wearing and he would reach down and play with this sidearm with his hand. Now I might be a little hard hearing, but I wasn't that hard hearing. I could hear that hammer going clickety-click and then back off. . . .

"Finally my brother told him, he said, 'Now Bill, if you don't quit this—you know, this aggressive manner towards the citizens —you're going to die. Somebody is going to do you in.' "

Earl Chapman, a man of about fifty, verified the quotation. He said that he'd known Pogue for ten or twelve years and his reputation was "quite bad." He said that Pogue "played with his gun like a child. . . . He would get it and finger it and play with it and lift it up and down. . . . His mental attitude was very dominatin' and very forceful. . . . I was afraid he would lose his mental stability and just shoot somebody."

With the Chapmans' invaluable testimony, the defense rested. A letter appeared in the *Idaho Statesman:* "Now that the trial for Bill Pogue is over, and he has been found guilty, when does the jury selection begin for the Claude Dallas trial?"

The two Michaels rang down the curtain with hotly controversial closing arguments. For almost four hours the experienced murder prosecutor Kennedy and the brilliant rookie Donnelly addressed the jury. Kennedy pointed out that Dallas's testimony conflicted with that of Jim Stevens and the Nielsens, three of his best friends. "Frankly," he told the jury, "Claude Dallas sounded good on the witness stand until you lined up what some of his friends said about him. But if his friends had heard one ounce of information that would have helped him, they would have told you about it."

The deputy attorney general argued that "the defendant lived in open violation of game laws and Bill Pogue and Conley Elms were down there symbolizing those laws and protecting our wildlife. They had handcuffs and were going to arrest him. That's why he killed them."

He asked the jurors if they didn't think it odd that Dallas could remember exactly where he buried the body nearly two years later, "but for some strange reason he could not remember where he buried Pogue's gun—the only piece of real evidence that could have confirmed Dallas's story."

In anguished tones the other Michael said that he wished he had it in his power to produce the gun. "After burying Mr. Pogue and while he was going across that desert," Donnelly said, "somewhere in that expanse, ladies and gentlemen, the weapon is buried that could prove our case." Courtroom spectators shushed one another. "And God," Donnelly said, "I wish I could find it for you!"

The defense lawyer beckoned toward his client, nursing the flu—another reminder of his human vulnerability—and called him "a good law-abiding peaceful individual with a reputation for truth, honesty and integrity." The prosecution, he said, "wants you to believe that Claude Dallas is a habitual violator of laws—giving Pogue and Elms the righteousness to draw their weapons on him."

He took note of the Idaho statute that mandated first-degree murder convictions for anyone who killed peace officers acting lawfully. "A peace officer using excessive force or threatening to kill is no longer a peace officer in the eyes of the law," Donnelly argued. "He is a citizen like you or I. He is an individual without authority to act in that manner. Do not be suckered in on this case by all of the rhetoric of the State that these were peace officers . . . because ladies and gentlemen, they weren't." He claimed that Pogue had taken away only one of Pogue's guns because "he was looking for an opportunity to utilize his own gun." In turn, Elms was to blame for "not taking action to cool the situation."

The indefatigable defense lawyer summoned up fate, the right of privacy, freedom of action and freedom from unwarranted assault or threat. Dallas, he argued, "was in fear for his life, and he did the only thing a reasonable and rational person can do at that point—preserve his existence. Pogue and Elms are dead at the hands of a man who has never committed a violent act in his life, a man who sought only the protection of his home, his property and the preservation of his life." Dallas, he said, "acted with passion that negates malice. And when you negate malice, you eliminate murder."

He quoted brief testimony by Dallas that Pogue had once left his card with the words *I'll take care of you later.* He lowered his voice and said, "And indeed, faithfully, that was to pass."

He told the jurors, "Ask yourselves when you consider motive: is there evidence in the record that the defendant has ever been arrested for a Fish and Game violation before? If there is, would the State have presented that? Does that comport with the statement that Jim Stevens attributed to the defendant, that he would never be arrested again?"

Tim Nettleton blinked and thought, Am I hearing things or did Donnelly just claim in so many words that Dallas was never arrested before? That's bullshit! Everybody in the courtroom knows better—the judge, the prosecutors, the defense, the jury . . . No, wait a minute, the jury doesn't know. Why don't Clayton or Kennedy say something?

Damn, Clayton Andersen raved to himself, that's misleading! *God damn, that's unfair!*

The young lawyer squirmed in his seat and started to object. Prosecutors seldom interrupted closing arguments; the state had the first and last word, and any falsehoods could be corrected, denied, attacked or even ridiculed later. But this particular distortion was as uncorrectable as a smashed egg.

Donnelly raced ahead, and Andersen's opportunity was gone. Angry at himself, he tried to assess the damage. By planting the idea that Dallas had never been arrested, the defense had finished the wrecking-ball job on one of Jim Stevens's most important claims, that Dallas had said, "I swore I'd never be arrested again, and they had handcuffs on."

Andersen tried to recall the defense attorney's exact phrasing. It was artistic, no doubt about that. It was technically correct that there was no "evidence in the record that Dallas had ever been arrested for a Fish and Game violation before"—he'd been cited, not arrested. But he had been arrested for draft evasion and transported halfway across the country in handcuffs and later in chains, and he'd been furious about it and said so. To the uninformed jurors, the final part of Donnelly's question must have hit home: "Does that comport with the statement that Jim Stevens attributed to the defendant, that he would never be arrested again?" Without that statement, where was the motivation for premeditated murder?

Andersen barely heard the rest of the defense argument. He conferred briefly with Kennedy before the special prosecutor stood up to rebut, and the two men agreed that they were stymied. The record of the draft evasion arrest was no more admissible now than before; the merest mention could result in a mistrial. Kennedy repeated the Stevens testimony in slightly different form in an attempt to restore it to life: "Counsel has stated that this was all a matter of fate. . . . Well, was it fate when Jim Stevens asked him why, and he said, 'Because I will never be arrested again and put in handcuffs'?"

He corrected Donnelly about Bill Pogue's calling card: "It didn't

say, 'I'll take care of you later.' It said, 'I'll *check* on you later.' "
He told the attentive jurors that the defense wanted them to believe
that Bill Pogue "was the kind of man that would go down there for
the purpose of having a shoot-out in front of two eyewitnesses.
That is simply preposterous. And that he would draw from five or
six feet away and shoot and miss. Incredible!"

After the case had gone to the jury, Dee Pogue walked to the
front of the courtroom. "Mr. Donnelly," she said, "would you ask
about Bill's watch and star sapphire ring? I'd really like to have
them back." The lawyer promised to check.

After the widow had walked away, Geneva Holman strode up
and asked Donnelly, "What does *she* want?"

When Donnelly told her, the Basque eyes flashed as she set the
record straight. "Let me be the first to tell you that regardless of
what came down here, Claude *doesn't* go around stealing people's
rings and watches. Wherever they are, they're there. What's buried
is buried. Claude does *not* have those in his personal possession."

Later Dallas confirmed the statement, and word was passed to
Mrs. Pogue.

52

GROWING UP IN Mississippi she'd been known as a "cute li'l thang," but Jimmie Gayle Hurley was having some very uncute thoughts about Claude Lafayette Dallas. She'd listened closely to the judge's instructions, especially when he'd explained that the killing of peace officers constituted first-degree murder if the officers had been acting in the lawful discharge of their duties. For the free-lance writer and PR person for the Snake River Stampede rodeo, that made everything nice and clear.

The jurors elected secondhand dealer Milo Moore foreman, and Jimmie asked, "Would it offend anyone if we had a prayer before we start?" After the Lord's Prayer, each of the ten women and two men spoke briefly. Apart from a few minor charges like concealing evidence, four major verdicts were possible: guilty of first- or second-degree murder, guilty of voluntary manslaughter, and justifiable homicide.

The first speakers said they weren't sure where they stood, but seemed sympathetic to Dallas. Farmer Bill Lewis, who'd kept reminding everyone that he had to leave on a moose-hunting trip in seven days, slapped the table and said, "I'll never go for first-degree if we're here six months."

Jimmie Hurley folded her arms across her chest and said, "Then you're gonna have trouble with me, 'cause that's where I stand."

At least three of the others went along with Marlys Blickenstaff's outspoken contention that the killings were in self-defense, and others seemed willing to be convinced. Jimmie Hurley said, "I can't believe you're so down on these lawmen."

Someone said, "Well, they went there looking for a fight."

"Two lawmen looking for a fight don't get caught that far off guard," Jimmie Hurley said. "The worst thing Bill Pogue ever did was to be firm and authoritative and do his duty as a Fish and Game man. Was this reason enough to be shot? It's ridiculous to say it was self-defense when Dallas shot them in the head. They weren't a threat to him when they were dying on the ground."

Doris Rhodes, a forty-seven-year-old grocery checker, said in a pleasant Ozark twang, "Well, Jimmie, me and my husband trap all the time and we always shoot the animals in the head."

Jimmie was surprised at how upset the remark made her. "These were not animals," she said loudly. "These were men!" She took in a deep breath; she had a lot of convincing to do and she couldn't do it at the top of her lungs. "These two men are our responsibility, yours and mine," she said. "We sent them down there to enforce the law. They were doing what we paid them to do. And because we sent them there, they'll never be husbands again and they'll never be fathers and they'll never see their grandchildren." Her voice faltered and she started to cry. She wasn't as tough as she'd thought.

Marlys Blickenstaff was coming to a boil. It was no picnic to be sequestered just when her husband was harvesting the seed corn and needed her help more than any other time of the year. She was more than willing to do her civic duty as long as the process made sense, but it very definitely did not make sense for this Hurley woman to babble about grandchildren and cry in her hankie like a character from Margaret Mitchell.

Marlys remembered every word of Judge Lodge's omnibus instructions. He had specifically ordered the jurors to rule on the basis of law and evidence, and the law and the evidence were clear. It might be true that Claude Dallas had murdered Pogue and Elms in cold blood, but it had been up to the state to prove it—and they hadn't. The law said "beyond a reasonable doubt." This one wasn't even close. The judge had said, "You should place yourself as

260

nearly as possible in the shoes of the defendant." Marlys told herself, Okay, I'm Claude Dallas and it's January fifth. Here's this Pogue playing with his gun, reaching for it every time I move, telling me I can go easy or I can go hard. Wouldn't I feel that he's going to shoot me if I make one wrong move? And if I end up shooting him, isn't that self-defense?

She looked at Hurley, still rattling on about how believable Jim Stevens had been and how Claude had made up a story to protect Stevens so why wouldn't he make up a story to protect himself? All right, sweetie pie, Marlys said to herself, let's get with it! All the rest of us are gonna use the judge's instructions, so by George you better do the same thing.

She turned toward Hurley and said, "You can't do this. It isn't fair to us, to the families, to Mr. Dallas. It isn't fair to *anybody.* We're all gonna follow the same rules!"

Someone said, "Well, I'm not sure the defense proved Dallas is innocent."

Marlys said, "The defense doesn't have to prove a damned thing!"

Others chimed in. One said, "Pogue was a bully." Another said Dallas had come across as "a kind man, a gentle man." Milo Moore said his mind was open but he was convinced that "Pogue went too far."

Jimmie Hurley backed up and tried to score some points with a series of questions. "If you were a lawman and handling someone and they were resisting you," she asked, "would you pat them on the back and say, 'We'll forget it'? Do we want these men to enforce the laws or not? If you turn Dallas loose you're declaring open season on lawmen. Did they go down there enforcing the laws of the state of Idaho? Were they acting in the line of duty?"

A few women nodded their heads, and she began to think she was making a little headway. "The only reason you have for believing self-defense was the testimony of Dallas himself," she went on. "He had the advantage. He knew he had another gun and they didn't know it. If this is self-defense, then every person who kills another person can yell the same thing. Dallas said he was law-abiding. We know for a fact that he was not."

"He certainly *was,* " someone spoke out.

Jimmie remembered short testimony about Dallas's problems with game wardens, and months ago she'd read about his draft evasion arrest in the papers, although she'd forgotten about it till Stevens had restored the thought to mind. But she didn't think she should mention that. The jury was supposed to stick to the courtroom evidence, and the draft evasion arrest hadn't come up. She wished she knew why. For the moment, she sat back and listened.

Donna Deihl, wife, mother of three sons and furniture clerk, was thinking about Jim Stevens and how he'd bumbled and fumbled around, correcting himself and telling God knew how many different stories about the shootings. He'd seemed so out of it. What a contrast Claude had been! He'd told one story and he'd told it straight.

She tried to remember how Stevens had quoted him: "I'll never be arrested again and these guys had handcuffs," something like that. She thought, Arrested *again?* Who ever said he was arrested *before?* It didn't fit in with anything about Claude. If he was arrested before, why hadn't the prosecution brought it up? That's exactly the point Mike Donnelly had made, and he was so right.

She decided that she couldn't take Stevens's testimony seriously. Claude had character. He'd had his traps taken away from him before, and he'd gone in and paid his dues and gone back out and done the same thing again. It's like traffic tickets, she thought. The Fish and Game has a warped outlook because there's so much poaching—it's like speeding on the freeway. And here come these environmentalists with police duties and they assume that every person they come up against is a criminal. They're just biased. Claude was pleading for a citation; he wasn't resisting arrest. He was right to feel threatened. He had a right to defend himself.

She thought about the shots he'd fired into the wardens' heads. That wasn't as easy to understand. She decided to withhold judgment on that, though she leaned strongly toward justifiable homicide.

The jurors shared four pizzas and soft drinks and worked through the lunch hour. Frank Dallas, the defendant's look-alike twenty-eight-year-old brother, waited in the courtroom for a verdict; brother Stuart had returned to his job in California. Dee Pogue told a friend that there were only two possible verdicts. "I don't want the death penalty," she said. "I want him to spend the rest of his life in prison because I think that's the worst thing that could happen to him." The Dallas Cheerleaders spelled each other in shifts, and one of them said they were planning a party for Claude when he was freed.

The jury deliberated for nine and a half hours and adjourned to its lodgings at the Sundowner, a highly visible motel at a main intersection in Caldwell. Donna Deihl was surprised by the number of Nevada license plates in the parking lot.

The first thing Thursday morning, jury foreman Milo Moore informed the judge that the jury needed a review of certain parts of the testimony and a clarification of jury instructions. He hinted that some jurors were being led by their emotions. The judge declined to repeat instructions that had taken him forty minutes to deliver two days before. "I don't want to be selective in rereading the instructions," he said. "You'll have to follow the law, and not your emotions. Go back and look at the instructions, and reread all of them."

When the foreman asked for portions of Dallas's and Stevens's testimony, Lodge said, "The court has to be very cautious about giving you any particular testimony. I don't want to emphasize any particular testimony." He told the jurors to review everything the two men had said. "This may take you some time," he added, "but that's better than retrying this case."

The jurors gave up at 6:00 P.M. Thursday and returned to the motel. Writer Jimmie Hurley was keeping a running account of the deliberations, and she checked her notes. After two days, six jurors were firm on justifiable homicide. Her motel roommate, the bright young schoolteacher Norma Schafer, had come up to first-degree on Elms and second-degree on Pogue. Jimmie was holding at first-degree on both counts, although she was beginning to realize that a split verdict—harsh on the Elms count, lighter on Pogue—might make practical sense. The other jurors stood somewhere between acquittal and second-degree.

Tempers flared on the third day when most of the jurors refused to yield to the idea of a split verdict. Dark-haired Marlys Blickenstaff spoke for the majority:

"Once you're in self-defense, you're in self-defense. Pogue and Elms went in there as a team. Whatever Pogue is gonna do, Elms is gonna do right along. So if Pogue was trying to kill Claude, then

263

Elms would do the same. If I'd been in Claude's shoes and I had these two guys coming at me, I wouldn't think, Well, this one's just gonna stand over here and pick his nose while that one shoots me. So if I'm gonna try and kill one, I'm certainly gonna try and kill the other."

Norma Schafer spoke up. "If there were twenty officers there, would it have been right for him to kill twenty officers? Where does it all end?"

A bank officer named Connie Tolmie said that Dallas hadn't killed twenty officers, just two, and that he'd been justified by the way Bill Pogue acted. Someone else thrust the judge's instructions at Norma Schafer and said, "Can't you read a single goddamn sentence?"

The blonde schoolteacher didn't answer. She was one of the few college graduates on the jury, and the only one with a master's degree.

Judge Lodge cosseted his jurors when they trooped into the courtroom in the afternoon to ask more questions. "You shouldn't change your minds merely to bring about a unanimous verdict," he counseled them, "but make every reasonable effort to reach a verdict."

Every reasonable effort produced no results on Friday. There was slight momentum toward a compromise verdict of voluntary manslaughter—defined under Idaho law as "the unlawful killing of a human being, without malice, upon a sudden quarrel or heat of passion"—but Jimmie Hurley and a few others held firm on murder. A trial watcher grumbled, "What can you expect when you've got ten women and only two men on the jury?" Such sexism wasn't entirely unexpected in the potato-growing state, where overderriered women (but not overderriered men) were known to some as "spudbutts."

The grocery store checker Doris Rhodes related a story to her fellow jurors. She'd been sitting in her motel room wondering how anyone could think that her fellow trapper Claude Dallas was guilty of anything, even manslaughter. It was beyond all understanding that several of the jurors were holding out for second-degree murder. And the Hurley woman—well, she was hopeless, still insisting on first-degree.

Doris Rhodes told the jury that she'd knelt on her motel room floor and prayed for guidance, any kind of sign. When she was finished, something made her open her Bible at random. Her eyes fell on Matthew 13:15:

> For this people's heart is waxed gross, and their ears are dull of hearing, and their eyes they have closed; lest at any time they should see with their eyes, and hear with their ears, and should understand with their heart, and should be converted, and I should heal them.

She continued reading to Matthew 13:16:

> But blessed are your eyes, for they see: and your ears, for they hear.

She said the motel room epiphany made her firmer than ever for acquittal. A few of the jurors seemed a little put off by the story, but Donna Deihl was thinking, Why not? Our pledge of allegiance is to one nation under God.

Saturday arrived with no verdict in sight. The judge said it was the longest deliberation he'd ever presided over, and the newspapers said it was the longest in Idaho history. Mike Donnelly said, "I can't fathom what's taking them so much time." Clayton Andersen confided to friends that things didn't look good.

When the jurors filed back into the courtroom for more help on the instructions, one was in tears. Judge Lodge patiently tried to dispel the confusion and added, "A defendant is never to be convicted on mere suspicion or conjecture. The defendant begins with a clean slate, and the presumption of innocence alone is sufficient enough to acquit." Once again he listed the possible verdicts, and added, "You can only convict a defendant of the highest degree of which you have no reasonable doubt."

Every now and then the spectators heard that one juror or another had been walked around the courthouse to cool down. Outbursts could be heard through the heavy doors. "We're taking turns having nervous breakdowns in there," a juror confided to her husband. "We're fighting screaming fits, crying, migraines." By

Saturday night, they'd deliberated thirty-four hours and were as far apart as ever.

The judge ordered a day off on Sunday, although the jurors remained sequestered. Bailiffs escorted Milo Moore and Bill Lewis to a private home and the females to a movie about a mountain man, *The Man from Snowy River.*

Afterward Donna Deihl said, "That movie helped us understand. We gave Claude credit for wanting to live and enjoy the mountains." Juror Shielda Talich, the teacher's aide who'd been agonizing over her responsibility, told a friend, "The hero was the type of person who reminded us all so much of Claude. We all sat there seeing Claude, seeing the beauty of the mountains and why a man like Claude would choose to become a mountain man."

On the way out of the theater, one of the jurors put her arm around another and said, "See, Jimmie? One man jumps on him and he had to defend himself against that man, and another jumps him and he had to defend himself against that man, too. *Don't you see?*"

Jimmie Hurley was almost asleep when the same woman appeared at her door. She recounted the conversation later: "She complimented me on being a writer. She told me that Dallas had been set up by the Carlins; they wanted him killed so they could get his trapping territory. I asked how she'd found that out and she said she'd been talking to some people. I said, 'Well, you're not supposed to be talking to people. You're supposed to be sequestered,' and she said they'd blurted it out before she could stop 'em.

"Then she told me that Stevens and Nielsen had lied on the stand because the prosecution would've sent them to jail otherwise. She didn't tell me where she'd heard that. She said Stevens had lied when he quoted Claude. So I told her that I'd read or heard a long time ago about Claude's arrest for draft evasion, and therefore I believed what Stevens said. I went to bed and didn't think much more about it."

53

ON MONDAY MORNING, Judge Lodge took note of the trial's cost —an estimated ninety thousand dollars to date—and ordered the jurors to continue. "I want to push them as long as possible because of the time and expense involved," he said. A Dallas Cheerleader named Debby Harris received a thank-you note for a letter she'd sent her hero the week before. "My birthday is Wednesday," she told reporters, "and the best present I could think of would be to see him get an acquittal."

At the reopening of deliberations, the woman who'd visited Jimmie Hurley's room spoke up. "Jimmie, remember what you told me last night? Don't you think you should tell the rest of us?"

"I'm not denying it," Jimmie said. "I haven't brought it up because I didn't want to influence anybody." She added, "It's not influencing me either. I'd still be at first-degree murder."

After a short discussion, another juror said, "Jimmie, if you'll swear to us on a stack of Bibles that you can put this out of your mind, we'll go on."

"Of course," Jimmie said. But soon the subject bubbled up again. By now most of the jurors felt that the rodeo secretary was all that stood between them and an acceptable compromise of voluntary manslaughter, a finding that could lead to Dallas's immediate release. They decided on a note to the judge. Jimmie insisted on sending one of her own, but she was voted down. She charged, "You want to get rid of me because you can't change me!" The note simply said that one of the jurors was using "extraneous information" and asked what to do about it.

Waiting for a response, the jurors split into little groups. A few read magazines, some played cards or looked out the window. Bill Lewis said, "Let's get this over with. I want to go hunting." Marlys Blickenstaff wandered to the corner where the exhibits and physical evidence were piled up. "Hey," she said, "let's look at this stuff." Three or four others joined her.

Near the bottom of a stack of papers they found complete information about the draft evasion arrest. It had been ruled inadmissible but left in the file. Connie Tolmie picked it up, then said, "Oops! I don't think I'm supposed to read this." Word got out, and soon everyone knew.

That evening foreman Milo Moore went from room to room. From the beginning he'd been the gentle patriarch of a matriarchal jury, playing the role of arbiter, seldom expressing an opinion of his own. But now the secondhand dealer began to sound impatient. "We're trying to get home," he said as he made his rounds. "Let's grow up." In the strictest sense, the visitations were a violation of the sequestering procedure, but the rule had been so honored in the breach that it no longer mattered. One juror had described the contents of a newspaper report, strictly forbidden. Roommates discussed the case at night, sometimes with outsiders. Husbands slipped in and out. Marlys Blickenstaff observed later, "By the end, half the people of Caldwell were involved in the decision."

By Tuesday morning, the sixth day of deliberations, the last holdouts for murder began to crumble. It was an inherent part of the jury system—"the strong wear down the weak," as Jimmie Hurley complained to the press later.

Sixty-seven-year-old Wanda Pence dropped to second-degree. Once she'd said, "I'll never leave first-degree on Conley Elms. He was an innocent bystander."

Jimmie Hurley, who'd borrowed a few tranquilizers from the

older woman from time to time, asked, "Wanda, can you live with this?"

"I have to," she answered. "I won't live at all if I don't get out of here."

Now there were nine for manslaughter and three against. The holdouts were Cheryl Knox, a thirty-year-old pediatric nurse who insisted on second-degree on the Elms count, and the roommates Schafer and Hurley, both of whom had compromised down to second-degree on Pogue but were first-degree on Elms.

Jimmie caught a few baleful glances and told herself, It might cost Owyhee County another hundred thousand, but I'm not changing. I'll sit here! They can't hurt me physically. She told the group, "I can't live in Idaho with a manslaughter verdict. You're gonna be run out of the state."

She knew she was no longer at her best. Sometimes she would ask herself what's the use and sit in a corner with a book, refusing to talk for hours. Later Donna Deihl accused her of raving that Dallas would "go to Alaska and kill people" and other wild charges. The truth was that neither Jimmie Hurley nor some of the others were quite themselves. After seven days, the Dallas jury had hit the wall.

Marlys Blickenstaff told what happened next: "Jimmy went to the chalkboard with a bunch of notes she'd written the night before. Right away she referred to the draft evasion arrest. She said, 'Knowing what I know . . .'

"That's what did it. We let her finish and we all looked around and were quiet. And when she was finished, she denied that she'd said it again and we told her she had; Connie read back her notes. Then Milo said a few nice words about Jimmie. I thought, You naive man, you can be taken in by this little southern belle with her little sweet talk."

Shortly after, a note went out to the judge:

> Your Honor. During our deliberations it has come to our attention that one of us had previous knowledge concerning the defendant (before being sworn in as a juror) that is influencing her judgment in regards to factual testimony. We feel we have reached an impasse because of the issue so stated.

Jimmie Hurley was called before the judge. As she was escorted out of the jury room by a bailiff, she heard voices: "Look what she's put us through!" "What'll they do to her? She's committed perjury." "She'll go to jail. . . ."

She shook her head and thought, They're willing for me to go to jail, but they want Claude Dallas to go free. Her English comp teacher back in Mississippi would have called that irony.

Clayton Andersen didn't like what was happening. The judge had called in both sides to question a juror. Criminal trials were supposed to be public, but this supplemental voir dire was scheduled for another courtroom behind two locked doors, with a deputy sheriff in front of each. There was something about closed sessions that made the young prosecutor uncomfortable. The people of the state of Idaho were involved in this case too, and deserved to know what was going on.

He read the note from the jury foreman again. Jimmie Hurley was marched in; he remembered her from the trial. She was the writer, the one they'd nearly bounced and then accepted when they learned she was a military wife.

At first the questions from the bench and both sides were deliberately vague. The presumption was that the jury stood eleven to one and that she was the holdout; any confirmation of her position would give one set of lawyers an intolerable advantage. She admitted that she'd "read or heard" something that bore on the case, but she insisted that she was prepared to make her decision based solely on the evidence. She said the other jurors were "pretty hostile at this time because they all want to go home, so they're looking for a scapegoat. So they won't believe me even if I go back."

Under close questioning by Michael Donnelly, she said that the extra information had come to mind during the testimony of Jim Stevens. The judge asked, "You don't recall whether you read it or heard it?"

"I either read it or heard someone say they read it." The questioning went back and forth. She kept insisting that what she'd learned wouldn't affect her decision. All of the jurors had read and heard about the case and had said so in the voir dire. The question was whether the information they'd absorbed would keep them from rendering a fair and honest verdict. The judge said he was satisfied and told her to step down.

Donnelly said, "Your Honor, I have a few more questions."

Andersen added, "I have one I could ask."

The judge said that the matter was closed.

"Your Honor," Donnelly persisted, "we request the opportunity to further question the juror."

"Denied. I'm going to have the juror return into the jury room for further deliberations."

The earnest Bill Mauk took up the argument. "Your Honor," Donnelly's partner said in a calm voice, "she indicated that she formed an opinion during the testimony of Jim Stevens, and that she has kept that opinion throughout the trial. . . . Had we been permitted to ask the juror a few more questions, Your Honor, I think it would have been appropriate to ask the juror . . . if the opinion or information she had assisted her or helped cause her in some way to form an opinion. . . ."

The judge said Mauk was asking the impossible. "You cannot take something out of your mind that is there. But she has also indicated to you under oath that she has been able to set that aside and that she would have arrived at the same conclusion with or without that recollection."

Mauk said that he wanted to ask her "whether the information caused her to form an opinion as to probable guilt or innocence. If it did, and if she has held that opinion and it tends to support that opinion, and she has relied on all the things that she has said, then it is tainted."

The judge looked exasperated. "Very well," he snapped. "We will call her back and ask that question. And if it is a mistrial it is a mistrial. Mister bailiff, please bring Mrs. Hurley back."

When she returned, Donnelly asked, "Did the opinion that you formed after hearing this or recalling this extraneous information cause you to form an opinion in your mind as to the probable guilt or innocence of the defendant?"

"It doesn't even go that far," the woman answered. "It just caused me to believe something that Jim Stevens said."

Clayton Andersen's heart sank. If she believed Stevens, she disbelieved Dallas, which meant that she was holding out for a conviction, probably first-degree murder. And the other eleven were set on something less, maybe even justifiable homicide. And now the defense knew it.

Donnelly pressed. "Did it cause you to develop your ultimate opinion as to a critical element or issue in the case?"

"That's hard to answer."

"Is the information pivotal in your decision?"

"No."

"Did the information cause you to give less credibility to the testimony of one witness."

"Yes."

Andersen shuddered. It looked as though Donnelly wasn't going to quit till she was removed from the jury.

Donnelly asked, "Because of that, did you carry that lack of credibility through the entire trial?"

"Probably. . . . It was there. I couldn't forget it was there. But I think I have said I would have felt that way anyway."

"Can you say that, truly knowing that information is in your mind?"

There was a long hesitation. Andersen felt sorry for the woman; she looked exhausted. He heard her answer in a resigned voice, "No, I guess I can't."

"Because of that information," Donnelly asked, "do you believe that one witness is lying and the other is not?"

For an instant a touch of fire returned to her voice. "Yes," she snapped. "When two people contradict each other, one has to be lying."

Donnelly said, "No further questions."

The judge asked, "Mrs. Hurley, from what you have said here, you also somehow arrived at the conclusion that what you read or heard is true?"

"Yes." Her voice had dropped off again.

"So the source had to be believable in your mind then?"

"Yes."

Lodge looked at Andersen and then back to the woman. "I'm going to ask, Mrs. Hurley, that you step down as a juror."

After Jimmie Hurley had been escorted out, Andersen stood up, enraged to the tips of his reddish-blond beard. He felt that both he and the court had been bullied, and not for the first time. It was no one's business where Jimmie Hurley had stood in the deliberations, and having teased the information out, Donnelly shouldn't have been permitted to bludgeon her with questions till he forced the answer he needed.

Andersen moved for a mistrial. "There's no choice to resolve this matter," he told the judge. He noted that two alternate jurors had been released at the beginning of deliberations and by now were tainted by exposure to the outside world. "There's no way anyone can determine what effect that would have on the jury deliberations," he added.

Bill Mauk argued for an eleven-member jury. "Our sole objective," he said, "is to continue with the trial to the point of a verdict." He said the defense would agree to a mistrial only if the prosecution would drop all charges permanently.

After a short conference with his lawyers, Dallas was questioned by the judge. Did he want to proceed? Yes, he answered. "I would waive the right, Your Honor, to a twelve-member jury. I would like to continue with an eleven-member jury regardless of the outcome. I have no idea how the jury stands at this time."

The judge denied Andersen's motion for a mistrial and said he would try to come up with a solution.

When Joyce Blanksma came home from teaching school, she found a note from her daughter: *Emergency. Call Judge Lodge.* The young widow was afraid she knew what was up. Earlier that day she'd sent a message to the two men and ten women she'd sat with as an alternate juror. "Tell them I'm thinking about them," she'd told a bailiff. Now she knew good and well she'd be joining them.

The prospect made her nervous. When the two alternates had been dismissed, they'd been told not to discuss the case, but she hadn't taken the warning seriously. Now she thought, Oh, why didn't I just shut up?

Clayton Andersen glared as the alternate was brought in and questioned. She admitted that she'd read about the case in the papers and discussed it with her mother and friends.

The judge asked, "Can you set this aside and base your decision solely on the evidence?"

"Yes, I can."

After Blanksma was accepted, Andersen railed at the judge, "This is absurd!" Driving home, he told his wife, "He wants to get this case over with. He made an economic decision. He's gonna have to live with it for a long time."

A dazed Jimmie Hurley packed in her room at the Sundowner. The judge was a fellow horseman, and they'd been on first-name terms for years, but it seemed to her that he'd allowed those lawyers to whipsaw her till she hardly knew her name. She thought about the other jurors. They know exactly what I know, she said to herself, and some a lot more. All kinds of propaganda's been coming into the motel night after night from husbands and friends and newspapers, not to mention dumb movies like *The Man from Snowy River*. If she was tainted, weren't they all?

She called her husband to drive her home. She couldn't think. She was so tired.

When Joyce Blanksma walked into the deliberation room, several of the women cried with relief. They'd been worried that the other alternate juror, postman John Rogers, would be named; he'd always been strong on first-degree murder. They asked where she stood, and she said, "Somewhere in the middle." Bill Lewis gave a loud sigh of relief, and Joyce thought, Well, at least I'm close to somebody.

The judge ordered them to back up and start over. "I know it's a terrible imposition to ask of you," he said, "but I'm sure you realize the importance of this case. This is a terrible thing that has happened, but it's something we could not avoid."

On Wednesday morning Joyce Blanksma let it be known that she perceived Dallas as "essentially a decent person" and would accept a manslaughter verdict. After two more hours of discussion, nurse Cheryl Knox came down from second-degree. "It's not what I want," she explained wearily, "but it's close enough."

That left the schoolteacher Norma Schafer. When her roommate had been summoned before the judge, she'd expected her to return. Nobody'll believe this crap, she'd told herself. Jimmie's in there because she knows Claude was arrested before, but these other people know even more about it and they're still here. It's crazy.

Now she felt abandoned by the court and the system. She stayed firm through another hour of bitter stares and then said to herself, No way I'm gonna change their minds. Not in ten years. She dropped to manslaughter. It was noon on Wednesday, October 20. After forty-five hours, the longest deliberations in Idaho history were over.

Everyone except a few of the jurors seemed unhappy with the verdict. Clayton Andersen called it "a tremendous injustice." He said, "I thought it was first-degree murder or I wouldn't have

274

prosecuted. . . . I think he lied on the witness stand. The Claude Dallas who was in the courtroom and the Claude Dallas [at Bull Camp] are two different individuals."

Tim Nettleton said, "Bill Pogue was a personal friend of mine. He was an officer doing his job, and he was killed in the line of duty." He gestured toward the courtroom. "And that's the support he gets. . . . When we go up to someone to arrest them, and they say, 'Go to hell,' are we supposed to say we're sorry and walk off?" He shrugged his narrow shoulders. "I just don't know."

Mike Donnelly and Bill Mauk emerged from the courtroom to the applause of the Dallas Cheerleaders. The smiles changed to frowns as Donnelly reported that Claude was "not satisfied" with the verdict. "He wanted a not-guilty verdict on all counts, but when you are dealing with a law enforcement official or a police officer in an altercation that ends in a shooting, there is a tendency to give more credit to the prosecution's case. My perception of the verdict is that if we were dealing with other individuals, the verdict would have been not guilty on all counts."

The gracious Mauk called Dee Pogue and Sheri Elms "innocent victims," and added, "We all hope this closes the book on this unfortunate situation for each of them and that they can now get on with their lives."

Eddie Pogue lashed out at everyone. "If you want justice in this country, you have to do it yourself," he hinted darkly. "I said Dallas wouldn't be allowed to get away with it, and he won't." He was enraged at Judge Lodge. "You've got a judge who allowed my brother to be put on trial from the beginning, rather than the defendant. I think the credibility of the judge has to be examined." Bill Pogue's younger brother added, "It's open season on game wardens. If you don't want a hundred-dollar ticket, you just have to put a hole in one."

Foreman Milo Moore patiently explained the verdict. "We just figured Pogue drew his gun and Dallas was a better marksman, that he was put in a position of self-defense. Dallas was a faster draw. He won out." But, said the secondhand dealer, Dallas had used excessive force when he shot both men in the head. If it hadn't been for those two acts, the verdict would have been justifiable homicide.

275

Juror Shielda Talich said she was especially pleased with the way Dallas had stood up under the news. "He took it with squared shoulders," she told friends. "He's not the kind of man to do anything except grit his teeth and stand there. Because he's not gonna be a baby about it." Later she added, "Many western men are too independent to be pushed. They're gonna react by protecting themselves. I won't minimize what he did—it was wrong. There's better ways to handle things than the way he did. But I would hate to see the world get into the situation where all the men were afraid to stand up for their own rights."

Marlys Blickenstaff was as outspoken as she'd been from the first day. "Game wardens are employees of mine," she said. "I pay their wages. Why are we having aggressive brutal men like Pogue on the force? Why didn't they remove him? Why did they retain this fella and allow him to go around with guns ablazin'?"

Old Bill Lewis said that the wardens had been "overbearing" and Dallas had fired in self-defense. Then he went off to hunt moose.

Dee Pogue and her teenage daughter Kathi were in a candy shop when they heard the news on the radio. They broke into tears. "I couldn't believe it," Dee said. "It was *so* destructive to me." She tried to analyze the verdict. "There were too many women on the jury," she decided. "Women tend to be maternal, and Dallas is a master at bringing out the maternal instinct. I don't know how he learned it, but he did." Later she made a short statement to the press: "It's ironic that a man who had so much respect for the law should in turn have the court system fail him."

Sheri Elms was visiting a friend. The phone rang and her friend answered, then turned to Sheri with a horrified look. Sheri was afraid her mother had died. "What's the problem?" she asked.

"I just can't tell you."

"Jo, I'll find out somewhere else."

"The verdict was . . . manslaughter."

Sheri felt numb. The situation was unreal, dreamlike. She thought, I'll have to take a few minutes to sort this out, because it can't possibly be true. It's science fiction. . . .

After a while she decided not to feel angry or vengeful. It was against Conley's philosophy.

* * *

That night, Dallas wrote home again. In neat block printing, he told his parents about the verdict and again praised his attorneys. "It was just an uphill road with these two fellows being law enforcement," he wrote. "Also, having an eyewitness didn't help." He assured Jennie and Claude Sr. that his spirits were good. "I'm a long ways from whipped." He said he wasn't planning "on staying with these bastards any longer than I have to."

54

THE JUDGE'S DOG was shot and thrown on his lawn. Jurors were threatened. Newspapers rang with editorials and letters: "The most prodigious miscarriage of justice within the annals of civilized jurisprudence." . . . "The police officers all over our state might as well paint a bullseye on the front of their uniforms." . . . "I have heard of the defendant pleading insanity, but never have I heard of a whole jury being insane. . . ."

A few jurors answered back. Donna Deihl said, "People are saying we were infatuated with Dallas. What cracks me up is—every single one of us were married. All but one had children!"

In an unsigned article for the *Idaho Statesman,* juror Deborah Ross called the verdict "true and justifiable." She reminded readers that Pogue had warned Dallas he could go easy or hard and "I'll carry you out." The twenty-eight-year-old housewife wrote, "If you were Dallas, what would you think if a man said that to you? He thought he was going to be killed! . . . Mr. Elms standing by did not have time to stop and consider these facts. He just saw his partner going down and went for his gun. . . ."

Dallas Cheerleader Jennie Shipley wrote: "I feel Jimmie Hurley's conduct was totally unacceptable. . . . Mrs. Hurley should have disqualified herself as a juror or at least discussed the problem with Judge Lodge at the time she suddenly regained her memory instead of waiting until five days into deliberations."

Jimmie Hurley, hard at work publicizing the 1983 Snake River Stampede rodeo, said she would just as soon forget the whole experience. "I'll clean toilets in the jail, but I'll never serve on a jury again."

A TV station polled its viewers and found that twenty to thirty percent thought Dallas should have gone free. But most people were outraged. Game wardens and their fellow law enforcers spoke the loudest. John Dawson, a California warden, told a newspaper reporter, "A little bit of America crumbled in my mind when I heard. We're very much in shock down here. We feel like our lives aren't going to be valued for very much." Gene Weller quoted a colleague: "Now I guess you know what the world thinks of game wardens." Idaho Fish and Game Director Jerry Conley claimed that the verdict "cheapened and jeopardized the lives of all peace officers."

A few cool heads pointed out that extreme reactions were premature. Dallas could still draw fifty years, enough to satisfy all but the most bloodthirsty, or he could go free and attend the Cheerleaders' victory party. It was up to the judge.

Claude Dallas Sr. and his oldest son Will spoke up in speech and print. The State of Idaho was to blame for what happened, Sr. wrote the *Statesman*. "If the role had been played out as planned, Claude would have died on that mountain with one paragraph on Page 8C stating that he was a criminal who had resisted arrest. . . . Evil men, who themselves are criminals, have used the law to bring righteous men death or imprisonment since the beginning. Any man who uses the court to destroy his fellow man commits treason against the state and destroys all that should be held sacrosanct."

Will, the charterboat-fishing captain, was quoted in a letter that ran alongside his father's: "I am proud that my brother took a stand against all law enforcement corruption that January day. . . . I hope that we all will have the courage that it must have taken to make the decision to survive in the face of the terror that Claude must have felt when the deadly purpose of those two officers was realized."

Will Dallas described himself as "an avid conservationist" and

279

put in a word for his father: "Claude L. Dallas Sr. raised his six sons to respect nature and to love the freedom of the outdoors. Above all, he instilled in all of us the respect of the law. . . ." He called on the newspaper's readers to laud his brother "for a heroic act of self-defense."

The family's voices were heard in an interview over Boise's KBOI. Dallas Sr. pointed out that all nine of his children had been raised on venison, and "killing and eating a deer . . . isn't any more wrong than if you went to a store and bought a roast beef." He said he knew that Pogue and Elms "went in there with the intentions of probably if not of killing him of manhandling him. I don't want my boy manhandled. I wouldn't stand for it. . . ."

He argued that his son hadn't been tried by a jury of his peers. "I don't know how a man that's never been hungry can try a hungry man that has committed an offense while he was hungry. I don't know how a man that's lived in the mountains the last fifteen years can be tried by schoolteachers."

He attacked corrupt lawmen again and cited Tim Nettleton as an example. "Claude's last night in jail, Nettleton put Ed Pogue in the cell with Claude. That's horrenyous! . . . Ah cain't believe a sheriff would allow that to happen."

When the interviewer asked how he could justify his son's final shots, Dallas Sr. said it was standard trapping practice. "You wouldn't let an animal lay there and suffer. . . . He put those men outa their misery."

Then it was an act of humanitarianism? The interviewer sounded dubious.

"Using that twenty-two was, I know that. He was taught that."

On the same show, Will Dallas said he would have done exactly what his brother Claude did. "There's no man going to violate my rights and not give me a way out. . . . To let you know that they're not gonna let you outa the place alive, how are you going to respond? Are you going to just die? . . . I would try to get to the man before he got to me."

He agreed with his father about the finishing shots. "They were probably dead before he did it. You can't murder a corpse. I can imagine his adrenaline flow after that gunplay. . . . He's standing there holding on to an empty gun with all of this still running through his head. I would go look for something else, a club or something, you know, and if they twitched I'd probably hit 'em with it."

Never one to ignore an opening, Mike Donnelly picked up on the idea of murdered cadavers. He announced to the press that he intended to ask the court to vacate the manslaughter convictions on the grounds that the state "had not proven beyond a reasonable doubt that . . . the victims were alive at the time of the final shots." Some were reminded of the man who murdered his parents and threw himself on the mercy of the court on the grounds that he was an orphan.

A Boise woman named Jodi Rupe wrote to the *Idaho Statesman* after listening to the Dallases and reading their letters. "I now better understand why Claude Dallas has the paranoid anti-law enforcement attitude that he plainly displayed in the courtroom. . . . I can hardly believe that his family not only condoned this murder but think of it as a heroic act." Jodi Rupe was Bill Pogue's daughter.

55

BACK IN SOUTH Carolina, it was a time for prayers and second thoughts and memories of Claude. Every member of the family was standing by him, but there was a feeling that he might not have chosen the most reasonable way to handle his problem at Bull Camp. Still, it was far more blessed to kill than be killed—they all agreed on that.

Dallas Sr. decided against any more interviews. The KBOI newsman just hadn't seemed to get it. Maybe nobody did. You couldn't understand Claude unless you understood the way he was raised and maybe the way his mother and father were raised and so on, ad infinitum. The Dallases chewed incessantly on Claude's history, from the diaper to the cell. The brothers checked in by long-distance telephone. A few times the family shared thoughts with outsiders. As usual, Sr. was the main spokesman. Gone were the jokes and japes. He tried to tell the whole story and tell it fair, as he knew fair.

"My grandmother had the bluest eyes I ever seen," said the patriarch of the clan that stretched from Carolina to California to New York to Texas. Approaching seventy, suffering from gout and heart problems and a hundred pounds of overweight, he often evoked his grandparents in explaining his son. "They were farmers in east Tennessee. Seventy-two acres of hard ground. How the hell they made it, I don't know. I loved my grandmother, spent more time there'n home. That woman never had to raise her voice to me. I'd hang on to her apron strings. I'd stand beside her and she'd milk a cow right into my mouth.

"My grandfather taught me all I know." He cleared his throat with a deep gurgling cough. "I'd love to be able to go back to my granddaddy and put my arm around his shoulder and say, 'Grandpa, I love ya.' But I'd've never said it when he was alive. We weren't people to touch or express anything. Parents didn't hug their children or talk about loving them in those days. That would've spoiled 'em or made the boys effeminate—that's the way they thought. It would've embarrassed my grandfather if I'd've told him. And I *did* love him. I've still got tools of his."

He talked less about his own parents. "Claude's mother was the coldest woman I ever saw," Jennie Dallas put in. "She never held a one of my babies."

"My daddy was a Brethren," the father went on. "The Mennonites are an offspring of the Brethren. He converted to Babtist just like Jennie and I converted to Catholicism. Clode's a Catholic, always was, though he don't work at it. My daddy was raised on a farm and he raised me on a farm. It gets in your blood. I ended up doing a lot of things in my life—making guns and knives, shooting men with a BAR in World War Two, tool and die work, inspecting bridge welds, other jobs—but I never wanted to be anything but a farmer. I just love the smell of working cattle. I *love* cattle!"

He smiled as he took in air. "I drove a farm truck when I was thirteen years old, picking up milk from dairy farmers of a morning. I'd go out at four A.M. and then I'd go to school. I got paid three dollars and two pounds of butter a week, and a quart a milk a day. That was a lot of help to my mother and my daddy. Wasn't much money around in twenty-eight, twenty-nine. That's how I started loving the dairy business."

"Good glory," Jennie said. "He wishes he was still in it. He wishes our boys were in it with him."

"*Yeah* I do," Claude said. "Seems like our best times was when the kids was growing up. Little Clode, he learned a lot on our farm. So'd Will, Jim—hell, we *all* did."

283

* * *

It took both Dallases to explain how their secondborn son came to be a Jr. "Claude only wanted one boy," Jennie started. "He already had daughters from his first marriage. When I was having Will, our firstborn, he told me all the way to the hospital, 'It's gotta be a boy or I'm not gonna pick you up!'"

"I had her believin' it, too," Dallas said.

"That's the truth," Jennie said in her mellifluous voice. "So I had Will in Louise, Virginia, in a little country hospital."

"I got drunk that night on a jug of whiskey," Claude said. "Went out and bought all the flowers out of a flower store. That hospital looked like a mortuary. I was proud to have a boy. Named him William Joseph Dallas after a second cousin in Ohio that was closer to me than my father. You cain't believe what a wonderful man old Will Dallas was. Died in my arms when he was sixty-nine years old. I'd named my first daughter Billy Jo after him. I wanted a William Joseph so bad I couldn't stand it."

Jennie said, "So I just kept having 'em till I had six boys and a girl. Claude was the second. He was skinny at birth, the only skinny baby I had, and his nose looked big like his daddy's."

"I took one look at him," Claude said, "and I told her, 'That's Junior!' My boys used to set on my lap and go to sleep at night till they was three four years old. I've had two of 'em at a time, one on each knee, and they'd be sound asleep. Jennie, remember that time I took li'l Claude to Waukesha?"

Jennie said she remembered.

"We'd started him to school when he'uz four," the father said. "It was a two-room schoolhouse with six classes. Claude was always a finicky eater, and one day Mrs. Goldthorp asked Jennie, 'Why doesn't he eat peaches? He tells me they're too fat.'"

The parents laughed at that one. "He didn't like slick food," Claude said, and laughed again. "He wouldn't eat meat. It was quite a problem gettin' that little fella to eat. So one day when he was five, I had some cattle to sell at a big sale over in Waukesha, Wisconsin. I took Claude and five head to the show. Little fella went to sleep at the banquet that night settin' next to me. His little head fell over, so I put it against my shoulder."

Jennie Dallas turned away as he continued. "The next morning, we went downstairs in the hotel for breakfast. God, he was a good-looking boy! Shy, but not too shy. I said, 'Well, what're ya gonna eat, son?'

284

"He said, 'Anything.'

"I knew he'uz just trying to be nice, so I said, 'No, no. Order!' He said he wanted ham and eggs.

"I said, 'Now if you order the ham, Claude, you'll have to eat it.' It came and I cut it up for him, but I took the fat off. *He ate every bite!* I'uz so proud of him I coulda busted." Sitting in the corner, Jennie Dallas smiled at her son's old triumph.

The storytelling went on for hours. Through all their travels, the Dallases seemed to have stored up more pleasant memories in the Upper Peninsula of Michigan than in all the other places. "It was the poorest farming country I ever seen," the father recalled. "We were under snow seven eight months a year. We didn't get but one cuttin' of hay. It's amazing how fast things grew when they grew. Strawberries as big as your fist. Alfalfa jumped out at'cha. I had a mower with a big crusher on it. I'd put Will on that, and Jim on the rake, and Claude on the baler. It'd do your heart good to see 'em out in the field, them three li'l kids."

"And mom in the truck," Jennie broke in. She was more interested in talking about Claude. "By seven or eight he was very strongheaded. He knew what he wanted to do and he did it. Like his daddy. He had a lot of Claude's characteristics."

"We had a hundred and twenty Brown Swiss," Sr. went on, "and the only way we kept the farm going was to work the family for noth' ' Had a milker and a field hand. The milker milked one side of : .rn and my boys the other. I'd spell 'em all off, and I did the feeding and cleaning up behind the cows and all the doctor work. The vet was ninety miles across icy roads in Sault Sainte Marie."

He got the boys up every morning at four by shaking their big toes. "They'd hit the floor with their eyes closed, but they was up. When they was four years old, I'd start 'em running the cows out. That was all of 'ems first job. As soon as you milk cows, you got to drive 'em out or they'll stop and smell the other cows and dawdle and splash droppings on the floor. My boys'd be barefoot, and I'd tell 'em, 'That stuff'll make you grow!' They'd run the cows out with a rubber hose, or they'd grab her tail and twist it—that's why you see a lot of dairy cows with kinked tails. Some mornings they'd cry and cry—'We're gonna miss Walt Disney on the TV!'—and I'd say, 'All right, go on back home.'

"When the boys were six or seven, I'd have 'em start milkin'. I

285

liked to have the boys milk because a cow'll give ten percent more if a child or a woman milks 'em. It's the gentleness.

"Around seven-thirty, they'd come back to the house to eat and catch the school bus. After the evening milking I'd send 'em to the store to buy a quarter-pound Butterfinger bar or a box of ice-cream sandwiches, and they'd all sit around licking their fingers and feeling like men.

"I was never hord on 'em like I was on the hired men. I always told the hired men, 'There's two things I require: If you haven't anything to do but turn around, do it quick. And second, no goddamn back talk! I tell you to do something, you better move.'

"I never had to whip my boys. Yeah, I whipped Bob's ass one time for throwing darts at the ceiling. But Will, he never had a whippin'. I took a broom and run him out the house one night, but they were laughing about it by the time dinner came round. Claude never had a whippin'. *I* did when I was a kid. It's useless."

When the father left the room, Jennie Dallas begged to differ. "He just forgets," she explained. "He hit 'em. Sure he hit 'em. I never was stern with my childen. My job was to bring them up right and give them love. Claude was stern enough for the two of us. They had to be perfect. He used to be that way about how I kept house."

She confided, "The thing I don't understand about my son is he never had a hot temper. He was always so calm and good to everybody. He got into trapping when he was seven or eight years old, brought me a mink one day, wanted me to have it made into a scarf. I told him, 'No, you sell it.' He'd worked so hard. He was always such a kindhearted little boy. I cain't understand what happened out there. . . ."

The father took over the narration. "He was a gutsy kid—he'd do things the other kids wouldn't. But he didn't like to fight, except with his brothers. When he was thirteen, a boy three years older was talking nasty to a girl. Claude told him to stop and the boy knocked Claude's eye all to one side and broke his nose, but Claude whipped him. It was the only fight he ever had."

He paused, then said, "My boys never did wrong. Never smoked pot, never even smoked cigarettes. Even now they hardly take a drink. I'd never let anybody do them wrong, either. One day the school bus driver made Claude set on the step for talking, and he come home with his little pants frozen. The next morning I went out and stopped the bus, and I told that driver, 'Don't you ever put my boy on that wet step again, cold or hot! If you do I'm gonna take you off this goddamn bus and beat the hell outa ya.' I don't want nobody to put their hands on my kid. It's one thing I don't tolerate. No way!"

He stopped for a breath, then started again. "One day a teacher tore Claude's shirt jerking him out of his cheer. I went to the teacher's house and I said, 'Do you know how hord I work to buy a shirt?' I said, 'I want you to buy him a shirt or give me the cash to pay for it.' He said, 'Well, Claude was flipping a bobby pin against a girl's arm.' I said, 'No! *He didn't do that!* Claude told me he didn't and if Claude says he didn't, he didn't.' So the teacher bought the new shirt, and I took Claude outa that school and put him in another one."

"He always did well in school," Jennie said in a faraway voice. "His teachers wanted him to go to college, but he wasn't planning on it. He wanted to go west instead."

"Had an IQ of a hundred and sixty-three," Sr. broke in. "His teacher told us, 'Mr. Dallas, if you don't have but one child that you could educate, it should be Claude. He's the smartest boy we got.' But he wanted to be a cowboy. I think it started with that horse."

"Oh, that horse!" Jennie exclaimed.

"When Claude was five or six, I bought him an Oklahoma cutting horse named Blue Roan—part quarter, part Arabian, and *fast*. A big heavy-necked beautiful horse; I raced him later against other farm horses. A lot of my men would go out with Blue Roan and come back walking. But Claude could ride anything with four feet. I always told him, 'I don't give a damn what happens to the horse, but when you come back from being thrown, you better have a piece of the bridle or something to show you tried to hold on to him. Don't come back empty-handed. You cain't do any better'n that.'

"One night when Claude was eight or nine I sent him out on Blue Roan after cattle. After a while I saw the horse turn the corner of the barn and come down the lane holding his head sideways, laying his feet to the ground as hard as he could. The bridle was broke, and Claude was gone.

"I jumped on the horse and took him back out. Claude was walkin' in when I turned the corner. He was staring at the ground, and when he looked up, it sent chills through me. That horse had run a half a mile through the woods with tree limbs beating

Claude's face. His mouth was cut, his nose broke. The horse had run away, and Claude was just too light to hold him. But he'd obeyed my rule: he had a piece of leather in his hand. And he wasn't crying. So I told him, 'Get back on that horse and ride him into the barn.' Claude rode him on in. I'd killed that horse if he'd hurt my boy again."

Looking back, the parents thought that Claude had been happiest on the northern Michigan farm. "He didn't take to Ohio," the father said. "Kept talking about going back to the Upper Peninsula, and when he stopped talking about that he talked about going west. Never had a date in his life. He worked after school for a bachelor farmer down the road, raising money to leave. Claude liked that cheap old bastard, worked for him for a dollar and a quarter an hour when he coulda got two-fifty anyplace else. He'd take on a man's job. He'd say, 'I got to get this done,' and he'd do it. He pushed himself. You could always depend on him. I took Jennie to the doctor in Green Bay when he was a little fella, and a cow kicked him right in the mouth. When we got home, his lip was hanging half off, but he'd finished milkin'. Still has the scar. *Grit!*"

"That boy never had to be told to work," he said after a while. "None of my boys! I told 'em, 'I don't give a damn what you do, but do the best you can.' There's nothing evil or degrading about work. I always said, If I can't leave my children but one thing and that's the will to work, I think I've done enough by 'em.'"

Hard work wasn't enough to keep the family farm solvent. The short growing season meant that there was never enough protein. "We ate venison and anything else we could kill," the father said. "Either that or go hungry."

He handed Claude Jr. a .30-.06 and put him on his first hunting stand when he was eleven or twelve. "It was just getting dark," Sr. recalled, "when I heard 'Bam!' He'd killed a doe deer. The local justice of the peace was working for me at the time and I had that deer and several others hanging in the woodshed. The JP wouldn't go near there. He was an honest old man."

For a treat, the boys liked to pile into the family car for an evening of jacklighting game. Sometimes they sold racks to unsuccessful hunters for twenty dollars a point. "We put up thirty to fifty deer a year for meat," the father related. "Our first year, the Can-

288

ada geese come in by the thousands and landed in our fields. I saw these heads sticking outa the tall grass. I thought they were snakes, honest to God!

"I drove right up to the geese in my low-slung Packard, took my walking stick and started beatin' hell outa them. Will grabbed one that I'd knocked his head purt' near off—one of 'em I did knock his head off and the other'n just hangin'—and it nearly beat him to death before I got to him."

The next year the whole clan was ready when the honkers came off Lake Superior on their annual migration. With his sons hanging on, Claude parked the tractor alongside the field and watched till the last of the exhausted flock had landed. Each time he fired, he killed five or six. The family spent the day plucking and cleaning. "We lived off wild game," Sr. said. "I don't know any natives that didn't."

He awarded rifles to his sons for not smoking before their sixteenth birthday; Claude's was a .30-.06. He'd had a 16-gauge double-barreled shotgun from the age of nine. "That boy never let loose of a gun," Claude Sr. said. "When those sons of bitches went through his bus out west, they took guns he'd had since he was a kid. I think that bastard Nettleton's still got 'em. Those guns meant something to him. We like guns in this family. Knives too. We're not ashamed to say so." The former knifesmith showed his collection of blades, each oiled and honed to a sharp edge. He took a belt buckle from the box and with a jerk converted it into a gleaming double-edged knife with a three-holed grip.

"Tell ya somethin'," he said, his voice dropping till it wasn't much louder than his wheeze. "When Claude was arrested for the draft and I went to the Federal Building in Columbus to pick him up, I'uz wearing this belt knife. Hell, I'd made 'em by the thousands, and as far as I'm concerned they're legal. I took it off and told Claude, 'Here's what you oughta have.' This marshal was standing there. Son of a bitch musta weighed three hundred pounds. He says, 'No goddamn way you can wear that in Ohio.' But he didn't make me take it off. Hell, I'd've used it on him!"

Neither parent liked to discuss the day Claude left home for good. "Jennie made him promise to finish high school," the father said. "He hung around a few months to raise money, and then he got into the 1941 International pickup I'd titled over to him and he left."

Jennie said, "We thought he'd stay away a year and come back, really and truly. 'Cause he's very close to his brothers and crazy about his little sister Mary. But we got fooled. He loved it out there."

"He went to see one of my daughters in California," the father continued, "and tried to raise a little money on a dairy farm. He lent his first month's pay to some nigger and he beat him out of it. So he had to work two more months to get enough money to leave on. He said he never did anything he hated worse than cleaning up after those calves. Well, a calf does stink. Then he took off. Next thing we knew he was a cowboy."

56

THOSE WHO FELT that Judge Lodge had been too lenient with Dallas were even more put out at the bail hearing. Clayton Andersen argued against bail, reminding the court that Dallas had no stable home or ties in the area and had been a fugitive before his capture. The judge noted that Idaho law required bail and set the figure at $100,000. Mike Donnelly and Bill Mauk were elated. "We anticipated that it may be higher," Mauk said. "It's within a realm we can reach. . . ."

A week later, reporters were tipped that Dallas had pungled up the money. A sheriff's deputy said, "All I can tell you is he is out." Bill Mauk was quoted as saying, "We've had a number of threatening calls on a regular basis from different people. The judge placed a number of restrictions on Claude's release regarding his conduct. That's all I'm going to sa

The judge ordered that the identity of the persons securing the bond be kept confidential unless the bond should have to be forfeited. The court has sealed to protect any parties from harassment, contact or interference with their lives."

* * *

Some were angered about the release, but others had learned a measure of philosophical restraint from the case. Humboldt County Undersheriff Steve Bishop commented, "In view of the verdict, so what if he's released? How much more of a mockery of justice can it be?"

Dee Pogue said that killers shouldn't be set free. Juror Connie Tolmie was "concerned about injuries to Claude." Cheerleader Madaline Meeks said it was only fair to let him out "since he never did a damned thing wrong."

Constance Wilson Ickes admitted that she was "cross." A TV station had reported that she and husband Millard had secured Dallas's bond. There'd been big headlines: WIFE OF CALDWELL VETERINARIAN PUT UP DALLAS' BOND; SHE'S CONFIDENT KILLER WILL SHOW UP FOR SENTENCING; CALDWELL COUPLE ENABLES DALLAS TO GAIN FREEDOM. It wasn't the kind of publicity that would please an alumna of Miss Chapin's School.

"I called the TV station up and told them off," Coco Ickes told a friend. "When we'd put up the property bond the judge said nobody had to know, but they found out and they showed a map of eastern Oregon with our ranch on it. Well, I have a son and grandchildren down there. Why bother them? Enough awful things have happened."

She still blamed Bill Pogue for Bull Camp. "I can't understand why they had somebody like him out in the field all these years," she said. "It's ridiculous." She was more forgiving of Elms. "I would guess he just happened to be there, though I've heard a few things about Conley Elms, too. I thought he was just sort of a big dumb character who got in the middle of it."

She said she had no idea where Claude was spending his spell of freedom, but the judge had confined him to Idaho, Oregon and Nevada. Claude was tired, she said, and needed a rest. She said she was "very fond" of the young man and wasn't at all nervous about the bond. She'd backed him before and never lost a dime.

Geneva and Herb Holman were also glad to help. "We lent him our red Citation so he'll be incognito," Geneva explained. "It'll go like hell if anybody gets after him." They supplied him with cash and credit cards and told him to have a good time.

* * *

Not long afterward, reports came in on the Nevada Fish and Game Department's 800 number that Dallas was at a private "be-hind-the-gate" hunting club at Willow Creek, a short drive from Paradise Hill. Members were said to include George Nielsen, Herb Holman and Frank Gavica. One of the callers said Dallas had set out illegal traps. Another accused him of shooting a lion.

Nevada wardens like Gene Weller and Rick Davidsaver were trying to decide what to do about the reports when another anony-mous caller warned their Reno headquarters, "Whatever you do, stay away from Willow Creek."

The front office ordered the wardens to butt out. Not even Claude Dallas would be foolish enough to trap illegally and poach big game in the face of a fifty-year prison sentence. And even if he was that crazy, what was the point of a confrontation? He was already in the hands of the courts. What were they going to do, write him a hundred-dollar citation? There was also a slight suspi-cion that the Paradise Hill gang had set a trap.

Hoyt and Mary Wilson welcomed their old ranch hand back to Steens Mountain, installed him in the trailer house and assigned him a good horse. "The place is yours," Hoyt told him. Of course there was the problem of the Oregon Fish and Game man up on the ridge with the spotting 'scope—or so Hoyt's mother suspected. Coco Ickes was usually right about such things.

They didn't talk much about the case. Claude had hopes that he would be put on probation because the jury had pulled so hard for him. He said he would return to Caldwell for sentencing—his time on the run had been "the worst fifteen months of my life."

He scrounged some gear and began trapping bobcats up above. Hoyt Wilson couldn't believe it. He told what happened next: "He goes up to where a band of prize bighorn sheep were hanging around, maybe a hundred of them, planted about twenty years ago. The state's been carefully building them up. They issue maybe six or eight tags for the whole mountain. You have to win one in a drawing.

"He shoots a mountain sheep! Then he puts it in our cold room and says we're gonna eat this thing, you know? Well, we couldn't have eaten it if we'd wanted to. It was a typical winter sheep, no fat, no nothing, tough as could be.

"I was appalled. So was Mary. I don't think he'd've done that eight or ten years ago. He was so tickled, and that was more appalling than anything—at a time when you'd think he'd be on his best behavior. But all he could think about was now he's got this trophy ram. . . ."

Geneva Holman couldn't discuss the prize sheep without giggling. "When he brought it down here, I said, 'What am I gonna *do* with you?'" She laughed a big Basque laugh, every shiny white tooth showing. "He brings it in the house and he says, 'Here's a little present.' A quarter of mountain sheep!" The tears slid down her round cheeks. "All stringy and lean!" She couldn't go on.

Later she said, "Just before he went north for sentencing, he told me he had to do something for me. I said, 'Someday you can bring me a bobcat.' He said, 'I can do that!' I told Herb, 'Oh, shit, we're gonna come home some night and find our door propped open with a dead bobcat or a bear or something.'" Both the Holmans laughed at that one.

Claude Dallas strolled up to the Canyon County courthouse on January 4, 1983, healthy and fit after nearly two months in the open. He walked through the fresh snow in a typical western outfit including a blue neckerchief, but he wore a tractor cap instead of his old trapper's hat.

Mike Donnelly had advised the press that his client was "willing to go in and take whatever sentence is imposed. He's realistic about it because there were law enforcement officers involved." The outrage over the verdict had scarcely died down. Just a few days before, Tim Nettleton had been quoted as saying that he hoped the judge did his job: "I don't think it's any secret that I've been discouraged by what's happened so far." Clayton Andersen said the State intended to take "a very hard line."

A presentence investigator had talked to Dallas family members, including several of his brothers, and informed the judge that the family had been "regularly involved" in poaching. She noted the parallel between the closeness of the family and Claude's behavior as a member of the Paradise Hill in-crowd. She said that Dallas was the type who would be loyal to those that he knows well and have very little regard for anyone that he does not know well or allow into his circle."

Judge Lodge was deluged by other information about Dallas

294

from the ranches and bars of the I-O-N country, most of it written in response to a form letter from Herb and Geneva Holman that enclosed two sample encomiums and closed with, "We urge you to write a letter today for a great cause."

Gene Weller told friends he was surprised by the way Dallas strolled into the courtroom "as if he owned it." Weller wasn't sure he would be called as a witness. "They want me to testify that Claude was a maggot," the enforcement warden told a friend. "I can't do it. Within the warden's meaning he *is* a no-good scrotebag maggot. But he beat me at a game. Maybe he was poaching and I had some suspicions, but he beat me at the game." To the highly moral Sunday School teacher, fairness was everything.

The courtroom was packed with Dallas's fans—defense witnesses in lace-up boots and ten-gallon hats, the neatly-turned-out Dallas Cheerleaders, and half the female members of the jury. "My husband told me not to come," said Shielda Talich. "He said, 'Let it die, let this thing rest.' But I couldn't."

The first witnesses belatedly tried to correct the record about Bill Pogue. A Fish and Game biologist testified that he'd accompanied the senior warden to the home of the irascible Chapman brothers, who'd capped off the defense testimony. The biologist said that the short interview had consisted of light conversation and that Pogue hadn't shown hostility or touched his gun.

Idaho C.O. Gary Loveland testified that he'd interviewed recent recipients of citations from Pogue and Conley Elms and found no one who suggested that either warden was quarrelsome, threatening, or dangerous.

Fish and Game Director Jerry Conley swore that the killings had made his department's job "much more difficult." State Trooper Rich Wills, a veteran of the Bull Camp investigations, testified that the public's "general consensus towards game wardens is now one of animosity." Gene Weller recalled the time Dallas told him, "You're welcome in my camp, but don't bring that badge in."

After Clayton Andersen had put on his final witness, the defense responded with its customary blitz. Hoyt Wilson testified that Dallas was "a sobering influence on the other guys." Born-again Christian Cortland Nielsen, George's brother, said his daily thoughts weren't complete until he talked with Claude. Top buckaroo Gary Rose called his old friend "a good all-around guy." Nevada rancher Richard Holbrook told how Dallas had "gathered and branded cattle, did some irrigation work and helped around my store—and didn't request any compensation."

When a middle-aged rancher named Harold Chapin stepped down after praising Dallas, a voice called out, "That's the best cowboy in Nevada!" It was colorful Waddy Mitchell, adorned for the occasion in muttonchop whiskers and a black-and-white cowboy suit. Willis Bland of Kings River, Nevada, testified that Dallas had "a good reputation." Larry Hill, manager of the Nevada Garvey ranches, called him "a good worker." Brother Bob Dallas spoke with his father's simple eloquence. Claude, he said, "was always working. All of the brothers were. He was the nicest one of the bunch, very polite and easygoing. . . . None of us has ever known of anything that he's ever done wrong. Claude wouldn't gun anybody down, not unless they were going to kill him."

Sentencing hearings were usually tedious formalities, since most judges had already written their verdicts. But Judge Lodge seemed to be listening closely, nodding, frowning lightly, flicking a smile when his bespectacled eyes found the face of a friend. After a while he told the lawyers to pick up the pace, a request he'd made more than once at the trial. For a man who'd managed to displease both sides and most of his constituency, he seemed self-assured. All agreed that he was playing a tight hand.

During the final intermission, juror Shielda Talich was pleased to see Claude heading her way. "Thank you for coming, Shielda," he said in his soft voice. She was surprised that he knew her name till it dawned on her that she'd become as much a part of his life as he'd become of hers. She said, "I couldn't stay away. I don't really want to be here."

"I don't either," Dallas quipped.

When Marlys Blickenstaff walked over, he thanked her for coming and she answered stiffly, "You're welcome. I hope you enjoyed your time off. I was very glad that you had this time to be with your friends and your family."

He nodded and stepped away, and she felt stupid. You know

everything about him, she berated herself, and here's your chance to say something bright and witty—and you say something dumb like that!

Juror Deborah Ross stood just outside the circle around Dallas and his counselors. She'd spoken to him briefly as he came into the courtroom. He'd smiled and asked, "Didn't you get enough of this before?" and she'd answered, "Evidently not."

Now she had an important question. "Claude," she said nervously, "I'm Debby Ross. As you know, I was on the jury. I'm planning to write a book about it. I just wanted to know how you feel about that."

He looked startled. "I really don't want anything to do with it," he said, shaking his head rapidly. "Nothing! I just don't want a book written about me." He seemed so emphatic that she dropped the subject, mumbled a good-bye, and stepped away. She thought, What a nice person he is, even when he's saying no. I think he'll like what I write.

Her working title was: *A Man Called Dallas.*

57

THE JUDGE'S TIME had come. As the onlookers climbed to their feet to honor his return from chambers, they studied his face for a hint. His soft features were set, his lips tight. He looked grim enough to sentence a nun, but most spectators figured he'd look just as serious if he were planning to set Dallas free. His judicial career would be over.

He spoke from notes, separating his words, making sure the court reporter and everyone else got the straight of it. He started like a man who was disturbed that he'd alienated only half the community. The jury, he said, "has been castigated, threatened and verbally abused by people who did not even attend the trial." The press "has advocated a state of emotional hypocrisy. . . ." The court's integrity "has been challenged without foundation. . . ."

He stared through his glasses at the defendant. "Nevertheless, Mr. Dallas," he said, "I feel in my heart that you know that you have been given a fair trial." His voice gained timbre and his black robes rippled with his gestures. "That jury, after seven days of deliberation, returned a verdict of voluntary manslaughter, and I am satisfied that even though you would like to feel differently, you know that their verdict is supported by the evidence."

* * *

Dallas Cheerleader Jennie Shipley thought, All through the trial the judge appeared to be so fair, so pleasant and cordial, but look at him now: gruff, stern. He's a totally different man, completely out of character. She feared the worst for Claude.

"I have lived with this case every day since that verdict, almost on a day and night basis," the judge intoned. "I have reread the transcripts, considered the presentence investigation, had the assistance and arguments of your attorneys, of course, and the State's attorneys, in an effort to refresh my memory. After having done all of that, Mr. Dallas, I can consciously tell you, *sincerely* tell you, that I do not believe the issue of self-defense arose at Bull Camp."

A stir went through the courtroom. In five or six minutes, His Honor had reached the heart of the matter. "By saying that, I do not mean by any stretch of the imagination that I think you are a bad person," he added as though to palliate his words. "The evidence is to the contrary. People that know you think very well of you, very highly, and would trust their lives and their money with you. And you have been responsible to the court while you were out on bond. So I am not critiquing you as an individual."

He explained his reasoning about self-defense: "You had been warned by Ed Carlin that law enforcement people and peace officers might be in the area and that they might come out and check your camp, and you then indicated . . . that you would be ready. And you knew at that point and during that period of time that the worst thing you had done, if anything, was commit a misdemeanor in violation of the game laws.

"When you were being taken down from the rim by the peace officers, you knew that they thought they had disarmed you when they took the gun from you.

"When they got to your camp at the bottom, Mr. Stevens came onto the scene, and to me it is contrary to common sense to believe that peace officers of Mr. Pogue's and Mr. Elms's experience would ever attempt to shoot anyone over a misdemeanor in the presence of not only another officer, but a third person, Mr. Stevens. . . .

"Your subsequent actions and statements corroborate, in my judgment, the fact that you did not exercise self-defense. Your own statement to Mr. Stevens shortly after the killing in response to his question, 'Why, Claude? Why did you do this?' or words to that effect, were that 'I swore I would never be arrested again and they had handcuffs on. I'm sorry I got you involved in this.' . . .

"I believe in my mind that [Stevens] is a friend of yours, or was during that period of time, and that . . . the last thing he would do is try to make things worse for you. Nobody else was there and he could have said anything he wanted to say and nobody could have disputed it. . . .

"When I take into consideration the expertise that you had with firearms and what you could do with firearms and the close range that you were in, it is my judgment that you drew that gun because you did not want to be taken in and you fired and you hit Mr. Pogue before he ever drew a gun. You did that and you could do that because of the fact they did not know that you were armed.

"And then, of course, you did turn to Mr. Elms and you fired and killed Mr. Elms. . . . At the very most, all he was doing was going for his gun with his hand inside his jacket after the first two shots had been fired. Again, with your expertise, the fact that you knew the position of the officers and did not give Mr. Elms an opportunity to have either dropped his hand or dropped the gun— if he actually got the gun drew—is totally inexcusable, and you are not in a position to argue that you had to kill him to secure your own life."

Donna Deihl was thinking, I can't believe this! That's not the way it happened at all. Didn't he listen to Claude?

"Mr. Pogue by this time had already been shot backwards and had not pulled his gun," the judge continued. "You had your gun drawn and were in a cross position and in a position to do him in at any time. In addition to that—and I do not like to dwell on the ugly—but you did go into the camp, you took your rifle, the twenty-two, and you came back and you shot both officers, prone on the ground, in the head, both in a motionless position.

"Mr. Stevens, who did not shoot a weapon, who did not kill anybody, was so shaken up by what transpired there that he had to sit down to gather his composure. I am convinced in my own mind that if he thought that there was any possibility that the incident which occurred could be construed to have been self-defense, he would have jumped on it. First, you were his friend, and second of all, he needed to convince you that that is what had happened to make sure that nothing else happened. But that didn't go through his state of mind. What went through his mind was that 'I have got to load my gun, I may be next.' And he even thought about the fact that he might have to kill you, in words to the effect that he couldn't do that because you were his friend. . . ."

In her seat of honor in the jury box, Shielda Talich wanted to stand up and say, Your Honor, don't you think that we went over every point you're making again and again and again? Why do you think it took us so long? Stop and think! You sound like a first-day juror. We covered those things in the first two days. It was much more subtle, complex. . . .

The judge stared at Dallas and said, "He described you, with the exception of a little hurried speech, as being still very collected and quiet and basically calm, particularly considering the incident that had just transpired. And your thought processes were very orderly, well organized. You immediately thought about what you were going to have to do and what was going to be necessary as far as removing the bodies, disguising the camp and the scene that had occurred there. You gave directions with particularity to Mr. Stevens of what he was to do, and these are not indicative of a person that is out of his mind. . . .

"Practically all of those acts at the scene at that time, particularly going and getting the twenty-two and coming back out, were offensive, not defensive, acts. . . .

"Again, in testimony of Mr. Stevens particularly, he said that you said to him, 'I would have took 'em on the rim but they would have killed me up there.' I can't imagine a friend or somebody that was even close to a friend making something up like that. . . . You are talking about almost premeditation. If that did transpire up on the rim, there was all the time period coming down the rim that you were thinking about the situation. . . .

"Then again at the time when you were putting Mr. Elms in the river and you came back and told Mr. Stevens . . . 'This is murder one for me. I didn't weight the body.' That is your own judgment of what transpired. And, again, I can't imagine anybody that would be a friend concocting something up like that . . . unless something like that *was* said and did in fact happen.

"You said at a later time, 'This gun,' meaning Pogue's, 'is going into the ground with this guy. I can't imagine anyone working that many years with Fish and Game,' and I think that is very relevant in this case. We have had testimony concerning your good character and what type of person you are, but there is some kind of a resentment or antigovernment philosophy in your thinking . . . probably because of the way you were brought up. . . ."

By now he had talked for nearly thirty minutes and made it abundantly clear that Dallas would serve time. But how much? Spectators hung on every syllable. He spoke of the "excellent people" who worked for the Fish and Game Department. He repeated that Dallas had shown no remorse for his victims or their families. Then he turned to the delicate subject of the bodies:

"You not only dragged [Elms] feetfirst, but you turned him around and dragged the body face first. I have seen those pictures and you know what I have seen. And then just dropping the body in the river—what effect is that going to have not only on the people that find that body, but the families that are involved?

"You buried Mr. Pogue's body in a shallow grave and you, more probably than anybody that I can think of in this courtroom, knew that that would not be sufficient. There was no testimony that it was covered with rocks or that any other type of precaution was taken to make sure that animals did not reach that body. It is very difficult for the court to understand how you can be described in the manner in which you are described and which I want to believe, and then do these types of atrocious things.

"Worse than that is the time period we are talking about, before you revealed the whereabouts of this body. Once you were free or had been removed from the scene and had not been discovered, there was ample time for you to have let somebody know the general location of that body for the sake of the family. That has been a puzzle to me all the way through this trial. I have never been able to figure it out, knowing you the way you have been described. You come from a close-knit family. You are a Catholic. You know what kind of pain and suffering that family would go through. . . ."

Donna Deihl resented the way the judge shook his finger at Claude. He was so emotionally involved that his face was red. No wonder he wasn't making sense. . . .

Jennie Shipley was enraged. She thought, Claude doesn't deserve this. It isn't fair, it isn't right, it isn't according to the feelings of the jury. She thought of walking out, but she had to hear the sentence.

The judge circled back to the central puzzle: Dallas's persona. "Obviously, as you have been described, you are a well-read individual. You are an intelligent person. . . . That is, again, a dichotomy for the court. I don't understand. You are intelligent . . . compassionate, thoughtful, well-liked, honest, loyal. . . . I am sure that that is one thing that puzzled the jury for seven days, trying to decide how these things could transpire with this type of person."

He called the killings "extremely violent type crime: not the sudden burst of bullets that went out and killed . . . but the taking of the gun . . . when they were in the prone position, obviously incapacitated, and shot again in the head. You cannot equate that with the killing of an animal like maybe you have done in trapping." He raised his voice. "The court cannot do it and you cannot do it!"

He spoke of the months in hiding, the leap through Craig Carver's trailer window, the wild ride across the desert, "the state's evidence that you fired certain rounds and nobody, fortunately, was hit if you did. . . . You had weapons in your possession and you were ready to use them, and everybody connected with the situation believed that you would use them. A person does not carry around the type of ammunition that you had and the number of guns that you had, particularly when you are being wanted and searched for by the FBI and other law enforcement officials, unless you intend to have some kind of use or defense with those weapons."

Rehabilitation, he said, wasn't an issue. "It is not your character to do what you did. . . . I think you do not necessarily have to rehabilitate a person that for all intents and purposes is a very capable, honest, moral person other than for the crime that he committed. We are not talking about somebody that had been disadvantaged all of his life, had been on drugs and dope and abused and mistreated all his life, and then try to bring him around by rehabilitation."

But Dallas and the public had to be shown that "if we kill a person who represents a public official, we are going to be treated more harshly than if we maybe kill somebody else, and the reason that must happen is because these people are put in jeopardy every day of their lives and they need that extra protection. We need to get that message out, that when it comes to law enforcement we do

303

not argue about whether the officials have the right or we have the right. We do that at a later time, in a court of law."

The judge had spoken for almost an hour. He cleared his throat and took a sip of water. When he started up again, his voice was muted, his gestures restrained. It was time to pronounce sentence.

"The court finds that the killing of Mr. Pogue was totally unjustified and that you killed Mr. Pogue with little or no remorse," he announced. ". . . It is further the judgment of this court that the killing of Mr. Elms was morally reprehensible and without justification. Your actions were void of any remorse or feeling. . . ." The sentence was thirty years.

Reporters ran for the phones. The judge rapped once with the gavel and then explained what the sentence meant in practical terms: "If you carry forward with what your character is normally described as, the parole board is in a position to exercise its discretion as to whether or not you would spend the full thirty years. However, if it is to the contrary, they can parole you short of that, by whatever number of years, but not very likely to be under ten."

He insisted that he did not like to play God. "No way can I bring back the lives that have been taken, and my heart goes out to those families. But two wrongs do not make a right. It is going to be difficult for you to be paroled—you might just as well face facts —because of the public opinion and feeling that exists. But . . . people should not be judged by public opinion.

"There is no way I could live with my conscience, knowing the sentences that I have imposed over the years that I have been involved in law enforcement, and justify in my mind any lesser sentence for the taking of human life than the sentence that I have imposed. I am going to remand you to the custody of the Canyon County sheriff to be delivered to the proper authorities at the Idaho State Penitentiary."

Dallas didn't react till the deputies approached him with shackles. Then his body tightened. When a deputy touched him, he jerked an inch or so away, then took off his blue scarf and held out his hands for the cuffs. A court officer said later, "It was the only time I ever saw real emotion on his face. You could see the frustration about going back inside."

Shielda Talich shaped a "Good luck" with her lips as he was led

304

quickly away. Madaline Meeks sobbed aloud. "He doesn't deserve it," she said to the other Dallas Cheerleaders. "Oh, God, he doesn't deserve it."

Clayton Andersen had to sit down and think. Somehow, he decided, justice had been done, in its own convoluted way and in its own good time. It wasn't perfect, but then it seldom was.

He joined a few of the jurors. Later he said, "I should have known better. They weren't in a good mood. They'd just heard the trial judge tell 'em that what they believed was bullshit."

One by one they told him off. Marlys Blickenstaff said he had a hell of a nerve approaching them after what he'd had to say about their verdict. Shielda Talich politely called him "too emotional" for his job. Donna Deihl said a man like him could never understand a man like Dallas, and neither could the judge.

Deborah Ross had started for the door, but a TV cameraman inhibited her exit. She turned and saw Andersen and the other jurors. She thought, Look at that—they're chitchatting with him all nicey-pie! The prosecutor saw her and said, "Debby, how you *doing?*"

She said icily, "I'm just fine." Then she told him, "I didn't like your insinuations in the papers. You said we didn't do our job. Jimmie Hurley wouldn't *let* us do our job. You said we were unjust. We were *not* unjust."

After a few more observations, she left. It was time to write *A Man Called Dallas.*

Tim Nettleton transported his prisoner in Owyhee County's official patrol car, the old white Chevy that he'd bought from a rental agency. Canyon County Sheriff John Prescott and Deputy Jack Arbaugh rode along. Dallas didn't say a word on the twenty-five-mile trip. When they parted company at the prison barbershop, Nettleton stuck out his hand and said, "Well, I've thought of a million ways to harass you on the way over here, Claude, but I think too much of myself for that. Best of luck."

Dallas shook, looked him in the eye, and said, "We'll be seeing ya." The sheriff had used the same expression for years. It was the old cowboy good-bye, from a man and his horse.

Epilogue

AT LEAST THREE songs were written about the mountain man's fate. When a local country and western singer applied at the Owyhee County sheriff's office for a driver's license and offered to sing a few bars of "Ode to Claude Dallas" by Gary Bill Page, Tim Nettleton told her not to bother. After she'd left, he snapped at the dispatcher, "For two cents I'd've told her to get her goddamn license somewhere else."

A book called *Outlaw*, subtitled "The True Story of Claude Dallas," reached the marketplace while Debby Ross's study was still in the typewriter. Colorado author Jeff Long presented Dallas's version of Bull Camp as though it were undisputed fact:

> "You can go hard," Pogue warned. "I can carry you out."
> "You're out of your mind," Dallas pitched back. "You can't shoot a man over a game violation."
> "I'll carry you out," Pogue said.
> In the following instant, the dream of the old West, the legends and machismo and mean truths caught them tight. "Hard," said Dallas. "That's only one way. That's dead."

"I can carry you out." Dallas was sure he saw Pogue reach for his gun. . . .

Outlaw depicted its hero as an idealistic young man who arrived in the high desert country "holding close to him the myths of the raw West," a "mountain man" blessed with "good breeding," and finally a "shining vaquero" in the eyes of his fellow convicts. The *Portland Oregonian* reviewer agreed with several others that the work fulfilled the promise of its flyleaf, which declared: "Claude Dallas and Bill Pogue were two extraordinary men who lived in the West of today but were ruled by the ideals of the previous century. Joined together by the land, diametrically opposed in faith, they were bound to clash in battle."

A colorful Nevadan named Leland York, former Fish and Game commissioner, thought of the killings as a slaughter, not a battle. Several months after Dallas had been shaved and shorn and assigned a cell, York told friends, "Anybody in a uniform would've got it at Bull Camp. A streetcar conductor. A scoutmaster. Dallas was ready. He'd rehearsed for years. Those two boys never had a chance."

York ordered plaques made up in honor of Bill Pogue and Conley Elms and donated one to the Winnemucca city council in memory of its former police chief. A few weeks after the presentation ceremony, he stopped at the Paradise Hill Bar with a friend from Canada. York liked to tell what happened:

"We ordered soda pops. George Nielsen looked at me and said, 'Get outa here.'

"I says, 'What for?'

" 'You're wasting the taxpayers' money with that damned plaque. Now get out!'

"I says, 'Why don't you throw me out?'

"He come down to my end of the bar and I tried to grab him. He says, 'I own this place.'

"I says, 'Come on outside. You don't own the outside, do ya?'

"His wife jumped off the barstool. He wouldn't come out from behind the bar and I kept rapping him with my finger, trying to get him mad enough so I could slap the soup outa him. I says, 'You're saying *I* wasted the taxpayers' money? Why, you dirty rotten lying cottonpicker, you're just like Dallas. The only difference is he's got guts enough to kill a man and all you do is lie.' I says, 'Look what

307

you did that night. You burn up the clothes, you give him a hundred dollars, you give him your pickup. You cost the county thirteen thousand dollars looking for Dallas. *And you accuse me of wasting the taxpayers' money?'*

"I walked out. My Canadian friend says, 'It's a good thing you didn't push him any further.'

" 'Why?'

" 'He had a gun on you. Under the bar. In his right hand.' "

Sometimes Sheri Elms felt vengeful. While chopping kindling one day, she thought, This is probably one of the things Dallas enjoyed, being out by himself, making a fire. She smelled the woodsmoke pouring from her chimney. "I felt real good," she told Dee Pogue, " 'cause that little son of a bitch isn't gonna chop kindling or smell a wood fire for a long, long time!"

She'd canceled the *Statesman* a week after Conley's death. Her TV stayed cold. "The least little thing I hear about it," she said, "it ruins the week."

Every day she needed to tell Conley something. Two years after his death, she still heard his pickup truck and ran to the window. Then she would say to herself disgustedly, "What are you doing? You know he's dead."

She remained on antidepressants. Once she'd been outgoing, almost garrulous, but now she had trouble thinking of things to say. "I've lost my confidence," she explained. "I'd given and received Conley's love, and when that was taken away, something happened to my balance. I haven't got it back."

Dee Pogue intended to spread her husband's ashes over his beloved Owyhee Desert but changed her mind. "We didn't want to make it a sad place for us or for Jerry Thiessen either," she explained. "So Tim Nettleton took us up in his airplane—my son, Steve, my daughter Kathi, and I—and we headed east toward another spot that Bill liked. It was a terrible day—high wind, a snowstorm—so we spread his ashes in the Sawtooth Mountains. He liked them, too."

Seeking distractions, she enrolled in a course called "social justice." On the first night the instructor explained that the death penalty hadn't been applicable to Claude Dallas "because of the overbearing authoritarian attitude of one of the wardens." Dee didn't comment.

While driving out of Boise almost three years after Bill's death, she asked her daughter Linda, "Have you noticed that those are just the Owyhee Mountains now? That it doesn't hurt to look that way anymore?"

Linda had to think. Then she said yes.

Jennie Dallas found it impossible to accept what had happened to her second-born son. "I keep busy," she said as she sliced ham in the kitchen of the neat home on Green Bay Trail. Claude Sr. was remodeling the bathroom with loud drillings and hammerings and outcries about his gouty foot. "But you can't be busy all the time," Jennie went on. "I can't stay at home long without thinking about all the things we should've done differently. But"—she turned up her hands—"I don't know what."

She was pleased that Claude Jr. had sent two Mother's Day cards. Years ago she'd had her children's baby shoes bronzed; then she'd given one to each as they left home. Claude's shoe turned up in his gear at Paradise Hill. "Stuart phoned up and told me, 'You're gonna cry when you get my package,' " she recalled. "Now I have *both* Claude's baby shoes." She'd also hung a couple of Charlie Russell prints from her son's collection, although she seldom looked at them. She didn't feel nostalgic about the West.

The father talked about death and old age. For a while he'd occupied himself running the Myrtle Beach Trap & Skeet Club, but illness had finally retired him while Jennie was still active in real estate. He spent $2,600 dollars on funeral plots after angry negotiations over the price. He sold his grandfather's tools that he'd held onto for fifty years, including a drill that swiveled around corners. "He was *so* proud of that," Jennie said.

"When you start failing," Sr. said, "you're no damned good to yourself." He settled into a kitchen chair and picked at a platter of cheese that Jennie had set out. "It's a shame. I'm in constant pain from my foot."

On a visit to his favorite greeting card shop, he'd noticed a beautiful card with the message: *For You, Son. It's so easy to be proud of a son like you. Happy Birthday.* The family had always loved cards. Frank's birthday was in three months and Jim's in five, so he'd mailed one to each.

"Frank called and asked why I sent it so early," Claude Sr. said later. "I said it was because I liked him and I might not be here for his birthday. Jim just said, 'That's all right, Daddy. Anytime you want to send me a card, you send me one.' "

He dwelled on his recent stroke. "When I woke up and couldn't move my arms, I knew I'd had a stroke. I called Jennie in her bedroom."

"I asked him did he want the rescue squad," Jennie said in her resonant voice.

"I said, 'Hell, no!' I could just see 'em coming here with the siren on and all the neighors saying, 'Well, the old bastard finally got it.' He gave a raucous Appalachian laugh, ending in a string of hee-hees like Snuffy Smith in the old comic strip.

"He would *not* let me call!" Jennie said.

"I said, 'Jennie, just phone the doctor.' My right hand to God, I'm tellin' you the fact. She called him at four A.M. He said to take two aspirins and call him back in twelve hours. I got me a new doctor."

After a while he mused, "Your kids don't give a damn about ya. Hell, they just use ya. If you was t'hell outa the way, then they'd think, 'God, I wish I'd've known him better.' " He left the kitchen, dragging his foot.

Jennie said, "He doesn't mean it. He loves to come out with crazy statements like that. It makes him different from everybody else." She opened a kitchen cabinet and displayed a shelf of prescription medicines. "If he wanted to die so bad, would he be takin' all this?" She raised her small nose, sniffed and said, "His mother's ninety-five."

A little iced bourbon revived the old man's spirits and returned him to the subject of his son and namesake. "I'd push a peanut to Seattle with my nose if I could bring Pogue and Elms to life. But it was something Claude had to do. He wasn't drunk and he wasn't pilfering. He was protecting hisself.

"I wonder, Why'd he carry Pogue out and not Elms? He musta thought he'd done something right or he wouldn't've drug Pogue out here. Hell, you can't eat him! He shoulda left 'em both." He squirmed as he tried to put himself in his son's boots. "I think he's gonna turn him in! 'Hey, this man was gonna kill me and I had to kill him. Here he is.' That's Clode! He's honest!"

He clinked the ice against the sides of the thick glass. "If it'd been me, I'd've killed that Stevens. And then I'd've said, 'Well, I wasn't there. Stevens killed these men and they killed him. I don't know any more about it.' No way they coulda proved that I killed 'em.

"The one I feel sorry for is that Mrs. Elms. That woman was caught in the middle. He'uz just a big dumb old boy. Didn't know what the hell the score was."

He led the way out the back door to show off his pickup truck, glossy in the radiant Carolina light. "That son of a bitch'll blow most other pickups off the road," he said. He pointed to the family Chrysler with its National Rifle Association sticker on the back. "It's air-conditioned," he said with pride.

He limped into the house. "There's never a day that I don't think about my boy and pray for him," he said, reaching for another snack. "It's a sad thing. Claude's a convicted felon now. He cain't ever own another gun."

When Jennie stepped out, he returned to his favorite subject, the miscreants who'd wronged him and his family. "That goddamn Nettleton is a dirty son of a bitch," he said. "Somebody oughta get that man. And that fuckin' Carlin, he's the one that set this up. There'uz bad blood between Carlin and Claude."

He took a thoughtful sip and said, "Claude says he knows who turned him in, but I think he's got the wrong dude. I think it's Nielsen. I don't trust that man and I don't like him. He turned Claude in to keep his own ass outa the penitentiary."

He hinted that he might put a curse on Nielsen and several others. He knew how. "I cursed a doctor," he said, chortling. "He died the next day. I cursed another guy and he fell over in his yard and died in six inches of water. My son Will knows how to do it." A typically prankish twinkle came into his eye. "I told Will, I says, 'Those Idaho Fish and Game are barbaric people, I'm gonna put a curse on 'em. Let 'em wake up every morning with a hard-on, and both hands asleep!' " He laughed so hard he had to wipe his eyes.

"My boys," he said, turning serious again, "we're tight together. I send out the alarm and everybody bristles. When I had a set-to with a cop down here, three of my boys wanted to come here and take care of him. *No shit!*"

311

* * *

Jennie returned, and the two of them reminisced as she prepared dinner. "That was about the time of the murders," she said.

"The *killings,*" Claude corrected her.

Jennie said, "I think somebody oughta write a book about that durn Pogue. Go way on back."

"That man was a hard'n," Sr. said. "He was a nasty bastard." He leaned back and cupped his foot with both hands, trying to ease the pain. "Claude's a man you can't push around. I think that's character. I think it's a credit to ya."

Jennie piped up, "Nobody's gonna push me around."

Claude said, "My granddaddy was that way. My father was that way. And *I'm* that way."

Jennie said, "My father called that spunk. He didn't like wishy-washy people."

Claude said, "I'll do anything for a person that's reasonable or a person that needs. But by damn, ain't *nobody* gonna tell me what to do. I just don't like it. Personal freedom is the most important thing in the world."

A few days later, while motorcycles from conventioning clubs spat and snarled and spewed blue smoke a mile or two away, a visitor inadvertently intruded on a crisis in the family home. A grandson, Dallas Sellers, had been beaten by Claude Sr. Now the two of them were patching things up on a trip to the market.

Jennie paced the kitchen. "My *gosh,*" she said, "he spanked that li'l boy so hard! I grabbed him to keep him from being hurt. Claude's two hundred and seventy-five pounds! Little Dallas was screaming. He's just a baby goin' through a stage. He's gotta be told, but he hasn't gotta be hit and knocked senseless."

Dallas Sellers turned out to be the three-year-old son of their daughter Mary Dallas Sellers, recently divorced and living nearby. "Precious li'l boy came along just at a time when we needed him, with the trouble and all," Jennie said. "He's given us something to hold on to, something to do. We love him to death. Claude tells him, 'If we adopt you, you'll be Dallas Dallas!' He just laughs!"

Grandfather and grandson returned home and entered the kitchen as Jennie left, casting stern glances behind. The child was a poster boy, blond, small for his years. His face bore three parallel reddish marks under the left eye, and both eyes looked swollen from crying. He carried a bag of chocolate chip cookies.

Dallas Sr. confided, "I don't know where he's picking this shit up. Of course, he's in nursery school." He winced as he dragged his foot across the floor. "I guess you heard," he said. "Little Dallas, he told me to shut up. Man, I cain't stand that! I never had one of my own children to tell me that. It's a *shock.*"

He scratched his balding head and lowered his voice: "Jennie got on me about it. I got ever'body in the world tellin' me what to do."

The boy sheltered behind his grandfather's thigh. "He's a nice lad," Dallas confided, touching the child's thin hair. "He's the closest to me of all my grandchildren. I'd like to influence his life in the right way, but I haven't had any influence yet. I'd like to steer him just like I raised my own."

After a while, the visitor got up to leave. Dallas Sellers shook hands shyly and said in a voice just above a whisper, "Come back." Under the shade trees along the driveway he climbed on a trike and pointed his finger. "Bang," he said. "You're daid."

ACKNOWLEDGMENTS

FOR THEIR WILLINGNESS to discuss the complex subject of Claude Dallas, Jr., sometimes halfway into the night, I thank Clayton and Cathy Andersen, Jim Bagwell, Dale Baird, Joyce Blanksma, Marlys Blickenstaff, Harry Capaul, Joann and Eddie Carlin, Jerry Conley, Wayne Cornell, Randy Curry, Jennie and Claude Dallas, Sr., Jim Dallas, Will Dallas, Benny Damele, Rick Davidsaver, Donna Deihl, Dale Elliot, Sheri Elms, Charles Fannon, Irene and Walt Fischer, Frank Gavica, Allen Granum, Geneva and Herb Holman, Jimmie Gayle Hurley, Constance Ickes, John Hart Kennedy, Cheryl Knox, Bill Lewis, Noel McElhany, Madaline Meeks, Santy Mendieta, Charlene and Tim Nettleton, Cortland Nielsen, Tommy Ormachea, Tom Pedroli, Wanda Pense, Dee Pogue, Kathi Pogue, Stan Rorex, Deborah Ross, Jerry Sans, Lynn Schild, Norma Schafer, Sam Seals, Jennie Shipley, Sandra and Jim Stevens, Gary Strauss, Shielda Tallich, Jerry Thiessen, Connie Tolmie, Gene Weller, Mary and Hoyt Wilson, Leland York, and certain others who have requested anonymity.

I also acknowledge a great debt to my friend and colleague John McCormick Harris. His journalistic skills contributed to this entire book, but especially to the portions about the Paradise Valley and its inhabitants.

Jack Olsen
Bainbridge Island, Washington

Find out what kind of woman could drive her son to kill his grandfather

NUTCRACKER
Money, Madness, Murder
by Shana Alexander

A TRUE TALE OF MURDER

Frank Bradshaw was one of this country's wealthiest men—with a daughter who complained constantly that he didn't give her all the money she needed.

If killing him would release his fortune, then Frances Bradshaw Schreuder was ready to murder. Or, more specifically, to brainwash her 17-year-old son into carrying out her twisted plan.

Shana Alexander, one of the country's foremost journalists, has also written *Very Much a Lady* and *Anyone's Daughter*, about Jean Harris and Patty Hearst, respectively.   16512-1-24 $3.95